B-ROAD BRITAIN

www.**rbooks**.co.uk

B-ROAD BRITAIN

Robbie Coltrane
with
Robert Uhlig

BANTAM PRESS

LONDON · TORONTO · SYDNEY · AUCKLAND · JOHANNESBURG

TRANSWORLD PUBLISHERS
61–63 Uxbridge Road, London W5 5SA
A Random House Group Company
www.rbooks.co.uk

First published in Great Britain
in 2008 by Bantam Press
an imprint of Transworld Publishers

A CIP catalogue record for this book
is available from the British Library.

ISBNs 9780593059906 (cased)
9780593059968 (tpb)

Addresses for Random House Group Ltd companies outside the UK
can be found at: www.randomhouse.co.uk
The Random House Group Ltd Reg. No. 954009

The Random House Group Limited supports The Forest Stewardship Council (FSC),
the leading international forest-certification organization. All our titles that are
printed on Greenpeace-approved FSC-certified paper carry the FSC logo.
Our paper procurement policy can be found at
www.rbooks.co.uk/environment

Typeset in 11/16pt Sabon by
Falcon Oast Graphic Art Ltd
Printed and bound in Great Britain by
Clays Ltd, Bungay, Suffolk

To Spencer and Alice

Acknowledgements

Many thanks to all the delightfully unselfconscious enthusiasts and eccentrics (they will choose which group they want to be in) who gave of their time, told their stories, and made this book possible. And a special thank you to Hamish Barbour, whose head holds more ideas than a MENSA suggestion box.

Many thanks, too, to Robert Uhlig, who sat for weeks with a tape recorder as I dredged (what is left) of my memory, and relived all the little incidents that made the journey so fascinating. He is excellent company and we sometimes talked for hours, just occasionally forgetting the book. I think that is called lateral research. Or possibly blethering. Google it.

Thanks, too, to Sarah Emsley who nagged me to the deadline, in the nicest possible way, and was extremely supportive, and to Stina Smemo for a fantastic PR campaign.

Introduction

The hour is late, the bottles empty and our bellies full. After-dinner conversation is turning to the marvels of the modern car – a subject closer to many men's hearts than the traditional trio of wine, women and song – when I have one of those unexpected thoughts commonly called a brainwave.

The glory of modern cars, my dining companions and I have agreed, is that you can step inside one, put your foot down and travel from Glasgow to London in five and a half hours, listening to all your favourite music on your iPod without ever having to speak to another soul.

But haven't you ever thought: isn't that frustratingly dull?

Am I the only one who sits in the sound-proofed cocoon of his car, gazing at passing church spires and signposts with funny names and wondering what goes on over there?

As we contemplate Britain's motoring culture, I can't help feeling something's been lost in the fifty years since the first British motorway was built. The need for speed has hardened the nation's arteries with six-lane tarmac and shut off any experience of the real country behind mile upon mile of hard shoulder. Maybe I'm a particularly nosey bastard, but I have a hankering for more local culture than I've found in the congealed offerings of a motorway service station.

Fortified with good wine and food, I declare boldly to my friends that I am the man to bypass the tourist fast-track, to venture off the motorways and take stock of our nation and its people, to unearth the impressive, the imposing, the unconventional, the traditions we cling on to and the new ones we've created. And maybe in the process, I say, I'll discover what we've lost, gained and fought to retain since the late 1950s.

The next day, when I've slept off tiredness and a wee hangover, I find myself still gripped by the idea. Fortunately, one of my dining buddies the previous night was Hamish Barbour, one of my oldest friends and a television producer of no small renown. Some of the best projects I've worked on started over dinner with Hamish. With him, I set about researching our idea. The more we look at it, the more I want to cast off the shackles of modern travel, where the destination is all-important, and delve back to the time when the journey was everything. Wilfully driving as far off the beaten track as possible, I decide I'll venture along a route few people would think of taking these days.

On this journey I want to discover for myself what it means to be British. Although not strongly patriotic (I always thought Samuel Johnson got it right when he said it was the last refuge of the scoundrel), I am fascinated about what exactly makes us British. After all, we've been a multicultural society for hundreds of years and I'm a classic example. Although Scottish, my father's roots go back to Ireland – hence the dark hair – and my mother's ancestors were Huguenot clay workers who escaped religious persecution in France in the seventeenth century. So for ages we Brits have been assimilating characteristics and customs from other cultures, thereby making us what we are today. But what exactly is that? In my quest to find out, the first step is to decide the route.

Most of my work is in London, I live near Glasgow and it's a trip I've made umpteen times, so a journey that takes me a different way from the usual M1–M6–A74 northbound combo seems most appropriate. Meandering satnav-free along B-roads, I want to rediscover the real Britain that has been bypassed, orbited and forgotten since the advent of the motorway. As long as I keep heading in a vaguely northerly direction, I'll let curiosity and the B-road network lead me the long way home.

Next up is the car. It's no secret that I have a passion for machinery and anything with an engine. The bigger, the better, as far as I'm concerned. Ships, aircraft, tractors, trucks, motorcycles and cars – I love them all. The thing that especially fascinates me about cars is that they conform so obviously to national characteristics. They're stacked with cultural clues. With their walnut fascia, leather upholstery and understated styling, British cars look as though they were conceived in a gents' club in St James's and, in the case of the classic Bentleys, as if they were built by a blacksmith and a genius. German cars have beautiful engineering and are extremely efficient, but their totally functional interiors are, in my opinion, quite un-attractive. French cars are very cleverly designed and original, but quite quirky and overcomplicated. My particular fancy is classic American cars and I can think of nothing more rewarding than restoring one of those beauties – turning a rusting heap of metal into something that can pass its MOT and carry five people from Glasgow to Edinburgh in style and comfort. Some people get their kicks climbing mountains, but

I get mine in a pair of overalls, bent over an engine in a garage. There's nothing better.

For this trip, however, only a British motor would be appropriate. It has to be a vehicle capable of making the journey before the first motorway miles were laid and it has to be a convertible for the simple reason that I insist on it. I consider using a Morris 1000, but soon dismiss that idea as an unnecessarily foolish hardship. After all, one of the most beautiful cars ever made was in its prime on the day in 1958 when Harold Watkinson, the Minister for Transport, inaugurated the London to Yorkshire motorway. Leading from Watford to Rugby, this was the first section of what would later be called the M1, Britain's first inter-urban highway. And, sitting in my kitchen, dreaming of the open road, I'm convinced there is no car more appropriate for avoiding the M1 and all its M-prefixed siblings than an open-topped Jag.

My choice is a Carmen red drop-head Jaguar XK150 S, designed by William Lyons, a genius engineer. The XK150 S, launched in 1958, was Jaguar's production sports car from the classic era of its Le Mans successes. Kitted out with leather seats, a manual gearbox and a de-tuned version of the engine that powered Jaguar's racing D-types and C-types, this will be travelling at the 250bhp pinnacle of 1950s style.

A few months later, I am ready to set off. Just the open road and moi. From London to Glasgow nothing and nobody will stand in the way of what I hope will be my rediscovery of Britain and Britishness. Except, that is, for a television crew and a producer with a schedule that makes the national railway timetable look accommodating and flexible.

In my glove compartment is the sketch I made of my ideal route. It will lead me west through the Home Counties and the

Cotswolds before turning east to the fens of Cambridge. From there I'll head north-west via the Midlands and the Peak District into Yorkshire, then take an abrupt sidestep west to the coast of the Irish Sea. The last part of my trip will lead me through the Lake District, then through the Border country into Scotland and ultimately on to Glasgow.

But so much for the best laid schemes. By the time the journey is over, scheduling problems, filming logistics and production restrictions will have all meant that occasionally I have had to backtrack, leapfrog, bypass or revisit some locations. None of this has detracted from the extraordinary people, places and events I've encountered on this fascinating journey of discovery. However, the upshot is this: the route that follows is the ideal journey I would have made had I not been pestered by a pesky producer for its entire length. If you watched the television series *B-Road Britain* you'll notice that this book contains many locations that were not shown on screen. This is because, for a number of reasons, and as is normal on a project of this nature, many of the wonderful people I met and places I visited didn't survive the editing process and ended up on the proverbial cutting-room floor. And that is why I decided to write this book. I like to think of it as the director's cut, the full, unexpurgated story before the strictures of programme-making turned my journey of discovery into three one-hour episodes with breaks for advertisements and brewing a cuppa.

And with that cleared up, let the journey commence.

Chapter One

As the Jag purrs effortlessly out of central London, my mind wanders to what lies ahead. The boot of the car is laden with some twenty pairs of clean underpants, but they are nothing compared with the weight of anxiety I'm carrying. Where will I stay each night? Who will I meet? What will I encounter? My greatest fear is that I am going to meet a lot of people with long-chop sideboards, some of whom will try to wrestle me to the ground, and that I'll discover villages where everyone has the same face and a virgin is a girl who runs faster than her brother.

Like many people, I'm a bit prejudiced about what lies beyond city boundaries. As a southern Glasgow boy, I'm more at home among the steel and concrete of a dockyard than the vales and hedgerows of the countryside. My hopes are not high, particularly as the producer has warned me not to expect an easy ride.

'We're going to keep you away from machines, Robbie.'

'But machines are what I understand.'

He raises his eyebrows. 'Exactly!'

To make matters worse, I am worried about the state of the roads. As far as I can remember, I've never driven from London to Glasgow by motorway without encountering at least 40 miles of contraflow. My most recent journey took me eleven hours – an outrageous state of affairs that led me to think that if our government isn't prepared to invest in the road network, then tolls might be the only answer. If the B-roads ahead are only half as bad as the motorways, my journey of rediscovery is going to take a very long time.

The short, 28-mile journey to my first destination leads me past the starting point of the M1, which I wilfully ignore, and close to the Ace Café, a motoring legend squeezed between the old North Circular and the west coast railway line from Euston to Glasgow. Back in the days before motorways, the Ace Café was where drivers filled up their cars and their stomachs before heading north, provided they could find a place between all the bikers and teenagers – a new phenomenon in the late 1950s – who, before the advent of Radio 1, flocked to fairgrounds and transport cafés to listen to the latest hits on jukeboxes. It was in this heady mix of bikes and rock 'n' roll that the bikers invented the practice of record-racing. This involved dropping a coin into the jukebox slot, selecting a record and racing to a given point and back before the music stopped. Foolish maybe. Dangerous most probably. But I bet it was fun and impressed the girls no end.

But I'm not stopping at this petrolhead temple. My route continues out of London via the Chiltern Hills to a market town exactly midway between London and Oxford on what used to be called the London Way. Only 24 miles from Charing Cross, it is a completely different world from the metropolis. In the eighteenth century, coaches and horses on the two-day journey to Oxford would rest overnight in High Wycombe. Known as Chepping Wycombe in the 1830s, when Benjamin

Disraeli fought and lost three elections to represent the constituency at Westminster, nowadays the town is regarded by many as just another dormitory in the bland commuter belt around London. But this sleepy county town is home to a unique and fascinating centuries-old tradition that is about to see its annual enactment.

My quest for enlightenment takes me first to the home of Darren Hayday, the outgoing mayor of High Wycombe and the most nervous person in town. Darren is breakfasting lightly, and with good reason. Sipping a cup of tea, he tells me that no one knows the precise origins of the upcoming ceremony that has got him in such a tizz. According to local legend, some 450 years ago Elizabeth I visited Wycombe and remarked on the corpulence of its civil officials. Suspicious that the bureaucrats were involved in skulduggery – a not unreasonable assumption, bringing to mind a Greek saying: He who deals in honey cannot help but lick his fingers – the locals seized on the Queen's comment and decided to hold the town's great and good to account. For Darren, that means today is Judgement Day.

Observed every year, except for a brief period in the seventeenth century when it was banned by Cromwell and the Puritans, the weighing-in tradition involves a set of giant scales erected at Frogmore, a square in the centre of High Wycombe, to weigh the outgoing and incoming mayors, as well as charter trustees, honorary burgesses, council officers and 'any other dignitary desirous of being weighed'.

Those who have not put on weight will be cheered for doing a good job without getting fat on taxpayers' cash. Those who have gained weight will be jeered at by the crowd for indulging in good living at the taxpayers' expense. In the past, the crowd would also pelt anyone who had gained a pound or two with fruit and vegetables, which in the days before tomatoes and soft fruit were readily available would mean a barrage of rotten turnips and potatoes.

So this explains Darren's minimal breakfast. Mindful of the potential humiliation that lies ahead, I ask him if he or anyone else has ever considered filling their pockets with lead before their first weighing.

'Oh no, we're always searched.' Darren looks anxious and takes another sip of his tea.

'You'll get a huge cheer if you've lost weight, though, won't you?'

'I'm hoping that's the case.'

Darren has little cause for concern. He's recently been on a diet and exercise regime, motivated by concerns for his physical health (although he doesn't make clear whether by that he means his treatment by the crowd this lunchtime or his long-term well-being).

Before I can find out if his hard work has paid off, I visit the incoming mayor, Valerie Razzaq, for whom the day has a different poignancy. Born, bred and educated in High Wycombe, Valerie is following in the footsteps of her late husband, Razz, who was mayor in 1988–9 and with whom she had three sons and four grandchildren. In an attempt to fill the large gap left in her life by his death, Valerie stood for selection as a town councillor in 2003 and was elected; she has been active in local politics ever since.

When I ask how she's prepared for her big day, she introduces me to what she calls a 'Bucksy saying' (meaning it comes from Buckinghamshire): 'I've been lolloping around like a tart.' Lolloping? What a wonderful word – one that reminds me why

I love the richness of the English language. Lolloping. I've been using it ever since.

Valerie outlines the agenda for the day, which involves a lot of exchanging of mayor's garments as well as handing over the chain of office.

'Valerie, you're avoiding the main event, aren't you?'

'You're right, Robbie.' She giggles anxiously like a school-girl. 'I'm scared to say it. Anyway . . . I'll take over the AGM from Darren.'

'And *then* you'll be mayor?'

'Yes. I'll be mayor.'

'Are you nervous?'

'Nervous? I'm terrified.'

Listening to her describe what lies ahead, *I'm* starting to feel nervous for her.

'So, Valerie. Any schemes up your sleeve for the weighing?'

'I'll be taking a brick.'

'A *brick*?'

'In my handbag.'

'Is that allowed?'

'It's traditional. Among the ladies, that is.'

A short while later, I watch as Darren, Valerie and various dignitaries emerge from the town hall for the long walk through the charming town centre to Frogmore, where a large crowd has gathered, including several men dressed in Civil War Roundhead and Cavalier costumes. With scant sympathy for the plight facing the anxious band of civil dignitaries, one of them shouts, 'Poor things! All those banquets!'

Listening to the crowd yelling I feel there's a wee air of the guillotine about the proceedings. I almost expect to hear the Town Beadle announce to a round of boos that the Countess of

Bologne will be the next under the blade. But the Beadle sticks to his script as he prepares Darren to take his place beneath a large brass tripod, from which hangs a chair with a plush seat – the gift of a local greengrocer – and a scale with a spring-loaded dial.

'Ladies and gentlemen. Welcome to the ancient weighing-in ceremony.' The Beadle pauses for effect as his cohorts, dressed in traditional costume, take their places. 'And now for our first victim . . .'

Darren looks sheepishly at me.

'Good luck, son.'

The Inspector of Weights and Measures examines the gilded dial, then whispers a few words to the Beadle.

'Councillor Darren Hayday . . .' The big moment has arrived and the Beadle is milking it for all it's worth, playing to the crowd as he waves the piece of paper on which he noted Darren's weight last year, then lifting his hat as he hollers the verdict: 'And no more!'

The crowd cheers. Darren looks relieved and smiles. All his time on the treadmill has paid off.

'All you got was "And no more"?' I say as Darren returns from his weighing. Having seen pictures of his jowly grin a year ago, I feel he deserves a bit more recognition for losing nearly 3 stone in his time in office. 'They didn't say: "And a lot less"?'

'Oh well . . .'

A few minutes later I realize the reason for Darren's quiet satisfaction when the Beadle turns to the crowd with a delighted grin.

'Councillor Jean Teesdale. And some more!'

The boos are loud and long. Behind the Beadle, Mrs

Teesdale, a delightful-looking woman in a floral dress, buries her face in her hands.

I don't keep a close tally of the number of cries of 'And no more' against shouts of 'And some more', but after several dozen officials, police superintendents, band members and their ilk have been weighed, it's clear that the 'no-mores' heavily outweigh the 'some-mores'. The system works. These officials have not gained weight at the public's expense – or if they have, they've shed it pretty damn quick before today's ceremony.

Although essentially a piece of theatre, the weighing appears to play a very worthwhile social and psychological role in the life of High Wycombe. It's all very good-natured nowadays, but I wonder how gentle it would have been in the days when many country people were suffering from malnutrition or were starving by the end of winter? I can imagine an unpopular mayor who had put on a couple of stone at the mayoral banquets getting the living daylights kicked out of him by the crowd.

Whoever introduced the ceremony was clearly very wise. If, as is widely thought, it was Elizabeth I, it shows she was just as smart as I've always believed she was. The ritual kept the officials in check and gave the local populace a nice day out, with the sense that they could hold their elected representatives to account in a very straightforward manner. It was also great entertainment, like a medieval version of *Big Brother*. Even this year there was a damn good turnout, although I couldn't help feeling sorry for poor Mrs Teesdale, who thanks to my efforts was going to have the humiliation of her weight-gain broadcast on national television. Poor soul.

I wonder why the ceremony has endured long after it

stopped serving a purpose? Where I live in Scotland, there are hundreds of standing stones in the middle of farmers' fields. It would be quite easy to remove them with a tractor and it would certainly make ploughing or harvesting the field easier, but there appears to be something that stops anyone from doing that. Maybe there's an instinct not to change something that's been in place for so many centuries. Like the standing stones, the mayor-weighing ceremony is something special and maybe for that reason alone they've kept it going. I like it so much I think it should be extended to MPs. But let's go the whole hog and make the chair electric.

Before I leave High Wycombe I seek out Valerie Razzaq. Dressed in her mayor's garb, with a red cloak, a three-pointed hat on her head, a gold chain and white ruffles round her neck, she is working the crowd, chatting to onlookers. I've already given Darren a large rich chocolate cake, into which he can now tuck with impunity after his weighing.

'Look at you, Valerie, going around town, kissing all the good-looking men. Isn't there some kind of law against that? Or is it part of the job description?'

Valerie laughs.

'I'm off now, but before I go: you're going to get weighed next year. Here's your lunch.' I hand the new mayor a bag with two carrots.

She gives a dirty cackle, then makes a lewd remark about the carrots.

'I just knew you'd get filthy on that. Well I never. A mayor with a sense of humour! It's every town's dream.'

From High Wycombe I drive through the Buckinghamshire countryside to a small and beautiful village near Henley-on-

Thames. Recorded as Thyrefield in the Anglo-Saxon Chronicle in 796, when Beorhtric of Wessex was king in these parts, it's now called Turville and is among the best-known villages in Britain. With only a few hundred inhabitants, Turville is little more than a blip on the map, yet millions are familiar with its church, pub and houses, simply because they've doubled as locations for the *Vicar of Dibley* and several other TV programmes and films, including the Daffyd Thomas (the only gay in the village) sketches in *Little Britain*, the outdoor scenes in *Goodnight Mr Tom* (which starred John Thaw), several episodes of *Midsomer Murders* and *Marple*, and *101 Dalmatians*.

At the heart of this quintessentially old English village lies the Bull & Butcher, a pub with dishes on its menu that shame-lessly cash in on the village's fame. Depending on your point of view, Steak & Dibley Pudding, Midsomer Burger and Chitty Chitty Bangers and Mash – the latter in tribute to the hilltop windmill that looks down on the village and featured in the film *Chitty Chitty Bang Bang* – will make you either wince or smile.

But I'm not stopping in this living film set. My next desti-nation is 60 miles further west in the heart of the Cotswolds. Driving through deepest Gloucestershire on the B4425 towards Cirencester, I pass along lanes lined with buttercups, cow parsley and dozens of species of wild flower. Stretching across the horizon are fields of wheat, barley and oilseed rape.

A few miles along an unclassified road, I pull into a driveway. As I go through a gate into a large field, a pair of biplanes buzz just feet over my head, their engines shattering the bucolic silence as they emit a dirty trail of stinky Avgas exhaust. I inhale greedily. Bliss.

Chapter Two

As I pull the Jag to a stop, two Boeing Stearman two-seater biplanes touch down on a stretch of lush green grass. At first glance, they look like any other Stearmans: elegant examples of military trainer aircraft from the 1940s that became popular as crop-dusters and sports planes after the Second World War. But above the upper wing is a strange contraption with a harness, and seated beneath the harness in the passenger compartment of each plane, ahead of the pilot, is a stunning girl in her early twenties wearing a tight red shiny tracksuit. I think I am in heaven.

Before I get a chance to introduce myself to the two young daredevils, Vic Norman, a man of sixty in red overalls, comes bounding over. With a faint Cockney accent, Vic explains how his fascination with flying led him to restore his own historic airfield and set up the world's only wing-walking team. Having been bitten by the flying bug at an early age – his father took him up in various De Havilland aircraft from when he was four – Vic started flying on his seventeenth birthday. To finance his passion, he put together an air show aerobatics team, teaching himself from a book how to fly loops and barrel rolls, and finding advertising sponsorship to cover his costs.

Then Vic stumbled upon an unexpected treasure. 'I was at home, looking through a book about the First World War that I'd got at a jumble sale, when I read about a training airfield at Rendcomb in Gloucestershire. I dropped the book with surprise. I couldn't believe it. It was only a few miles away from where I lived.'

Vic hared round to a farm he knew nearby. It was all ploughed fields, but in the corner of one of the fields he spotted a building. It housed cows, but Vic immediately recognized it as a standard First World War Ministry of Defence structure.

'I walked around the place. In some woods I found an old machine-gun butt, which the Royal Flying Corps would use to sight the guns on their aeroplanes. I was convinced this had been the site of the airfield I'd read about in my book.'

Extremely excited by his find, Vic knocked on the farmer's front door. 'Hello. Can I introduce myself? I live down the road . . .'

'You the young man that makes all the noise in the aeroplanes?'

'Well, yes . . . I am . . . But please – can you tell me about an airfield I've discovered you have on your farm?'

The farmer explained how the airfield used to belong to his grandfather and showed Vic some pictures of it in use in the early 1920s. Vic was gobsmacked. It was everything a flying enthusiast would dream of having on his doorstep. Determined to find a way to buy the land, but lacking funds of his own, he managed to attract interest from some partners and returned to the farmer a few months later with an offer.

'You've got to let us buy this airfield.'

'It's not for sale.'

For months Vic harangued the farmer until finally he agreed

to sell him the land, albeit at a price that was over the odds. He then set about restoring the fields and buildings to their wartime state, even constructing hangars to their original designs and installing a fleet of biplanes.

Standing on the rebuilt airfield, I think about all the RFC airmen who trained there. They often learned to fly on wooden mock-ups suspended on a gimbal, before being pushed out for their first solo flight on a powered biplane with only two engine speeds (on and off). I think what Vic has done is terrific. A lot of people dream of great things, but he's taken a risk and fulfilled this massive ambition.

'Would you like to have a go?' Vic points behind me at the two Stearmans, one of them dating from 1938, the other from 1944, and both built as primary trainers.

'In one of those? Try stopping me.' Then I remember the last time I tried to get into a tight cockpit and found myself wedged between cables, terrified that I would send the plane into a tail-spin if I touched them. 'But do you think I'll get in?'

'No problem. Let me introduce you to one of our team pilots, Martin Carrington. He got his licence last week you'll be pleased to hear. You'll be safe in his hands.'

Fortunately I know Martin has been flying since he was nine and I can laugh it off. 'And he's almost sober?' I turn to Martin, a noticeably more sylph-like figure than me. 'So what sort of things will we be doing?'

'A flight round the local area. And then a loop the loop. If you fancy it . . .'

'A loop the loop? Yeah . . . that bit would be fine . . . I wouldn't be scared at all.'

'How long ago was breakfast?'

'I was just thinking that, actually. Thank heavens I had the muesli and didn't go for the full English. Nothing too scary or stunty?'

'It's all done very safely. We'll dive into a nice positive loop . . .'

'Lovely . . .'

'. . . and you can watch the scenery go past . . .'

'Right then.'

'. . . upside down.'

Martin, I'm sure, has seen many more nervous passengers than me. 'Don't worry,' he says. 'It's a perfect day for flying. Let's go to it.'

'Shall we be off, chaps?' Half of me's as excited as a little boy. The other half is terrified. I try to put a brave face on it. 'Chocks away?' Then I notice they don't have any chocks.

Shoe-horned and strapped into the plane, I discover that sitting in front of the pilot is slightly unnerving. There's no way of telling what he's about to do. Every manoeuvre will come as a surprise.

A few feet in front of me roars a 450hp Pratt & Whitney. With the engine idling on the ground, sitting behind it is the smelliest, noisiest place on the planet. Fortunately, once we're airborne, the engine speeds up and the wind sucks the exhaust clear of my face.

For the first five minutes I'm petrified. Martin executes a series of daredevil manoeuvres and, flying upside down, I can't help thinking that my life depends on two relatively thin straps holding me into the plane. If they snap, I'm gone. It's scary. But I soon realize I'm in good hands and I relax into the flight, enjoying every minute of it. By the end, I feel I should have been doing this all my life.

The highlight comes when Martin pulls back on the joystick

to send the plane climbing high above the airfield, then points its nose straight at the ground, putting the Stearman into a terrifying vertical dive. The ground shoots towards us alarmingly fast. Just as I think Martin has a death wish, he pulls the plane into a loop and I realize the purpose of the dive. We needed the speed for the manoeuvre – but I have little time to think about the physics of aerobatics. My mind is now totally occupied by the alarming sensation that I'm going to be pushed through my seat. The G-force kicks in, my body feels as if it has increased in weight fourfold, and I slip down into the plane, my head disappearing beneath the windscreen into the fuselage as we climb high into the sky. There's a glorious moment at the top of the loop when I feel weightless and the world goes silent, then we return to the horizontal before Martin throws the plane into a couple of barrel rolls, executes a few corkscrew turns and touches us down back on the airfield.

I am as much amazed as relieved. 'How do you do that? How do you manage to know where you are in three dimensions?'

Martin shrugs. 'Just close your eyes and hope.' Liar! 'It's something you get used to.'

I love that cool, unruffled demeanour that pilots have. It's the same with racing drivers. All those modest shrugs when you ask them how they do it and all that talk of 'a little incident' or 'Monty's had an off' when you know they mean something really serious, such as a life-threatening crash.

It's been a fantastic experience, one that has left my organs in a completely different place from where they started. And to think Martin does it every day.

However, for Vic and Martin, stunt flying is just a means to an end. Their passion is wing-walking, which, as Vic explains as we stride back to the clubhouse, began shortly after the First World War. Young pilots were returning home exhilarated by their adventures in the sky, desperate not to go back to the dull jobs they'd had before the war. Some of them purchased surplus biplanes cheaply and went barnstorming. They'd travel the country, landing in villages, where they'd put up boards and charge locals for their first taste of flight. They took mechanics with them, who would often have to rebuild the engines overnight because of their unreliability. It was an era of daring young men in bug-eyed goggles, caps on backwards, flying flimsy machines through the air like erratic, colourful butterflies. Rooted in the carefree, happy-go-lucky tradition of show business, these daredevils slept in barns and were regarded as loveable rogues who would raise a storm wherever they went. Every village and provincial town offered rich pickings and any farmer's field could become an aerodrome. Buzzing the main street at low level was enough to have crowds following the biplane to the flying field.

'It was great fun,' says Vic, 'but after two or three years the villagers got a bit blasé about the visiting barnstormers. Then one bloke had a brilliant idea. He said to his mechanic, "You climb out on the wing and I'll fly down the high street." It worked. Every single person in the village turned up for a flight the next day.'

That's all it was. An attention-grabbing bit of open-air theatre and showmanship. As well as mechanics, girlfriends were persuaded to walk the wings, performing in-flight transfers from cockpit to wing with only the rigging wires to save them from oblivion. These airborne adventurers' ultimate stunt was transferring themselves from one plane to another – mid-flight. Really!

Vic leads me into the clubhouse, where there's a long line of vintage British motorcycles. And I think: an airfield with some wonderful aeroplanes and now a collection of beautiful bikes? Vic is clearly my kinda guy. Then he introduces me to three of his wing-walkers and I'm even more bowled over. Lucy, Sarah and Danielle are delightful. There's something very attractive about women who court danger – although being old enough to be their father, I make sure I keep my admiration well in check.

As I arrive, Lucy and Sarah are teaching Danielle, the newest recruit, the routines. Sarah and Danielle are sitting on chairs arranged one behind the other like the seats on a biplane. In front of them is a table on to which Danielle can step to emulate climbing on to the upper wing. Lucy stands beside the surrogate plane, leading Danielle through the moves, while Sarah pretends to be the pilot. Not only will Danielle have to avoid throwing up when she gets into the air, but she has to memorize her mentor Lucy's routine. I can't help thinking that being sick would be the easier option.

I watch the trio rehearse, then ask Danielle how on earth she came to the job of wing-walking. You can imagine the advert for this job: 'Must enjoy fresh air and exercise and have a care-free attitude to life insurance. No time-wasters, please.'

'My dad was in the RAF,' she says. 'We used to go to air shows and I always liked watching the wing-walkers. I wanted a job that I'd get up in the morning and be really excited about.'

'How many people think you're crazy when you tell them what you do?'

'Out of ten people who ask me? About nine or ten.'

'Really? Surely it's the ones who want to spend their working lives in front of computer screens who are crazy.' To me, Danielle seems eminently sensible.

Danielle had to audition against more than a thousand other applicants. They all had to be relatively light, less than 5 foot 6 inches tall, agile – Sarah, Lucy and Danielle all have a background in dance – and tough. The job can be physically and mentally demanding; during the season they often work fourteen hours a day. When it rains the raindrops sting their faces. They've even done their routines in snow showers. Having satisfied Vic and Martin that she had the physical strength for the acrobatics and the personality to deal with the pressure and the public, Danielle was asked to get up on a wing. 'They wanted to see if I liked it and if I looked okay. That was hard.'

Although it sounds surprising that thousands of applicants want to be wing-walkers, I remember what I was like when I was seventeen. Like many teenagers, I was an adrenalin junkie always on the lookout for the next fix, so I can relate to these girls. In that light, applying for a job in which you'd get your kicks under close supervision, after intensive training and with a multitude of safety checks, seems to be infinitely more sensible than the legions of boy-racers that I see getting their thrills by thrashing souped-up hatchbacks along country lanes, not always avoiding the trees. I am totally beguiled. Danielle, Lucy and Sarah are beautiful and so brave. And it's clear that wing-walking is not the kind of thing you do if you 'quite fancy' it. I admire that single-minded determination.

A few minutes later, I am back in the air, flying beside two other Stearmans, our wingtips at times only 18 inches apart. One carries Lucy, who has slipped on some white gloves and a red leather flying helmet. The third plane carries a cameraman in the passenger seat.

The pilot makes a 'T' sign with his hands to indicate to Lucy that it's time to transfer on to the wing. Watching her climb out of her seat and begin her careful ascent on to the upper wing, I think it's possibly the most dangerous thing I've ever seen. Having removed her straps, she waits for a signal from the pilot, then rises from her seat into a 100 m.p.h. gale. Teetering on her toes, she makes a grab for two handles cut into the trailing edge of the upper wing. She pulls herself upright into the full brunt of the howling wind, places one foot on a panel in front of the pilot's windscreen and steps up on to the wing. With one knee resting on the wing, she is at the most risky part of the manoeuvre, the wind rushing over the upper surface of the wing straight on to her torso. Clutching the rig with her right hand and grabbing one of the wires with her left, she hauls herself fully on to the wing and slips under the outrigger wiring. Lucy then stands fully upright, pressed by the wind against the rig, to which she straps herself before giving a thumbs-up to the pilot.

We perform a few simple manoeuvres, then Lucy starts to spin round like a Catherine wheel. At first I think something has gone horribly wrong. Has a bolt come loose? Then I realize it's part of her astonishing display.

We land, then Danielle takes my place in the Stearman and I watch with amazement from the ground as the two girls go through their incredible routines, often flying so close they can shake hands or pass a handkerchief. It's astounding. Two pretty women strapped to trapezes on top of two beautiful aeroplanes, performing stunning and daring manoeuvres. What's not to like?

It's the contradiction that gets me. Two huge machines race towards each other with big loud engines. On top of them are elegant, elfin creatures looking like the figures you see on top of art deco ashtrays. And then as the two motorized beasts almost touch, the two figurines spin round like windmills. It's absolutely stunningly wonderful. And like Sir Ralph Richardson said when he was asked why he liked fireworks so much, it's because it's completely unnecessary. The utter point-lessness of it is its beauty.

Fifteen minutes later they're back on the ground. Lucy is wiping the splattered flies off her face and I want to know if Danielle still thinks she made the right career choice.

'Oh definitely. I can't wait to get back up there.'

While Vic and the pilots retire to the bar, Lucy, Danielle and I are given paper towels and squeezy bottles of Mr Muscle aeroplane cleaner. The job may look glamorous, but at the end of each day it's the wing-walkers' job to clean the flies off the planes.

'Right, guys,' I say to the lads' backs as they retreat to the bar. 'Thanks.' I turn to the girls. 'So where does it get dirty, then?'

Lucy shows me the front of the wings: 'The leading edges mainly.'

I start scrubbing. 'I suppose a clean plane is a happy plane.'

Although it takes phenomenal guts to do what Lucy and the other wing-walkers do, it's clear the airfield is a very traditional place. But it's also somewhere to relish English eccentricity and single-minded determination. A tenant in one of Vic's barns has recently built a Fokker triplane just for the hell of it.

'How the fuck did you do that?' I say, astounded and uncharacteristically profane.

'I got the plans, didn't I.' He's a former RAF mechanic.

I love that can-do attitude, which everyone thinks is very American but is actually typically British. 'Where did you get the wood?'

'From America, of course. You can't get the right grain of spruce here.'

'You're joking?' I say, as though I knew Wales was previously covered in 'the right spruce'.

'No.'

As for Vic and his wing-walkers, it's nice to see people who have fulfilled their dreams. 'Living the dream' is a phrase that's bandied about meaninglessly these days, particularly in those painful television talent contests. But here was a man who got up one day and decided to do what he really wanted to do, taking a huge risk to achieve something no one could possibly guarantee would work, but in which he had a deep belief. I would have loved to have been a fly in the room when Vic suggested it to his wife.

'I've had an idea, darling.'

'Yes?'

'I want to build a First World War airfield.'

'. . .'

Yet Vic did it and it bloody worked. You can't argue with that.

My next destination, Woodchester Mansion, is less than 25 miles away, but first I need to refill the Jag. By good luck and coincidence, an excellent garage lies on my route. The Green Garage at Bisley near Stroud is the first petrol station in the country to sell bio-fuels, such as bio-diesel, made by blending traditional fuel with renewable rapeseed oil. And with all the four-wheel drives careering about this part of the country, it's probably just as well.

Unfortunately, a classic car such as the XK150 cannot run on environmentally friendly fuel yet, but I still make the most of the eco-friendly products on offer as I refill it with dirty old unleaded, washing my windscreen and headlights with harvested and filtered rainwater, wiping my feet on the recycled-tyre doormat and buying some eco-friendly car-cleaning products and organic food in the shop, which has been built from sustainable and recycled materials.

North America and Scandinavia are far ahead of us when it comes to using bio-fuels and building sustainable buildings, but hopefully we'll catch up. I admire what the people at Bisley are doing immensely. Again, it's people going against the flow by committing to something they think is right and in which they believe. And as Confucius said, the only fish that go with the flow are the dead ones.

Filling the car up and checking its water and oil – just like my dad taught me – makes me think that as a society we have become like the cargo cultists, those tribal societies that don't understand manufactured goods and believe they've been created by divine spirits. Because we don't make things any more and mechanical knowledge is no longer part of our culture, many of us these days don't understand the workings of even the most rudimentary machines, such as cars or toasters or washing machines. Twenty years ago, any working man knew how to service his car, change the brake pads and repair it. But nowadays few have the knowledge and many cars are like televisions – impossible to service yourself. That leaves us dependent on a culture that does understand how to do it. Perhaps it's all a grand conspiracy to make manufacturers rich.

But what is certain is that in the last twenty years we have lost what used to be a kind of general knowledge about how things work, and that's not a healthy state of affairs.

By chance, my next destination provides a perfect illustration of some of the vital skills that we have lost since we stopped making things from scratch ourselves.

Hidden in a valley in the Cotswolds, Woodchester Mansion is one of the most outstanding buildings in Britain to have been abandoned while in mid-construction. That's what makes it so special. Looking for all the world as if its medieval builders went off for a tea break and never came back, this Grade I listed building has been saved from dereliction but remains unfinished, which means modern stonemasons can study centuries-old building techniques and architectural details, then put them to use preserving churches, cathedrals and stately homes.

In 1845, William Leigh, an Eton- and Oxford-educated self-titled 'gentleman of leisure', bought the 4,000-acre estate of Woodchester Park from the Earl of Ducie for £100,000. Depending on how you calculate it, that's anywhere between £7 million and £213 million in today's money.

A devout convert to Catholicism, Leigh gave some of the land to the Congregation of Passionists for the construction of a Roman Catholic church and a monastery for the Passionist brothers. He then employed Charles Francis Hansom, brother of the designer of the hansom cab, to build him a grand Gothic mansion. Hansom delegated the task to his twenty-one-year-old assistant Benjamin Bucknall, who had never before built a house but showed a passion for Gothic architecture. He researched medieval buildings and building techniques, becoming an authority on the subject. The result was a masterpiece, even in its incomplete form. As near as dammit, it's a perfect medieval building.

Weird gargoyles dominate the exterior, all cut from yellow oolitic limestone from local Cotswold quarries. Interior ceiling bosses feature stunning carvings of ferns, vines and mysterious figures such as the Green Man, a fertility figure from ancient British legend. Domestic buildings, such as a brewery (which could make 18 gallons of beer a day – just imagine that!), a bakery and a laundry, are cheek-by-jowl with the monastic, including one of the most beautiful private chapels in England. In its heyday more than a hundred people of varying trades worked on the site. The clock tower was completed by 1858 and by 1866 the main building had been roofed. But then Leigh died in 1873 and, criminally, his son, who didn't share his father's religious vocation, abandoned the construction work, partly because the estate was now too small to support the costs of finishing and maintaining the mansion.

Successive generations of the Leigh family continued to live in parts of the mansion until the early twentieth century, when it was sold to a trust that intended to convert the building into a psychiatric hospital. American and Canadian troops used it as a base during the Second World War, constructing pontoon bridges over the lake in preparation for the D-Day landings. In the 1950s it became a field study centre, but was only saved from ruin in 1987 when Stroud District Council bought the house and carried out emergency repairs, aided by English Heritage.

In 1992, the Woodchester Mansion Trust, a conservation group set up by local people, signed a ninety-nine-year lease on the property and its 23 acres of surrounding pasture. As well as repairing the house, the Trust also provides training in stonemasonry, conservation and architecture, and is the only on-site training in stonemasonry available anywhere in Britain. So far the Trust has restored the grand staircase, rainwater system, west range and clock tower. The intention is to make it watertight and weatherproof, but otherwise to leave it unfinished, which is what I think makes it so delightful.

Touring Woodchester is like walking through a three-dimensional textbook of medieval building techniques. This Marie Celeste of buildings is absolutely mindblowing. Some of the rooms have no floors, so in places you can look up from the ground floor through three storeys, seeing among other features three beautiful, pristine fireplaces, bell pushes for servants and enormously heavy roof beams. It all looks brand-new, as if it were built yesterday.

The quality of the stone-cutting and grouting is so high that I am open-mouthed as I explore. A lot of the fine craftsmanship was designed to be concealed once the floor was installed, but it was still of the highest quality. It is an astounding eye-opener. If you have got to my age you seldom walk into a room and exclaim with amazement at the way in which it's been built, but that happens here with every room I enter.

Restorers from all over the world travel to Woodchester Mansion to examine the building techniques used. Mark Hancock, a master stonemason, has chiselled dozens of buildings and shows me around the house. Pointing up at the ceiling in what was intended to be the library, he tells me how Bucknall's determination to stick to Gothic building techniques and principles overrode any other consideration.

'See what I was saying about it being structural Gothic? Look at that arch up there.'

Looking up, I'm flabbergasted at the perfection of the detail. Even parts of the original scaffolding are still in place.

'That detail does nothing but hold the roof up. There are several ways you could have done that, but they chose the most expensive and most impractical.'

Years ago, a stonemason's job was highly sought after, but nowadays Mark is struggling to find apprentices. It's hard work and many of the young people he trains abandon the trade as soon as they finish the apprenticeship. Most of Mark's courses are attended by older people who have spent their working lives in offices and want an escape. I could weep over the skills being lost with each successive generation.

Mark has been working on the Cotswold stone at Woodchester for twenty years and wants me to have a go at carving a new block for one of the crumbling walls. When I was at art school about forty years ago – yes, it really was that far in the past – I made a lot of very pretentious rubbish out of any material known to man. I made things out of silver, wood, paint, canvas and plastics, but I never got the chance to make anything out of stone. Never something that would last for ever. My wife is a sculptor, so I have tried cutting stone before, but I've always found it incredibly difficult. If you hold the chisel too tight, it jars every time you hit it and you can pick up an injury called white finger. If you hold it too loosely, it flies all over the place and your accuracy goes down the pan. And if you don't hit at exactly the right angle, you can split the stone.

Mark explains that they are no longer allowed to use stone from the quarry that originally supplied the mansion, as the Department for Environment, Food and Rural Affairs has designated that quarry a Site of Special Scientific Interest. Instead the stone comes from a quarry near Bath that provides the next closest geological match. It's an oolitic limestone (its structure is a matrix of tiny balls), fairly soft and non-abrasive.

'First of all we need the saw,' Mark points into a corner, 'which is just over there.'

'Oh blimey! You mean this little thing?' It's a 4-foot-long blade with teeth like a pantomime crocodile.

Mark laughs. 'Yeah, that's the thing.'

'Do you cut it just like wood?'

'Just keep it flat and sitting in that little groove.' He shows me a thin line he has etched into the surface of the stone, which is about 6 inches thick. 'Then move it gently backwards and forwards.'

I start to saw. 'And a mere four years later . . .'

'It'll go quite quickly.'

He's right. The stone is softer than I expected – he describes it as being like a digestive biscuit – and I'm through the block in about a minute. Then it's time to give this smooth block of stone some distressing to make it fit in with the stones used in the mansion's walls. Mark gives me a chisel and a mallet with a neoprene head to knock a 5-millimetre channel around the edge of the stone, a technique that stonemasons call 'working a draft'. This thin edge protects the edge of the stone. That done, he hands me a claw tool – a chisel with a row of fine teeth on its cutting edge – to remove 5 millimetres of the stone from the rest of the top surface. Then I pick up a 2-inch chisel to even the surface, followed by a double-headed axe to put in a texture that matches the rest of the stones used on the house. Finally I carve a mason's mark into the stone with a half-inch chisel and a mallet. In this age of power tools, it's very satisfying and a real privilege to use traditional tools and methods to hew a block for such a posh building and then to put my signature on it.

Proudly carrying the stone I've cut and marked outside, I hope my humble contribution will be the centrepiece of the grand entrance. But no. Mark insists it has to go round the side, where it will only be seen by the odd squirrel.

None the less, I admire my creation. 'Well, that was very pleasing.'

'We may not be able to live for ever, but our work will.' Mark is being very generous.

'Or this time next week someone will say: "Who did that dreadful bit of work?" And I will cringe.'

'It's the closest you're going to get to immortality.'

From Woodchester Mansion, I cut across country, then head north-east, arriving 40 miles later in Stow-on-the-Wold, a breathtakingly pretty village that looks like a Hollywood interpretation of the Cotswolds. Nothing is out of place. But the surprise is that it's entirely authentic, if maybe a little too lovingly kept. Partly that's because, unlike the builders of today, who will happily use the cheapest materials they can find, Cotswold villages like Stow were made from local materials, in this case limestone. Consequently, the buildings look as if they rose out of the ground and always belonged there. Simple, really, but it makes a big difference. At the heart of the village is the Royalist Inn. According to the *Guinness Book of Records*, this is the oldest inn in the country. Built in AD 987 by Aethelmar, Duke of Cornwall, the building is thought to have been used originally as a hospice and as somewhere to overnight. With its easy access to ports and cities, Stow was a popular market town at this time, particularly for the sale of sheep, and it attracted many traders, who would use the inn for food, drink and shelter during markets, fairs, saints' days and pagan festivals.

Where the bar is now situated, a pit used to be the venue for cockfighting, bear-baiting and other blood sports on which the crowd of traders and locals would bet. Such sports were particularly popular in Tudor times, but the traditions continued for many centuries.

As the highest town in the Cotswolds, 800 feet above sea level, Stow was tactically important during the Civil War. On 21 March 1646, a Royalist army commanded by Sir Jacob Astley was attempting to join up with King Charles at Oxford when it was met at Stow by a Parliamentary force under Colonel Brereton. The fighting was fierce and deadly. The Royalists were defeated and more than a thousand men were imprisoned within St Edward's Church. The slaughter was apparently so great that ducks were able to bathe in the pools of blood that formed on the street leading away from the market square, giving rise to the street's name: Digbeth, or Duck's Bath. The final skirmish between the Royalists and Parliamentarians is said to have taken place on the street outside the inn.

From Stow-on-the-Wold my route takes me along the Cotswold Ridge past Broadway Tower, an eighteenth-century Gothic folly built for the Earl of Coventry. From the top of its ramparts it is possible to see as far as the Welsh mountains. With a view across thirteen counties, if I climbed it now I would be able to see right to the Vale of Evesham, where my next destination awaits me.

According to the speedometer, I've done a few hundred miles since I left London and yet I'm hardly any further north than when I set off. Going off the beaten track is leading me along a very meandering road and it's taking a lot of time.

But so what?

I've already been to places and seen things that I never knew existed. I'm having a blast.

Chapter Three

From Broadway Tower, the B4632 takes me further into Worcestershire until I come to the B4035, where I take a left turn. I'm heading for the tiny village of Bretforton to meet a man called Billy Byrd. Big, bearded and with a lovely thick Worcestershire accent, Billy is a real character who has lived all his life in Bretforton (and his family has been here for seven hundred years). Like dozens of generations of his forebears, he has grown asparagus for several decades.

I love asparagus and I've a bit of history with this wonderful vegetable. I first fell in love with it in 1984 while making a movie called *Chinese Boxes* in West Berlin. Before the fall of the Berlin Wall, land was extremely scarce in West Berlin and asparagus was one of the very few vegetables grown there. Everything else was flown in.

The Berliners force their asparagus, covering it in soil as it grows inside plastic tubes. As well as turning the asparagus white, this results in a sweeter, more tender taste. These *Spargel*, as they call them, are as thick as a good sausage or a Cohiba cigar and absolutely to die for. In Germany in May they have what they call the *Spargel* season and just about everything on a restaurant's menu comes '*mit Spargel*'. But best of all, I found, was *Spargel* on its own. A thick bunch about 4 inches across would come tied in a red ribbon. I'd untie it, watch the glorious pale shoots tumble down, then dribble them with hollandaise sauce and dust them with some freshly ground black pepper. Eaten with bread and butter, they were heaven.

So it was with considerable expectation that I arrived at Billy's farm. Blessed with perfect soil, the Vale of Evesham has a reputation as the best place in the world to grow asparagus, or 'spara-grass' as the locals call it. Thousands of years of erosion of the Cotswold stone valley floor has created a thick carpet of sandy loam ideal for asparagus, and the mild, wet climate helps it grow slowly, which gives it more flavour.

Bill is a lovely man with an easy grin, who talks about slugs 'buggering up' his crop of 'grass buds'. When I ask him if he means asparagus spears, he says farmers call it grass and 'posh people calls 'em spears and I ain't posh'.

Dressed in Wellington boots, jeans and a thick jumper, and walking along long beds of asparagus in one of his fields, Bill tells me why asparagus costs so much in shops and restaurants. The shoots grow from a crown that's planted several inches beneath the ground. Every day during the short, intensive asparagus season – which lasts only seven weeks, from St George's Day (23 April) to 21 June – a new shoot will start growing from the crown. If you let it grow to its full extent, the fern-like shoot turns into a flower with a head full of seeds.

'You can tell the ones that are going to be good breeders. Them you don't pick.' Bill points at a shoot. 'The others you got to pick before them gets too big.'

Suddenly the penny drops and I can see why asparagus is so expensive. It's simple. With the shoots growing up to 6 inches overnight, someone's got to walk along every asparagus bed in every field every day and pick them. It's astonishingly labour-intensive and if you miss a day, you'll lose some of the shoots because they get too woody. Because it's such hard work, many of the local farmers have moved on to easier crops, such as rapeseed, which produces two harvests a year, each of which can be brought in by machine in a single day.

Bill shows me his asparagus-cutting tool. It looks like a screwdriver. 'You sharpens him every so often,' Bill says, pointing at the half-inch blade on the tip. 'And then you puts a groove in there, usually four grooves, but three if you're thrifty.'

The grooves put a serrated edge on to the blade to help cut the asparagus, but with every shoot having to be cut by hand, I ask if there's any other tool that might speed up the toil.

'Just the blade,' says Bill. 'And you'd want no beer when you were doing this or you'd miss it all the while.'

Slipping the tip of the blade about 2 inches deep into the soil, Bill makes two quick stabbing movements and lifts the shoot. When I have a go, I realize how easy Bill's experience makes it look. It's not easy to get a clean cut first time and I tear at the asparagus. The base of my shoot is ragged and trails the thick soil, which is so rich that Bill never needs to fertilize it.

Tomorrow there's likely to be another shoot close to where I just removed my ragged-ended effort. Crowns usually last eight to ten years – 'then you knock it on the head and plant a new 'un,' says Bill – but some are forty years old.

Bill takes home the thinnest spears, called sprues, for cooking. Everything else (medium-thick is called best and the thickest of all is called special) is sold. Any really superior spears are allowed to go to seed to provide Bill with a continuing supply of crowns.

As for the harvested crop, a hundred years ago it would have been taken by horse and dray to the nearest station a couple of miles away at Badsey. Although served by the Oxford, Worcester and Wolverhampton railway, satirized as the Old Worse and Worse due to its construction problems and unreliability, the asparagus would have been on the restaurant tables of London by lunchtime the next day. In those days, railways provided the only reliable links between rural areas such as the Vale of Evesham and the metropolitan conurbations. But the advent of the car and the building of fast roads, and eventually motorways, put paid to local railways and, along with them, fast and cheap access to distant customers. Now Bill sells his asparagus only at his farm shop, the local train station having closed in the 1960s.

It seems ironic to me that for many people in Britain it's easier to buy Peruvian asparagus than the home-grown variety. It's a shame, because English asparagus is something really special, something we ought to cherish. And what's special about the English asparagus season is that it is just that: a season. It is a time of the year when the asparagus ripens and becomes absolutely delicious. Of course you can eat the stuff that's flown in from Peru, 6,500 miles away, any time of the year. But it doesn't taste like asparagus to me. And because it's not seasonal, it doesn't seem such a treat. And as for your carbon footprint? Don't ask . . .

Although worried that I'll trigger a horrible fit in Bill by mentioning Peruvian asparagus, I want to know what he thinks of the foreign interlopers. He is remarkably generous. 'As long as we ain't in the season, it doesn't matter.'

'Really?'

'It's a good thing they do it. Then when someone tastes the proper stuff, they know what it's about. They got to judge it with summat.'

'That's good thinking.'

I take a bite of the bud. It's absolutely delicious. 'Is it okay to eat it raw like this?'

'Oh yes. People slice them into salads. But they've more flavour when they're cooked.'

'Have you got any tips about cooking it?'

'No. The wife does that. A sprig of mint and a pinch of salt, boil it and you can add your own cack afterwards.' Bill likes his 'cack' – a dab of salad cream on the side – but I'm a hollandaise-on-top kinda guy.

'Isn't it supposed to be an aphrodisiac?' I say.

'Well I ain't done too bad on it.' Bill laughs.

'Seventeen kids?'

'Nooo. Three's enough.'

And are any of Bill's three children going to take over the farm when he retires?

'No.'

'But didn't you learn everything you know from your father?'

'Oh yes. Him don't ever talk to you. It's just things you pick up bein' with him.'

'So what's going to happen when you retire?'

'There won't be any farming around here. It'll be the end of it.'

'That's a shame.'

'That's the way. In all the funerals and the weddings away from here, they all been from market gardening.' The grass-growers are dying out and their children are marrying away from the Vale.

'I don't understand that. We've all got to eat.'

'But when you can import stuff, growing it yourself is stupid. We've got the ground to do it and the labour – them Poles, they're very good workers – but we can import it cheaper.'

To test for myself whether the Peruvian asparagus can rival our homegrown buds, I leave Billy and head for the Fleece Inn at Bretforton. Built in 1400, the inn is steeped in history. The current landlord, Nigel Smith, who greets me dressed in collarless shirt and baggy shorts, rents the pub from the National Trust, to whom it was bequeathed in 1977 by a woman whose family had owned it since it was built. Watching this very down-to-earth man working in his pub, greeting every customer and flirting with the barmaids, I can see he's a contented soul.

During the season, Nigel serves up to fifty boxes of asparagus a day, most of it steamed in his pub kitchen in a large stainless-steel cabinet the size of an American refrigerator. Until I visited the Fleece I didn't realize quite how central a role asparagus plays in these parts. Even the local cider-drinkers swear by it, saying it clears out your kidneys when you're hungover, setting you up nicely for the next cider session.

'I'm just looking at your menu. It's asparagus with butter, local asparagus with quail egg salad – there's asparagus with every single thing.'

'Absolutely.'

'That's fantastic.'

'Well it is asparagus season, so it's got to be done.'

There's no escaping the stuff. It's even in the ice cream.

At the end of May, the peak of the season, Nigel's pub hosts an asparagus festival in collaboration with the British Asparagus Association and the local district council, which is keen to promote the recently renewed culinary and health-related interest in the vegetable. Ten or fifteen years ago, asparagus growing was on the wane, but now the number of local acres devoted to its cultivation is growing every year. The highlight of the festival is an auction of prize buds in which the price paid for 'a hundred' (which, perversely, is 120 asparagus stems) usually tops £500.

Out of season, Nigel serves imported asparagus, a bundle of which he has provided so that I can compare it to the handful of buds I've picked in Billy Byrd's field.

With two dishes in front of me, both containing asparagus dribbled with hollandaise sauce, I feel ideally qualified to compare and contrast. It goes without saying that Billy's buds are outstanding. I take a bite of a stem with a piece of brown bread and butter. It's delicious. If this was the last thing I ever ate, I would die a happy man. Although how many firing squads could rustle up a decent hollandaise, I wonder?

Now on to the Peruvian asparagus. Nigel and I agree it's not bad. It does taste of asparagus, but it's not as sweet and full-flavoured as the English competition. It has a slightly bitter aftertaste and I think it isn't a patch on the homegrown.

'Whichever one you eat,' I say, 'it's quite hard to eat it elegantly, isn't it.'

'Yes,' says Nigel. 'But hey, who cares?'

I ask him if there's any truth in the suggestion, as first noted in the eighteenth century by a physician to the French Royal Family, that asparagus 'eaten to excess causes filthy and disagreeable smell in the urine'.

'Oh yes,' he says.

'During the asparagus season do you have to turn up the extractor fan in the toilet?'

'We have fans with two settings: normal and asparagus season. It is a pretty awesome smell. But making all that interesting aroma must be doing you some good.'

Asparagus is packed with vitamins A, C and B6, as well as glutathione (a powerful antioxidant), potassium and thiamine, and it's rich in fibre. It's also low in fat, cholesterol and sodium, making it extremely healthy. But unfortunately it's also packed with asparagusic acid (or alpha-aminodimethyl-gamma-butyrothetin as we call it down the lab), which breaks down during digestion into compounds from the same sulphur group that makes skunks smell. No wonder the stink can be so bad. (Interestingly, asparagusic acid kills parasitic nematodes and so protects the asparagus plant against them; it's just unfortunate that it has less pleasant side effects.)

However, not all of us are affected. And no one knows quite why. In some people, just a few buds are enough for the un-desired effect. Other people need to eat a kilogram or more, while some people never seem to suffer from it. Scientists (and I'm glad I wasn't among them) have conducted several studies but remain divided on why people have different responses to asparagus. One camp thinks only about half the population have the gene enabling them to break down asparagusic acid into its smellier components. Others think everyone digests asparagus the same way, but only about half of us have a gene that enables us to smell the skunk-like stink. Interestingly, nine out of ten Israelis and three-quarters of Chinese people cannot smell it.

The fascinating thing about the asparagus-urine conundrum is that it wasn't until the eighteenth century that anyone noticed it produced stinky pee, which coincidentally was when sulphur-rich fertilizers were introduced to improve the flavour and yield of asparagus, onions and garlic. Maybe there's a link?

Leaving Bretforton, these scientific questions remain un-answered as I retrace my route to where the B4032 meets the B4632 and turn left. A few miles further and I'm at Shakespeare County Raceway, where thousands of enthusiasts have converged on a converted aircraft runway that lays claim to being the very first drag racing strip in Britain.

Drag racing in the UK started in 1958, when Stratford folk who preferred changing gear to *King Lear* (sorry, couldn't resist that!) took over Long Marston Airfield, a Second World War RAF base. With rusting relics of aircraft nearby, the speed enthusiasts used the runway for two-lane sprints before drag racing officially found its way to England in 1963. Long Marston echoed to the sounds of exotic pre-war Bentleys and Ferrari sports cars, as well as Norton and BSA race bikes, as they hurled themselves in pairs down a straight quarter of a mile sprint track. Ever since then, petrolheads have been racing their cars against the clock at Long Marston.

The day that I turn up is billed as a 'run what you brung' event. It's a great idea. Your vehicle doesn't have to be dragster or competitive. You could bring the family car and run it up the strip. The timings don't go towards any kind of championship. It's just a bit of fun and that's what is charming about it.

Walking through the four rows of participants preparing and tuning their cars, I spot sons revving engines while their dads adjust the chain, an old guy who has brought his car every year for thirty-two years to try to beat his best time and, of course, a handful of wacky machines with huge rear wheels, gleaming chromed engines and custom paint jobs. Few of the participants are motor engineers. They're all amateurs indulging in their great passion. Meanwhile mothers are walking around pushing baby buggies between the caravans and tents, and kids wearing ear protectors are running between the cars, eating burgers from family barbecues and playing games. It's like a family day at the beach with roaring engines as a backdrop, and it's totally unlike most motorsport events, which have become very corporate. There are no huge adverts for mobile phone networks and no shifty-looking shiny-blue-suited men who have no interest in cars, only in corporate networking. These are the hardcore boys in '65 Cortinas, '57 Chevys and Pontiac Firebirds with stonking engines they've spent hours labouring over in a wee garage somewhere. It's sweet, charming and good-natured, with people lending each other tools and winding each other up – 'Oh he's brought that piece of shit. He'll never get it beyond the quarter mile' – and I think it's delightful.

Best of all, no one's paying any attention to me. I get no demands for autographs and no mobile phones are stuck in my face to take a photograph. I know it's because they know that, like them, I'm having fun and they don't want to interrupt it. The only question I get is someone asking me if I'm enjoying myself.

'Oh yes. You bet I am. What've you got there?'

'It's a motorbike. I've put a fifteen hundred c.c. engine on it.'

'Bet that goes.'

'Yup. You could say that.'

Looking round, I notice there's a real spread of ages. There are just as many youngsters with hot hatches as middle-aged men with customized cars from the 1950s to 1970s. There's even a junior dragster class for eleven- to sixteen-year-olds. Watching a young lad who's brought a Morris 1000 with a V8 engine crammed into it doing wheelies up the drag strip, I can't help thinking: good for you. He's not standing around street corners, nicking someone's mobile phone. He's doing something with his life in a wonderfully amateur (in the best sense of being done entirely not for gain but for the joy of it and without any professional training), carefree way. It's great.

Closer to the quarter-mile track on which the cars are doing their runs, a delicious smell of hot Castrol and ethanol hangs in the air. When they sprint down the strip, they're not racing against each other for bragging rights as much as competing against themselves because they're all trying to beat their own best times.

I meet an old boy called Gerald, an engineer of seventy-six who worked for Lucas engineering and, unable to kick the habit, has come to Shakespeare County Raceway every year since 1961. He's got a lovely old Berkeley sports car, unfortunately with a problem that makes his gearbox sound like a biscuit tin full of marbles. Firing up the glorious-sounding engine for me, he tells me the original had a two-stroke motorcycle engine that drove the front wheels. Gerald has built a new chassis and installed an MG Sprite engine that drives the rear wheels and speeds the car up the track at up to 120 m.p.h. And while Gerald's doing the ton on the strip, his wife Joan is in the pits, getting the tea on.

Moving on, I meet a racer called Roy, a Brummie who's preparing a couple of three-year-old lime-green dragsters under the Supercharged Outlaws banner with which he's won several championship races. With its emphasis on going very fast for a very short straight-line distance, drag racing has never particularly interested me, but I've always been fascinated by how they squeeze so much power out of the engines.

'It's the wife's car, actually.' Roy points at the vehicle he's working on. 'We've got two cars in the family – both labours of love – and the wife will be driving this one eventually.'

I'd wager that the car (if that's what you can call it) looks completely unlike any other wife's car in the country. The chassis is home-built. The V8 engine is from a 1972 Jensen Interceptor and the back wheels are 2-foot-high lumps of soft rubber pumped to such a low pressure for extra grip that you can press dimples in them with your thumb.

Although a weekend at the circuit costs Roy a relatively paltry £300 in wages for his assistants, food and travel, drag racing can be a very expensive business. Many of the engines in dragsters are on the edge of their capabilities and prone to exploding.

'The last time I took my car out it cost me eight thousand pounds,' he says. 'The flywheel came off the end of the crank-shaft and trashed the gearbox. It hurts when you've got a day job and you do this in your spare time with your own money.'

Like many dragsters, Roy's cars have only one meter for the driver (a rev counter) and a warning light that comes on when the engine reaches 5,500 r.p.m. and he has to change gear.

'You must have reactions like a ferret because it's happening so quickly?'

'It calms down after the second gear.'

'Does it?'

'In the first gear I'm pulling nigh on ninety miles per hour. I reach a hundred and forty-seven miles an hour in five seconds . . .'

'Jesus.'

'. . . and nigh on a hundred and ninety miles an hour in seven seconds. In the world of drag racing that's quite slow.'

'Is it?'

'The big corporate sponsored vehicles are doing three hundred and thirty miles an hour in four and a half seconds.'

These are mindblowing figures. So why does he do it?

'It's a childhood dream. It's a showman's sport and an adrenalin buzz. You're peddling your wares to the punters out there.'

'It's the cock strutting his stuff, isn't it?'

'Basically. But I like the technical side of it as well.'

'It must be fantastic to drive a car yourself.'

'It grabs your attention, that's for sure, when you're sitting in the car for the first time.'

I laugh. 'You're thinking: did I remember to . . . Did we remember to tighten . . .'

'Definitely. All that goes through your mind.'

It's all a bit of fun to see how fast your little runabout can go, but I was here to see something a lot slower and a lot bigger – a 14-ton fire engine that can pull record-breaking wheelies. By skilful control of power, acceleration, brakes and clutch, Steve Murty can drive a bright red fire tender with its front wheels 12 feet in the air for record-breaking distances.

The front half is a Leyland-built former army truck, of which a hundred were sent out to the Falklands to rebuild the infrastructure after the war in the 1980s. It's strong enough to tow three trailers and was used in Australia to tug road trains across deserts. The rear comes from a fire truck that was in an accident. In this 14-litre turbo-charged 600bhp Cummins diesel-engined monster, Steve is attempting to break the Guinness world record of 547 metres for a truck wheelie.

Flames billowing out of two chromed exhaust pipes behind

the driver's cab, the massive truck thunders up the strip, making it look so easy that I wonder if Steve ever drives it with the front wheels on the ground. For the last couple of hundred metres, the back of the tender scrapes the ground, leaving two trails of sparks along the road as Steve continues well past the 600-metre markers with the bonnet in the air. At 651 metres he drops the front of the engine on to the track, turns the fire truck round and does it again. Clearly a total pro.

Being a bit of a smarty pants, I'd thought it was impossible to make a truck wheelie. Either the axle would snap or the wheels would spin round. But Steve can clearly do it. Afterwards I ask him how.

'It's all an engineering trick. Everyone thinks it's a massive amount of weight in the back, but the secret is a custom-made gearbox.'

For many years Steve had a specialist car with which he set a 1-kilometre wheelie record. Eventually his reputation reached British Leyland, who asked him if he could help them make a wheelie truck. He said it was a simple equation: if you have lots of money and lots of time, anything is possible. Leyland had only six weeks, but fortunately they were in a quiet period between big orders for the military. They also had almost unlimited facilities and they were looking for a challenge that would keep their workforce from doing awful things to apprentices. Leyland turned over its entire workforce, from office staff to engineers and electricians, to the project. And now I was standing beside the fruit of that impressive effort, although one with a slightly depressing postscript. After all, if Leyland could do all that in just six weeks, why did the company go down the pan? But that was a bigger, more complicated political story.

'Here's the big question,' I say to Steve. 'Do you think I could get this truck to wheelie?'

He looks sceptical. 'My eldest boy took several weeks to learn and he was born with this vehicle in his blood.'

The secret, Steve says, is a subtle balance of brakes and power. With the brakes on and the engine revving, the natural physical response of the truck is to try to spin backwards round its rear axle. Provided I can harness that power, I'll be able to lift the front off the ground.

'It's impossible for me to explain,' says Steve. 'You've got to feel it through your bottom.' (This reminded me of a couple of incidents in my early acting career. Don't ask!)

'Is it worth a couple of pints?'

'There's a lot of wagers on this already and most of it is on you not doing it.'

With a reputation as a mechanical man, I'm honour-bound to accept the challenge.

Sitting beside me in the cab, Steve lets me take the fire truck for a spin round the airfield so that I can get a feel for it. She's nippy and manoeuvrable for a big girl. Then the moment arrives. Oh come on, I want to say, how hard can it be to get a 16-ton truck on to two wheels? Well, a bit harder than I'd first thought.

'Put your left foot on the brake, and then just give it some accelerator, just as a blip,' says Steve.

I try several times, but each time the truck moves off with all four wheels firmly attached to the ground. Then I manage to lift the bonnet slightly into the air, although the front wheels are still firmly on the ground.

'That's it, that's it,' shouts Steve. It seems I'm on to something. 'Keep it going, let your brake off, a little bit, a little bit.'

The skill, I find, involves revving the engine to build up power, then bouncing the front at the correct rhythm so that each bounce is progressively higher until eventually the bonnet lifts into the air.

'Yo-oh!' I can't help exclaiming like a child as I eventually raise the bonnet into the air and thunder down the tarmac. 'Oh my God.'

I jam on the brakes, then have another go. This time the front rises even higher. It's unbelievably exciting. My heart is racing. Beside me in the cab, Steve is wearing a big grin. 'Gets you going, doesn't it?'

'Phwoar. Time for my tablets. What a fantastic experience.'

'Again?'

'Yeah. Let's do it again. Come on – let's do it again!' This time I lift the front much quicker than before. 'Yo-oh! You'd think fire trucks were exciting enough already, wouldn't you? That's just amazing.'

I want one. But maybe it's a bit big for the B-roads and I've still got a long way to go before Glasgow.

'Can you do it again, Robbie?' shouts the cameraman.

Would you believe it? 'No! I'm going to drive around a bit and calm myself down.'

Back on the B-roads, I pass through Leamington Spa – I'm moving slightly further north, although still relatively slowly – and come to a stop in some pristine grassland between Leamington and Rugby. This is the unlikely home of a very unlikely pastime.

We Brits have a long tradition of embracing new activities and the countryside through which I'm driving has always been very much associated with sport. Warwickshire has one of the oldest cricket clubs in the world and the first lawn tennis club was set up here in 1872. Add to that the game of rugby, which is said to have been invented at Rugby school (although historians are in some disagreement about that), and it seems appropriate that I'm about to meet someone who's furthering the cause of a new and slightly insane sport.

My suspicions are first aroused when I'm presented with an outfit that looks quite familiar – think mid-seventies Tarbuck, or middle-aged white man dressed like a young black pimp – though the sport that awaits me is something totally new and unexpected.

Removing my baseball cap I sit down in my tank top and smart casuals beside Derek Robbins, the man behind an activity that bills itself as 'the best sport you've never heard of'.

So what is it?

Well, it's golf, Jim, but not as Tarby would know it. No bunkers, no holes, no balls. And not a Pringle sweater in sight. That's because it's disc golf, where players throw Frisbees from the tee into specially designed baskets in as few shots as possible. And if St Andrews is the home of traditional golf, then the home of British disc golf is here: Quarry Park, created by Derek, by day an IT consultant at nearby Warwick University, by night and at weekends a sporting hero. Now in his late forties and still single, Derek has dedicated his life, and all his savings, to this bizarre sport.

Disc golf began in the 1970s in America – unsurprising, as they'd make a competition out of putting ketchup on your chips – but for Derek it began at the tender age of seventeen when he became the UK Overall Frisbee Champion. The youngest person to have won at that time, his prize was to be sent on a trip to America to compete for the UK. He discovered disc golf during that trip and was immediately hooked.

'After that it became my ambition to build my own course.'

Derek was another man with a dream in his eye, just like Vic Norman at RFC Rendcomb. His parents tried to sow the seeds of doubt, but Derek was determined.

The first disc golf course in Britain was built in 1981 (there's even a course on the Isle of Mull), but Derek wanted one of his own. It took him ten years to save enough money for a 15-acre site, which even includes a stretch of the river Avon.

'It was just grazing land with no trees. I bought it at auction and planted about eighteen hundred trees. I planted them specifically to test certain types of shot and create out-of-bounds areas. The trees are the equivalent of bunkers.'

Now Derek's sights are set on building a proper clubhouse to replace the slightly shabby-looking tin-roofed lean-to shed full of empty wine bottles that's now in use, often by university disc golf clubs who come to meet Derek, undisputed hero of British disc golfers. Founder of the British Disc Golf Association, he's currently ranked number one in Britain and the man all two thousand active British players want to beat.

Like them, I want to have a go, but first I need a grounding in the rudiments of the sport. Where golf has a bag full of clubs – driver, putters, sand wedges and so on – disc golfers have a bag full of discs.

'These sharp-edged discs are drivers.' Derek holds up some very thin, very rigid and very hard Frisbees. They're much stiffer than the Frisbees for sale at petrol stations. 'They're very fast but they're not very stable, so to get them to go a long way is not very easy.'

Derek picks up a thicker disc. 'The putters have a rounder

edge. They don't fly quite as fast but they fly a lot straighter.'

It sounds brilliant to me. Well, brilliant if you're very good at it. And what attracts me to the sport as I look out over the course is that everyone is walking around in what I would call skater-boy outfits. There are none of the silly dress codes of conventional golf clubs.

Before I get to have a go, Derek explains the rules, which are mercifully short and simple. Like golf, the course usually has eighteen holes and each player begins by throwing from the tee. Instead of a hole, there's a target consisting of a pole with a chain basket affair on the top. The total score for a course is determined by totalling the number of throws taken to reach each of the chained-basket targets. And that's about it.

Now for the technique. If you're good you can make the disc bend around corners. Derek can reach such distant positions that it's quite scary. He points his finger at a far-off target.

'There are a couple of trees there with a basket just behind them.'

'But that's miles away.' From where I'm standing, the trees are about 80 metres away and the basket is almost hidden behind them.

'Yeah, but it might just be in range. We'll see.'

'Right . . .' I'm not convinced that Derek isn't overstating his skills.

'For this we'll take a disc that turns quite strongly left, so we'll send it out to the right and have it turn round to the left.'

If he gets it right, the disc should skim past the trees, then veer towards the target. He throws it with considerable abandon and I watch as it soars away, then veers left precisely as he promised.

'I've left myself with a little putt.'

'That's just fantastic. I don't believe it.' Feeling like a five-year-old, I pester Derek to do it again. His second attempt is just as good. 'That's extraordinary. I'm completely flabbergasted. I didn't know humans could do that kind of thing.'

To me, it seems Derek has some remarkable, God-given gift.

'What's your best ever shot?'

'I once got a hole in one from a hundred and eighteen metres. It was a complete fluke. The disc missed the basket, hit a fir tree, bounced back and went into the basket.'

'Perfect. The stuff of legend.'

Now it's my turn.

'You want to reach back as if you're pulling a cord to start an outboard motor,' says Derek, 'but follow through with your arm all the way to your other side. Keep the disc level with the ground as you release it.'

I give it a wee shotty.

'Nice. That looks good.' Derek seems impressed.

I'm deeply pleased with myself. I've never thrown a Frisbee so far, but then I've never thrown a proper disc like this one and I've never received instruction from such an expert. 'It wobbled a bit. Why was that?'

'Maybe it didn't come out of your hand quite cleanly.' Derek shows me the ideal throwing motion again. I wind up my body, then unleash the disc with all the force I can muster. It slams into the ground a few inches from where Derek is standing. He grins nervously, then giggles as I look sheepish.

'Oh blimey! I think I might have released that just a little too late . . .'

'I'm just glad I stepped back before you threw it.'

'You've still got two arms, haven't you?'

Preparing for my next attempt, I notice Derek stepping back and taking cover. No chances this time.

After some more practice, Derek introduces me to Sharon, who met her fiancé playing disc golf, and Frank, a local player. They happen to be on the course today and have been enlisted as our opponents in a foursome. Introductions made, Derek leads off the tee, selecting the Comet, his signature disc, for a par 2, 100-yard shot. Shazza takes her turn, then I'm up on the tee, selecting a disc that Derek calls the Beast. Much to my surprise, I don't disgrace myself.

To cut a long story short, I don't make a total arse of myself. With balletic grace, Sharon, Derek and Frank achieve par 2s. I take five shots. Not bad, I think, for a beginner and I've really enjoyed it. It's a delightful game that I could even see myself playing with my son. It's an excellent way to spend a few hours.

But what's intriguing about disc golf is that, although it was invented in California – probably by a bunch of stoners who thought it was cool and anti-establishment – and although the players all dress like they've just come from the skate park, it hasn't taken long for them to adopt that very male characteristic of 'establishing some rules'. Already there are regulations about which discs you can use on which types of shot, and how you're meant to behave on the course. Men are obsessed with establishing rules and I bet it won't take long for a dress code to emerge. For the moment, you can play it in T-shirt, shorts and a pair of crocs, but I wonder if you'll soon have to wear sensible slacks and spike-soled shoes?

I turned up at the course cynically wondering if there was an element of mental illness associated with disc golf. And now that I am leaving, my shallow preconceptions have been completely reversed. It's a lovely place and a delightful way to spend time. And in Derek I've met another man who has a passion for something, someone who puts his money where his mouth is and gets on with it. I admire people like him. And he's enabled a lot of other people to have fun. That's a very fine and noble thing.

Chapter Four

From Derek Robbins's disc golf course I drive east towards Banbury and Milton Kenyes. Surrounded by motorways and A-roads – these parts are bordered by the M1 and M40 and bisected by the A5 – I have to take a bewildering succession of B-roads to reach my next destination. Soon I'm passing signposts with intriguing names such as Deanshanger and Potterspury, then I take a right turn and drive into a busy, picturesque market town with a high street of attractive red-brick Georgian buildings.

This is Stony Stratford, which bills itself as 'the jewel of Milton Keynes' – a description that anyone who's seen Milton Keynes will know doesn't do justice to Stony Stratford. Whereas Milton Keynes is – how shall I put it? – an acquired taste and didn't formally exist until 1967, when the government decided to create a new town in Buckinghamshire, the area around Stony Stratford is beautiful and, having been in use since prehistoric times, is steeped in history.

Stratford means 'ford on a Roman road' and refers to the crossing of the river Ouse by Iter II, a Roman road (built along a Celtic track and later called Watling Street by the Anglo-Saxons) that led from Dover, via London and St Albans, through Stony Stratford and on, via Wroxeter in Shropshire, to Hadrian's Wall. Stony is thought to refer to stones on the bed of the ford, differentiating Stony Stratford from nearby Fenny Stratford.

That gives some indication of its beginnings, and it has been a significant place for most of its history. An important market town by the twelfth century, by the stagecoach era Stony Stratford had become a major resting place for coaches such as the Telegraph, which ran from London to Manchester, and the Irish Post, which started in London and crossed the bandit-infested wilds of North Wales to Holyhead.

I've come to Stony Stratford to investigate two coaching inns that served the stagecoaches and whose large, hand-painted signs dominate the High Street. One proudly proclaims itself 'The Famous Cock Hotel' (no sniggering, please). A hundred yards further down, an equally prominent sign advertises 'The InnFamous Bull' (oh go on, snigger then). And inside one of them a man is waiting to tell me the intriguing story that links these two hostelries.

Shafts of sunlight cut through the semi-darkness as I enter an oak-beamed bar. Sitting in the corner, a ponytailed stubble-chinned character is waiting for me, nursing a large brandy. In his camel coat, George Webley looks like an East End car dealer or bookmaker and, in his Cockney twang, he rabbits like one too. I get stuck in to the cup of tea he's got for me and then we're down to business. I want to know what's so special about this place.

'So, we're in the Cock, as only seems appropriate.'
'Exactly.'
'And the Bull is down the road.'
'Two doors down.'

'And we all know the expression "a cock and bull story" . . .'

'Well, this is where it originated.'

'It really is?'

'Oh yeah, without a doubt.'

It's a fascinating story (only there's a bit of a sting in the tail, but more of that later) and George is a fount of knowledge. Often it's the incomers who become obsessed with the history of their new home and George is the living embodiment of that adage. He's done a lot of research, much of which he wants to impart as quickly as possible.

'This used to be the crossroads of Britain. People would turn up here – the coach drivers – put the horses out the back and get everything sorted out, then they'd come in here and avail themselves of some liquid refreshment.' George is telling the story with some relish. 'And of course there'd be loads of them here, hundreds and hundreds of them.'

'Literally?'

'Literally hundreds and hundreds. So they'd turn up here and they'd start off, they'd talk about their boring, mundane day.'

George starts to get carried away, re-enacting the conversations between the coach drivers. It's a bravura storytelling performance, but how can anyone really know what the stagecoach drivers would have said?

Nevertheless, according to George, these coach drivers had a hard life and when they met up at coaching inns liked nothing better than to spin a few tall tales. And the more they drank and the later the hour, the taller their tales. If they weren't spinning yarns in the Cock Hotel, they would be two doors down at the Bull Inn, relating similarly fanciful tales.

Eventually these tall stories became known as Cock and Bull stories, says George.

'So I suppose they would talk about Dick Turpin and how many times they'd been held up?'

'He was here!' George doesn't miss an opportunity to impart – dare I say it – another potential cock and bull story.

'Was he?'

'In fact – this isn't a cock and bull story – in 1753 he came up here trying to evade capture. And they knew his horse . . .'

Like Turpin's horse, George is galloping off on the wind. Again it's a fascinating story. To evade his pursuers, Turpin apparently hid his horse in the upstairs room of a shop in the High Street. But as before, I'm not sure there's any way of verifying the tale. An entertaining anecdote maybe, but short on evidence. In other words: potential cock and bull.

George keeps me entertained for several more hours with stories about the Romans, Boudicca, Richard the Lionheart, Edward V, 'Bill' Shakespeare, Richard III, the planning of the Grand Union Canal – the list goes on and on – all of which supposedly were connected to Stony Stratford. Eventually it's time for bed.

Making my way upstairs, I ponder everything I've heard this evening. It was all very interesting, but if the essence of a cock and bull story is that it's either a lie or a gross exaggeration, then maybe the cock and bull stories were not invented here at all. And maybe the Cock and the Bull were built in 1946 by Charles Forte. And maybe the tale about the inns is like the ploughman's lunch: a blue-suited marketing man's invention. How do you decide what's true? Tossing and turning in bed, I decide this one needs further research.

In the cool light of the next day, I discover that the basic facts of George's story do stand up to scrutiny. The Cock Hotel certainly dates back to 1470, although most of it was rebuilt in 1745 after the Great Fire of Stony Stratford; and there are claims in Stony Stratford that the Bull Inn was in operation by 1600. If so, both were in business in the heyday of stage-coaches. Original timetables show the town to have been a stopping point on many stagecoach routes, including the Manchester Flier, which left London at 8.30 a.m. and stopped at the Cock for twenty-five minutes en route to Manchester, where it arrived at 5.10 a.m. the next day.

It's also entirely possible that Stony Stratford High Street would have seen several hundred coaches a day. After all, the area was deliberately chosen for the location of Milton Keynes because it is equidistant from London, Birmingham, Leicester, Oxford and Cambridge, all of which would have been stage-coach destinations.

But although these facts support George's claims, there are other equally plausible explanations, including that 'cock and bull' is a corruption of 'a concocted and bully story', with bully being a further corruption of the Danish *bullen*, which means exaggerated.

Other theories suggest 'cock and bull' is linked to ancient fables (such as those written by Aesop in the sixth century BC) in which animals talked. Or that it is derived from the French term for a tall story, *coq à l'âne* (cock to donkey), which in turn has a Scottish derivative, *cockalayne*.

Turning to the Oxford English Dictionary, I find it cites the first use of the phrase in 1621 in Robert Burton's medical text-book on depression, *The Anatomy of Melancholy*. In it, Burton writes: 'Some mens whole delight is to take tobacco, and drink all day long in a tavern or alehouse, to discourse, sing, jest, roare, talk of a cock and bull over a pot.' But I discover that even before that, John Day, a playwright contemporary with Shakespeare, uses the phrase in *Law-trickes or Who Would have Thought it?*, a comedy he published in 1608: 'What a tale of a cock and a bull he told my father.'

Elizabethan and Jacobean dramatists such as Day often staged their plays at coaching inns, so they might have been familiar with the vernacular in use at such establishments. We'll never know if Day picked up the phrase in this way, but the quotations from his play and from Burton suggest to me that the saying is rooted in animal fables and had been in proverbial use before that.

Continuing my researches, I find yet another explanation that does link the phrase to the Cock Hotel and the Bull Inn, but in a different way from George's story. In this telling, a gentleman whose coach had broken down with a damaged wheel managed to secure a seat on a mail coach. Taking his place, he discovered he was sharing the carriage with two men, one employed by the Bull and the other by the Cock. Eager to secure the gentleman's trade, these men spent the journey listing the advantages of their own establishment at great length, often nearly coming to blows. Four miles from Stony Stratford and unable to take any more of the two men's boasts, the gentleman is said to have drawn his gun, shot it through the roof of the mail coach and ordered it to stop before running off into the night, yelling, 'I've had quite enough of your Cock and Bull stories.' It's an appealing tale, but it's got one problem. Mail coaches weren't introduced until the 1780s, more than 170 years after John Day had used the phrase.

So where does that leave us? To me, the animal fables origin seems the most likely, although I find George's colourful explanation much more appealing. And if there's anything to be learned from my entertaining evening at the Cock Hotel with George, it's the adage so beloved of scurrilous tabloid journalists: never let the facts get in the way of a good story.

As I drive away from Stony Stratford, one of the many tales that George told me the previous night sticks in my mind, partly because I could recognize it was true and partly because it chimed with my journey to Glasgow.

Stony Stratford's busy stagecoach trade came to an abrupt end in 1838 with the opening of the London to Birmingham railway, part of what is today the West Coast main line. Passengers and mail immediately switched their allegiances from horse to steam and Stony Stratford went into decline. It was a severe and succinct lesson in the effects of transport links on a community. The town's fortunes changed for the better after the invention of the car, when Stony Stratford became an important stopping point on the A5 from London to the north-west, but the cursed M1 put paid to this resurgence when its first section, from Watford to Crick, opened in November 1959. From then on, Britain's travellers bypassed Stony Stratford in their pursuit of destination over route, missing out on its glorious history and the beauty of its High Street. What more could you ask for if you wanted yet another good reason to avoid motorways?

With a mix of Georgian and Gothic Victorian architecture, Northampton, my next destination, has a lovely town centre that looks as if it hasn't changed in a hundred years. Looming over the town and visible from most parts of it is the Express Lift Tower, a 127.45-metre Grade II listed concrete column built to test new lifts at the Express Lifts factory and, known to locals as the Northampton Lighthouse (Northampton is one of the furthest places in England from the sea) or the Cobblers' Needle.

Strangely, an interesting statistic links the beautiful old Jag that I'm driving and Northampton city centre. British men apparently spend twice as much on their cars as they do on their girlfriends. It's a pretty outrageous idea, until you think you could get a rebuilt Jaguar engine for about £1,500, which would also buy you a pair of the best Manolo Blahnik shoes. I know which of those I think is the bargain. And if you think I'm talking cobblers, in my defence I am in the shoemaking capital of Britain. (Sorry, last pun, I promise.)

An obsession with shoes is often said to be a strictly female thing. Let me overthrow that prejudice. One of my most beloved possessions is a pair of co-respondent shoes, those classic two-toned spiv shoes from the 1940s. I *love* them. I've been strangely attracted to co-respondents since first seeing the opening sequence of Alfred Hitchcock's *Strangers On a Train*. To the shriek of a whistle and the fanfare of Dimitri Tiomkin's brassy score, a Diamond Cab taxi draws up outside a train station in Washington. A porter opens the door and lifts out a suitcase. Then an immaculately shod Robert Walker steps out of the cab. All we see are his black-and-white co-respondent shoes as he walks away. Then a second cab stops and an equally immaculately shod Farley Granger steps out. This time the camera shows only his sensible brogues. At this point we know nothing about the characters or the plot, but just from their shoes we know that Walker's the bad guy and Granger the good.

Co-respondent shoes were so called not only for their two corresponding colours, but also because they were thought of as the shoes worn by co-respondents in divorce cases. In the days when the law allowed very few grounds for divorce, a married couple seeking to divorce would arrange for the wife to stay in a hotel overnight and leave two pairs of shoes outside her room: a woman's pair and a pair of distinctly men's shoes, such as the two-toned type regarded at that time as the philanderer's favoured footwear. A private detective, hired by the married couple to verify independently the likelihood of an adulterous act, would then testify that he had spotted the shoes and so the husband could claim adultery and be granted a divorce.

Walking down Jermyn Street one day, I spotted a beautiful pair of co-respondent shoes with thick leather soles in the window of Tricker's, a shop that boasted a Royal Warrant of Appointment to the Prince of Wales. My immediate reaction was that I had to have a pair, but I'd heard Jermyn Street shoes cost £1,000 for the last (or mould) and then a further £1,000 for each consecutive pair. Thinking it would be decadent to pay that much, I gingerly entered the shop expecting nothing more than the opportunity to have a closer look at the shoes.

'How much for a pair?' I asked.

'About three hundred and fifty pounds,' said the salesman.

It was less than I'd thought and they were fantastic shoes. I threw caution to the winds.

'Don't you make a last of my feet first and then make the shoes from that?'

'There's no need for that. The only complicated thing about feet is that most people have one foot larger than the other. We've got a mould of every size we make. You look like an eleven D.'

The salesman called out to an assistant to get a pair of 11D shoes from the stockroom. The left shoe fitted perfectly, but I have a high instep on my right foot, so the laces didn't run straight on that one.

'I think we're going to need a high-rise double-D for Mr C.'

The assistant scuttled off back to the stockroom. 'George, make it a size 12.'

Within ten minutes of entering the shop I was wearing a perfectly fitting pair of shoes and the salesman had taken full details of the peculiarities of my feet, including the size of hole needed, the width of my ankle, the height of my instep and the length of my big toes, and he had matched them to a mould. It made good sense. Because there isn't an infinite variety of feet shapes and sizes, the shop could narrow down its range of fittings to about fifty variations for each foot. A balance between excellence and common sense – a Scotsman's dream!

A few weeks later I had a new pair of shoes for £350, which still seemed a lot of money. But when I visit the Tricker's factory here in Northampton, I realize that not only will they last for ever like a perfect-fitting suit, but the amount of work that goes into each handmade pair warrants every penny of that £350 and more.

Before going to the Tricker's workshop, however, I stop at the Northampton Museum and Art Gallery, scene of the town's shoe museum and home to more than twelve thousand pairs – only a few more than in the average girl's wardrobe. Walking into the museum, I'm immediately drawn to a display case with a shoe for an elephant's foot. This was made by the Lotus shoe company for Jumbo (really!) when Hannibal's crossing of the Alps was re-enacted in 1959 for *Hannibal*, an Italian film starring Bud Spencer, Terence Hill and Victor Mature. They had to have boots for the elephants –

obviously – and I could just imagine the phone call to the shoe company.

'I'd like a set of shoes for an elephant, please . . .'

'Is that you, Terry? Stop messing about.'

'No, really.'

'A pair of shoes for an elephant? Whaddya think this is? April the first?'

Beside the elephant shoe is a pair of pink kid ankle-strap shoes made for a small girl in about 1890, and nearby there's a Roman sandal with great big hobnails on it. Looking at them I find it difficult to imagine going to war in a pair of leather-strapped open-toed sandals, but many historians believe that one of the major secrets of Roman military success was the design of their footwear, which allowed them to march for hours on end. The Romans recognized that shoes were machines for feet at a time when we Jocks were running into battle barefoot, naked and with paint on our faces. We might have looked a fright, and maybe that helped us scare off invaders, but to conquer Europe, the Romans knew they needed shoes to protect their feet.

It's no accident that Northampton Museum has the world's largest shoe collection (it includes General Tom Thumb's Napoleonic boots, Queen Victoria's wedding slippers, Margot Fonteyn's pink satin ballet pointe shoes, Elton John's boots from the movie *Tommy* and a pair of motor racing boots belonging to Emerson Fittipaldi). The town's association with shoemaking goes back to the fifteenth century, when the large cattle market here guaranteed ready access to cow hides, the river Nene and the woodlands along its banks provided the water and timber essential for the tanning process, and the town's location in the centre of England made distribution easy.

The defining moment in Northampton's shoe industry came in 1642, when sufficient shoemakers were working in the town for a group of thirteen of them, led by Thomas Pendleton, to tender for a contract to make six hundred pairs of boots and four thousand pairs of shoes to equip Cromwell's New Model Army to go and massacre the Irish. They won the contract and Northampton became the shoemaking capital of England.

By the early nineteenth century, the census registered more than 1,800 Northampton shoemakers, many of them employing a large number of freelance workers, who collected leather and other raw components from a manufacturer and then returned the finished footwear for payment. However, by the mid-1860s traditional shoemaking was threatened as mechanization arrived. Some factories were using steam engines to churn out 100,000 pairs of shoes a week. Only a few independent shoemakers remained, continuing to use traditional techniques to make shoes by hand. When the global search for cheap labour in the twentieth century took factory production abroad, these traditional shoemakers were the only ones left in Northampton, practising the techniques and skills that had been passed down through generations of family and craftsmen for more than five hundred years.

I get a chance to sample these skills when I turn up at Tricker's magnificent red-brick factory. Amid the terraced houses and shoe factories in Northampton's back streets, the words R. E. Tricker Ltd stand out in foot-high gilt lettering on the frontage of the Victorian building. Inside it, sixty-year-old hand-sewer Len Robinson is waiting to introduce me to the finer arts of bespoke leather shoemaking.

Len is not just any old shoemaker; he is reputedly the finest shoemaker in Northampton. Tricker's sends him to Japan each year to exhibit his craft to gobsmacked audiences, and if anyone were to refer to Len as a cobbler he would, he tells me, 'treat that comment with the contempt it deserves'. This makes me realize I've been insulting shoemakers for years – Len tells me cobblers are unskilled repairers of soles (they cobble things together), whereas a shoemaker is a true craftsman who never stops learning his trade. Point taken.

It's always struck me as amazing that shoemakers could take something as relatively simple as the skin of a cow and make something as durable as a shoe out of it. It's an amazing skill, but learning it is one of those things that you need to be shown rather than having it explained. And the terminology doesn't make it any easier. Each piece of the shoe seems to have a fantastic name – the vamp, the throat, the shank and, my favourite, the welt. But ironically the process begins with the last: a wooden mould of a foot.

With the correct standardized last chosen or hand-fashioned, the shoemaker can get to work. A clicker – that's a job title – carefully selects a piece of leather suitable for the shoe's upper, taking the weight, grain and colour of the leather into account. He then cuts it either by hand or by machine, depending on how much you're prepared to pay for the shoe. The shoemaker then sews the leather uppers to linings and stiffeners appropriate to the type of shoe being made. A brogue will have more stiffeners than a lighter shoe. These uppers are then stretched over the last, tacked with nails to a moistened insole that has been moulded to the bottom of the last and left for a couple of days so that all the stretching to the shape of the customer's foot has taken place before they even put it on.

In the final stage of the production process the shoemaker uses waxed and rolled linen thread (or flax) and a curved bristle that's as sharp and stiff as a needle to stitch the uppers to the insole on the welt, which is the leather rim where the upper meets the sole and which stops your feet from getting soggy in the rain. Len shows me how he uses a tool to punch a hole through the upper. He threads the waxed flax through the hole to pull the two parts together, removes the nail that's holding them in place and ties a knot to keep them secured to each other. As Len twists the flax, the wax creates a massive resistance that ensures the knot will never loosen. He then hammers the knot into a groove in the insole.

That demonstrated, he lets me have a go. I soon discover it's not as easy as it looks. It's dangerous work. If I slipped with the curved bristle I'd take a nail off, at least.

'Don't you wear any protection?'

Len's dismissive. 'I haven't hurt myself in bloody years.'

'Did you hurt yourself when you started?'

'Oh yes . . .'

His warning focuses my attention on the job. 'This seems like hard work to me. How long would it take you to sew a complete shoe?'

'About half an hour, give or take.'

'Half an hour? Really? It would take me that long to do one stitch.'

It reminds me of that story of the proud old cobbler who used to take six months to make just one pair of boots . . . so they sacked him.

I pull another couple of knots, then hand the half-made shoe back to Len, who finishes the job swiftly. Then, with the uppers and insole sewn to one another, the outer sole, usually made of thicker, tougher leather, is stitched on to the welt. All that remains is for Len to construct and attach the heel, tidy up the shoe and add any fancy ornamentation.

I'm astounded at the speed, intricacy and extent of the work that Len puts into the shoe. It makes me think I've been severely undercharged for my £350 co-respondents.

As with anything that people have been doing for hundreds of years, every ten years or so there's a breakthrough in skill or technique. The way it's done now is an accumulation of all those steps forward. It's the same with old cars. You can take them apart and work out exactly what each generation of engineers back to the Egyptians was thinking when they were developing metalwork or devising a vehicle. And when I think back to the Roman sandals I saw in the museum, I can see the shared heritage with the brogue that Len and I have stitched in the Tricker's workshop.

That accumulation of human knowledge is something very precious; it binds generations and communities together. I sometimes wonder if it explains why there seems to be more respect and better communication between generations in less-developed countries than there is in Britain. If you are going to spend your life doing what your father did and something goes wrong, you contact your father for advice. But if you leave home and go into a job that didn't exist when the previous generation was growing up, such as computing, then you won't have much to talk about with your dad when you come home in your fancy Armani suit. Simple, really. Discuss . . .

Tradition plays a very important role in any society, but the trouble with tradition in Britain is that it's endemically tied up with class. And when society started to break down class barriers – something of which I was totally in favour – a lot of babies were thrown out with the bathwater. People stopped living close to their relatives and communities disintegrated because the younger generation wanted to get away from the confines of their class and background. In itself that was no bad thing, but it means that nowadays parents emigrate to Australia, grandparents retire to France or Spain and the children are left at home. I'm not suggesting we put the clock back, but I have noticed that whenever I visit somewhere where the people seem contented, there does seem to be a merging of the generations. Traditions – shared occupations, shared activities and shared rituals – play a big part in holding generations together, and recognizing that doesn't mean you have to be reactionary or backward. It can mean you appreciate the value to all of us if two people born thirty years apart have something to talk to each other about. Thinking there should by default be a generation gap is an astonishingly shallow commentary on human nature.

Blessed with the most unbelievably beautiful weather, I drive on further east towards Cambridge. We all know that the Lake District, Devon and Cornwall are stunning, but in the short time I've been on the road I'm discovering that most of the bits in between these known beauty spots are just as remarkable. If I hadn't embarked on this journey I would never have realized that Northamptonshire, Warwickshire and Buckinghamshire are so picturesque. Like many Jocks, I expect only to be impressed by mountains and fast-running water. But travelling through the heart of England I'm surprised by the huge sense of space I get from the open sky and the way the landscape alters every few miles, the huge variety of crops creating a constantly changing texture in the land. And of course, it's particularly great in a convertable. Driving on a motorway through these parts sometimes gives you a glimpse of the countryside, but I find I'm usually concentrating too intently on the traffic to take it in. And six lanes of tarmac rarely allow anyone a real feel for the intimate nooks, crannies, contours and vistas of a landscape.

Already on this journey I've seen some fantastic natural sights, but midway between Northampton and Cambridge I come to something man-made and truly awesome. Just beyond Bedford is the tiny village of Cardington. Looming over the village, and dominating the skyline for miles around, are two massive green buildings, the sight of which can only provoke one sensible question: 'What on earth are these for?'

They're called the Cardington Sheds, but they're not really the kind of thing you could tuck away at the end of the garden. Once the biggest structures in Britain, they were built in 1918 and eventually housed the R101, the largest airship in the world. Nowadays they're wonderful industrial relics of an age when everyone was convinced airships were the long-distance transport vehicles of the future. After all, airships were filled with highly flammable gas, they were incredibly slow, dangerous to fly in a storm, and they could carry only a few dozen passengers. Strange, really, that they never caught on.

Incredible as it might seem, Cardington village was the Cape Canaveral – or, at the very least, the Heathrow airport – of its day. Britain was determined to have the best and the biggest. And Cardington was chosen to be the hub of that ambition.

And what ambition! Shed Number One is more than 800 feet long, 180 feet wide and 157 feet high. All of the aircraft carrier *Ark Royal* plus all but the last 40 feet of the *Titanic* would fit inside.

So much about these imposing structures is jaw-dropping. More than 4,000 tons of steel were used in the building of the two sheds, and several hundred tons more steel were needed to construct enormous windbreaks at each end of each shed, necessary to protect airships being moved in or out. The doors alone weigh 940 tons. They need to be that damned heavy because if they caught the wind, anything lighter would end up doing a Mary Poppins from here to Japan. Well, maybe not Japan, but you get my point.

Initially only one shed was built. The intention was to use it to develop a response to the German Zeppelin bombers, which attacked Britain in the first two years of the First World War. However, the first British ship, the R31, was commissioned only five days before the Armistice and by April 1919 the facility had been nationalized as the Royal Airship Works. In 1924 the Imperial Airship Scheme was proposed as a military project to design a dirigible capable of carrying two hundred troops or five fighter aircraft. To lift that quantity, the engineers calculated they'd need to build an airship of 8 million cubic feet. Work began immediately on extending the length and raising the roof of Shed Number One to house the R101, a prototype airship of 5 million cubic feet capacity, and in 1928 a shed at a secret airship base in Norfolk was dismantled and re-erected at Cardington. This became Shed Number Two.

At 6.30 a.m. on 4 October 1930 the Imperial Airship Scheme bore its first fruit when the R101, the largest vessel in the world, set off on its maiden flight for Karachi, now in Pakistan but then part of British India. Fifty-four passengers, including Lord Thomson, Secretary of State for Air, and Air Vice-Marshal Sir William Sefton Brancker, the Director of Civil Aviation, were on board. Three thousand people watched her leave, but tragically the R101 never made it. She crashed into a hillside in northern France; exactly why remains a mystery to this day. Only six passengers survived. The Imperial Airship Scheme was abandoned, and Cardington became a storage base and, later on, a testing facility for the Building Research Establishment.

Now, nearly eighty years later, Shed One hasn't been maintained and lies empty, rusting and forlorn. However, Shed Two, still used by the film industry, is freshly painted dark green and is in perfect nick. Recent films shot here include *Batman Begins* – Batman from Bedfordshire, who'd have thought it? – but it's now up for sale for a cool £6 million. Not cheap, but at least you'd never need an extension.

Like any des res up for sale, Shed Two is surrounded by a fence. Without a convincing reason for why I might want to buy it, I'm not going to persuade the local estate agent to let me have a viewing. But Shed One is a different matter. As you might expect, big notices surround the place saying DANGER. KEEP OUT. Wise words indeed, but show anything like that to a television director and you might as well wave a red rag in front of a bull. Inevitably the director wants me to venture into the rusting monstrosity of a building – while he waits outside, watching it all on his monitor, coffee in hand.

With doors as tall as a sixteen-storey building and as heavy as three fully laden jumbo jets, it's going to take more than a wee shove to get them open so that I can go inside. Like all major expeditions, my venture into Shed One's innards begins with a small step. In this case it's a small metal box with a handle located on a platform near where the two huge doors meet. Incredibly, the handle is all that keeps the two doors locked together, so I give it a whirl and they unlock. A few paces further along the platform is what looks like your average garden hut, only this one is built on to the platform tacked on to the front of each door. Inside the hut is a very large metal cabinet with a row of buttons and coloured lights. The red light indicates that the master switch is in the on position. All I need to do is press it and the doors open. They slide apart as smoothly as a ship easing down a slipway into the water. Well, a ship that moves very slowly: the door takes about fifteen minutes to inch its way open fully, rails creaking and sirens blasting all the way.

Inside, I'm overwhelmed by the sheer scale of the building. It feels even bigger than it did on the outside. Six thousand double deckers would fit in it. And (*Boy's Own* fact) Nelson's Column wouldn't touch the ceiling – not that you'd want to put it in here.

Looking around the building, I can see it's a simple structure of scaffolding covered with corrugated sheets, punctuated with glass for the windows. At first it doesn't seem that big, but then I spot parked to the side a truck that looks like a Matchbox toy next to the building and I realize its true scale. Yet, amazingly, when the R101 was housed here there were only about 8 inches of free space between the side of the ship and the shed. What a ship it must have been.

After the Imperial Airship Scheme's ambitious plans were scrapped, Shed One was used to build barrage balloons in the Second World War, but since then nothing that flies has left the building – until now. The observation that you could quite easily fly a small aircraft inside the shed is enough to have us calling in a man with a radio-controlled plane – Ally Machinchy, British Aerobatic Champion and World Jet Freestyle champion for radio-controlled aircraft. Ally's currently working on breaking the world airspeed record for these miniature marvels. Officially it's 255 m.p.h., but Ally's already logged 298 m.p.h. and intends to break 300 m.p.h. At that speed, it's flying so fast he's radio-controlling a speck in the sky.

Inside the shed, however, Ally flies a Super Cub electric plane with an electric motor and 1-metre wingspan, performing tricks and stunts. It's the largest indoor space in which he's flown; usually he flies in sports centres. He controls it with remarkable agility, chatting to me while he sends it speeding up and down the shed, performing loops and rolls with what seems like the greatest of ease. While I ask him questions, Ally buzzes the plane within inches of the top of my head. It's a bravura performance. Then he lets me have a go and, as with so many things, it looks a lot easier when you're watching it than when you're doing it. I manage to get the plane to take off several times, but it always crashes. Best left to the experts, eh?

Chapter Five

Experts are in no short supply at my next destination. It's a place well known throughout the world for brains, boating and beautiful buildings. Oh – and spies. No prizes for guessing it's Cambridge, home of the sporting Blue. But if I suggested going to meet a Cambridge Blue, what would come to mind? To most of us it would be a stout young man rowing up and down the Cam, or hearty rugger buggers kicking the living daylights out of each other in pursuit of an oval ball. You probably wouldn't think of a gang of intense, not particularly athletic chaps in polo shirts and tank tops playing tiddlywinks, but believe it or not, these are the Cambridge Blues I've come to see.

When the idea of visiting the World Tiddlywinks Championship was first mooted, my initial reaction was very predictable: Oh no, it's going to be a nerd's paradise. In my mind, tiddlywinks conjured up images of visiting the vicar for afternoon tea.

How wrong I was.

My childhood memories of tiddlywinks seem to revolve around plinking coloured discs on a square board into a cup in the middle. It was as dull as ditchwater and I always seemed to lose.

The game played by the world champions at Cambridge is something different entirely. Like snooker, at least half the game is about preventing your opponent from having an easy shot. And like croquet, it's a vicious and aggressive sport posing as a genteel upper-class pastime.

At Selwyn College, where the World Championship is being held, I meet Patrick Barrie, a lecturer in chemical engineering at Cambridge, chairman of the English Tiddlywinks Association, six times World Singles and six times World Pairs Champion. A vision in a blue England polo shirt who speaks with a slight lisp as he explains the rules, Patrick has played in five successive Varsity matches for Cambridge and can therefore claim to have three-quarters of a Blue. He insists it's a game of rare cunning and deviousness.

'It's not just about flicking winks into the cup, you know,' he says. 'It's a game with a bit of strategy, a bit of tactics, a bit of gamesmanship, a bit of nerve and it's actually quite fun. You need a good measure of dexterity, a steady hand, lots of practice.'

'Sobriety?'

'Sobriety sometimes helps, though some people drink at the lunchtime before the tournament. They find it steadies their hand.'

I want to ask Patrick if the rumour I heard about the game's origin is true or is it – see what I'm doing here – a cock and bull story: 'I heard it started because some chaps wanted to impress some girls with claims they were Cambridge Blues.'

'That's *almost* true. In 1955 a couple of students wanted to represent Cambridge as they thought it might impress some-body. They were no good at rugby, football or rowing, so they decided to take up tiddlywinks.'

These two enterprising chaps – I hesitate to refer affectionately to them as geeks because it's so often a derogatory term for anyone eccentric, imaginative or visionary – were called Bill Steen and Rick Martin. In the true tradition of British maleness, it didn't take long for enterprising Messrs Steen and Martin to establish a set of rules. That done, the next item on their agenda was to challenge a member of the Royal Family to a match. In 1958, they established the English Tiddlywinks Association as a rule-making body and, after an article entitled 'Does Prince Philip Cheat at Tiddlywinks?' was published in *The Spectator*, threw down the gauntlet to the Duke of Edinburgh, who responded by appointing the Goons (the radio comedy group that included Peter Sellers and Spike Milligan) as his royal champions to represent him in the match. Under the gaze of television and newsreel cameras from around the world, the Goons faced a university team at the Guildhall in Cambridge. A message from Prince Philip was read out: 'I wish the Cambridge team to lose and my incomparable champions to win a resounding and stereophonic victory. At one time I had hoped to join my champions but, unfortunately, while practising secretly, I pulled an important muscle in the second or tiddly joint of my winking finger.'

After a half-time break in which the two teams drank Babycham and the Varsity team presented the Goons with some rhubarb, and a minor diversion when the Welsh Goon Harry Secombe tried to auction a leek, the Cambridge team scored a resounding win of sixteen games to nil, a victory described by the next day's newspapers as 'one of the most dramatic sporting upsets for years'.

The Goons match caught the public imagination and triggered the formation of several new clubs, mainly at other universities and colleges. The Duke of Edinburgh remained an avid fan and every year since 1961, has awarded the Silver Wink trophy to the winner of the inter-University Tiddlywinks Championships.

Patrick tells me that Steen and Martin 'rescued the game from the Victorian doldrums in which tiddlywinks had become suitable for only the nursery, and created the modern adult game.'

'So what's the difference between the modern adult game and its Victorian origins?'

'Most of the modern game is about trying to cover up enemy counters. It's a game of capture and recapture.'

'So is it a wee bit like snooker?'

'In some ways it's like snooker, but a better comparison is chess. Like chess, you're trying to take out your opponent's pieces, but the differences are that captured pieces can come back on to the field of play and that the capture shot might not work. In tiddlywinks a lot of the game is recognizing the shot you want to do, but then realizing it's difficult and maybe you should do something else.'

These days the game of tiddlywinks is dominated by the acute rivalry between the Cambridge and Oxford University teams and by extremely intense competition between British and American players. In fact, the best American pair is in town to challenge the best British pair. I wonder how they prepare for these big matches. Hopefully no steroids are involved.

'The English pair has been known to employ significant quantities of alcohol for preparation and team building,' says Patrick. 'Historically, the American players have been associated with hippie communes and there have been suggestions that strategic substances have been used in the past. You'll have to ask the Americans.'

Each player starts with six counters at the corner of the mat. The process is very simple: players squidge off in an attempt to score the most tiddlies. Essentially, they must mash a squidger on a wink into the pot or squop an opponent's wink.

Confused? Allow me to explain.

To squidge is to press a small wink with a large one (the squidger), sending it flipping through the air towards the target cup at the centre of the table. To squop is to squidge a wink on to an opponent's wink, thereby temporarily retiring the enemy wink from play. A squopped wink cannot be squidged again until it is de-squopped, either by the original squopper or by a squopped player's partner who manages to squidge a third wink atop the second and spill the squopper off.

Concentrate now – here's the strategy:

There are blitzes (potting all six of your colour before any squops have been taken), bombs (squidging a wink at a pile, usually from a distance, in the hope of significantly disturbing it), boondocks, bring-ins and bristols (jumping a pile on to another wink). If you squidge a successful pot from the base-line it's called a Carnovsky, and if you destroy a pile completely you've scored a crud. If you've got a flexible squidger you can pot nurdle winks. There are also gromps, the brundle and the snoob, the junior birdman, a lunch, a Poss, the John O'Groat, scrunges and – my favourite – the John Lennon Memorial Shot, which is a simultaneous boondock and squop. And inevitably there's the Paul McCartney, which is a John Lennon Memorial Shot gone wrong.

All in all it's very different from the wet summer holidays I spent in St Andrews thinking I was playing tiddlywinks. As

I explain to Patrick, 'I now realize the reason I found it so boring was that we were playing a very simplistic version of the game, but this has all the sneakiness and subterfuge that makes a game interesting.'

'Oh yes,' says Patrick. 'It's a good intellectual game. There's a lot to it. People start playing it because it's something different and the people who play it have a sense of humour, but after a little while potting becomes addictive.'

The potting becomes addictive? Okay . . . I think we've found him, Sergeant.

Watching the game, I discover that very few shots involve putting a wink in the pot for the simple reason that every potted wink is one fewer wink on the 'battle area' as Patrick calls it.

'The battle area is where the fight is going on and a wink in the pot stays in the pot.'

I'm confused. Surely it's best to get your winks into the pot as soon as possible? But Patrick explains that, as in cricket, time plays an important role in tiddlywinks. A pairs game lasts twenty-five minutes plus five additional plays for each player. After that, scores are added up according to a somewhat complicated formula. A wink in the pot is worth three tiddlies and an uncovered wink is worth one tiddly. The player with the most tiddlies is awarded four game points, the player with the second most tiddlies gets two game points and the third-place player gets one game point. A partnership that comes first and second will therefore win a game by six points to one point. And there are fourteen games in a tournament, so a tour-nament can last a whole weekend. I'd never thought of tiddlywinks as a stamina sport.

When I try my hand at the game, I find that I've once again discovered a pastime that is a lot harder than it looks. With coaching from some of the best players in the world, I manage to pot a few winks, but only after several hundred have over-shot, gone wide, exited the playing table or dropped short of the pot. It's a damn subtle game that prompts me to plead with the producer: 'Just cut out all the winks that missed.' Some chance . . .

However, it's not until I play a pairs game with Patrick against Larry Khan, an American ranked number one in the world and holder of nineteen world singles titles, and Matt Fayers, ranked third in the world, that I really appreciate the subtleties of the game.

Although he's able to pot winks at will from anywhere on the felt-covered table, Patrick's strength is pile play, which means he's particularly adept at moving whole piles of winks else-where, or making sure only his winks emerge from a pile, or flipping or destroying piles. My strength is best described as taking instruction from Patrick, so perhaps unsurprisingly Patrick and I lose by one and a half points to five and a half points.

I'd arrived at Selwyn College sceptical about the attractions of tiddlywinks, but having played with some of the game's best practitioners, I'm hooked. If I only had the skill to excel at it, I could see myself getting seriously into tiddlywinks. It's a great game for teenagers; after all, the only equipment you need is twenty-five plastic discs, a cup and a felt tablecloth, and it's all about warfare, annihilation, intimidation and victory against the odds. If more people were aware of this demonic game, I'm sure it would be more popular. I can imagine televised tiddly-winks – it's just as exciting and just as skilful as snooker, bowls or darts, but only when you understand what's happening.

Tiddlywinks has a unique personality and character. Like the best games, it's easy to learn but difficult to master. Other than that, it's like no other game. It's cheap, portable, accessible, sometimes vicious, great fun, over in forty minutes, and you can't catch any diseases whilst taking part. What's not to like about it?

Also, before you decide it's just a game for over-educated Oxbridge propellerheads who lack social skills, let me set you straight: all the players were married and there were some stunning women playing too. I can just imagine the chat-up line: 'Why don't you come round to mine for a game of tiddly-winks?' It certainly promises something more intriguing than dinner. They're not daft, these lads.

There's a sad end to my tiddlywinks tale – these lads have to buy in their winks from Italy because they can't get any here of good enough quality. I ask you: how can a country that's invented such a world-class sport as tiddlywinks not provide our sporting heroes with the equipment to pursue their noble endeavours? Buck up, Britain's plastic-moulding community!

From the cerebral confines and arcane pastimes of a Cambridge junior common room, my journey leads me about 60 miles northwards to the venue of an intensely physical competition where brawn is much more highly valued than brains. Hallaton and Medbourne, two sleepy villages set in the rolling green countryside of south-east Leicestershire, are usually home to a few hundred people. They're typical rural England, pretty and quiet. However, once a year the bucolic bliss is shattered as the fields between the two villages are transformed into a battlefield swamped by marauding hordes of young men and a crowd of up to ten thousand spectators.

Keen to see the action, I pitch up in Hallaton and Medbourne on the very morning of this year's contest.

Informed that I'm about to witness what is best described as a kind of no-holds-barred rugby, I know exactly where to go to meet the principal participants. Sitting round a big wooden table in a back garden in Medbourne I find some twenty lads, all in rugby shirts, some of them carrying injuries from past years, such as bent fingers or cauliflower ears, all as mad as a box of frogs and all tucking into gloriously heaped plates of British fried breakfast washed down with beer – a perfectly balanced meal. Those artery-clogging calories will be sorely needed in a few hours, as I'm about to discover.

At the heart of the group sit John Burrows and his sons. Having taken part in bottle-kicking for more than eighty years, the Burrows of Medbourne are central to the event; last year they held breakfast for thirty-two participants. With interjections from the various lads around the table, John explains to me the rules of the roughest game in England.

The first rule is, there are no rules. That means no limit to the numbers in each team. Anyone who turns up can join in, although there's a hardcore of lads from each village who take part every year. Assorted visitors 'jump for a while into the free-for-all', I'm told, but they usually don't last very long.

'So how do you make sure it's fair then?' I ask the lads.

'It's not!' The lads laugh at the naivety of my question.

The only way to explain bottle-kicking is to go back to the game's origins. According to local folklore, either it harks back to England's pagan past, when hares were sacrificed to the goddess Eostre (hares were considered sacred animals and it's thought this convention was appropriated by Christians for the Easter Rabbit), or it goes back to an ancient local tradition of free food and ale being given to villagers at Easter. According to this tale, two Hallaton ladies crossing a field were saved from a raging bull by a startled hare that distracted the bull from its charge. These ladies donated money to the church to show their gratitude to God for sending the hare, on the understanding that every Easter Monday the vicar would provide a hare pie, twelve penny loaves and two barrels of ale for the poor of the village.

Of course, this food and drink was manna from heaven to the village's poor and needy. Unsurprisingly, everyone wanted a piece of the action and fights soon broke out. It didn't take long for news of free drink in Hallaton to reach the residents of neighbouring Medbourne, who joined the fray and stole the ale. The Hallatonians (breath mint, anyone?) fought to retrieve the spoils, thus beginning the village rivalry that continues to this day.

These days it's less about the free drink and more about village pride. Phil Allan, a veteran of the game, describes it as bigger than the Cup Final. In all its history it's been cancelled only once, in 2001, when foot-and-mouth closed down the countryside. During both World Wars, when the men were away fighting, the women of the villages continued the tradition. The only time bottle-kicking was seriously threatened was in 1790, when the rector of Hallaton, opposed to the tradition because of its pagan origins, tried to ban the event. It took only a day for the rector to relent after the words 'no pie, no parson' appeared scrawled on the wall of the vicarage.

Nowadays the event starts with a parade through the villages. Locals carry a large hare pie and the three bottles, which are actually small kegs, two of which are filled with ale.

Above: *Who wouldn't be smiling? A lovely car, a beautiful view and a bacon sandwich on its way!*

The Jaguar XK150 S. It's hard to imagine that anything this stylish came off a production line, but it did.

'And no more!' Mayor Darren Hayday might well look pleased with himself during the High Wycombe weighing-in ceremony. His impressive weight loss meant that he didn't have to face any abuse or flying fruit on his last day in office.

Right: On her first day as mayor Valerie Razzaq promised me she didn't have any lead in her hand-bag. This was a big day for her in more ways than one.

Lucy looked like an art deco statue until she started to spin. The wing-walking display at Rendcomb airfield in Gloucestershire looked most alarming from the air!

Right: *The picture says it all. I could never be a wing-walker – I look rubbish in red.*

Above: *Woodchester Mansion is the Marie Celeste of Britain's listed houses. It looks as if the tradesmen left for lunch 150 years ago and never came back.*

Concentration has to be total when cutting stone: one slip and hours of work could be ruined.

The National Trust owns the Fleece Inn at Bretforton and very nice it is too. With none of that 'theme' nonsense, it's a wee gem.

Right: Nigel Smith the landlord and Billy Byrd the 'spara-grass' grower enjoying the sunshine.

During the asparagus season the delicious stalks are in almost every dish on the Fleece Inn menu. Heaven.

Big, brash and American, right?
Wrong. Built by British Leyland in
England. A truly awesome beast.

Above: *Derek Robbins explains to me the mysteries of disc golf. It's a lot of fun, with no pimp shoes required!*

George Webley telling me a fascinating tale at the Innfamous Bull in Stony Stratford. But was it a cock and bull story about cock and bull stories?

The third bottle, called the dummy and made of solid wood painted red, white and blue, is sitting on the middle of the pub table as the villagers explain the day's events. The pie is blessed by the Hallaton vicar, then cut apart and some of it thrown to the crowd for the scramble. The rest is placed in a sack to be carried up nearby Hare Pie Hill. Meanwhile, the bottles are taken to the Buttercross, a monument at the centre of the village that was used to keep butter and cheese cool when the village was a market town. Here the bottles are decorated and the penny loaves distributed.

In the early afternoon, the remainder of the pie is placed on a sack in a dip at the top of Hare Pie Bank, a field flanked by two streams about a mile apart, and tossed out to the crowd. The Master of the Stowe (the chief bottle-kicker) throws the first bottle in the air three times. The third time that it falls to the ground, the waiting players leap on it and the game starts. The two teams attempt to move the bottle by any means possible across Hare Pie Bank, over ditches, hedges and barbed wire towards their own villages. Broken bones are not uncommon and emergency services are on standby.

Whichever team manages to carry the bottle across the stream nearest to their village wins it. Some years the streams are in full flow and the villagers have to swim across them to get the bottle home to their village. In those years, Hare Pie Bank ends up looking like the Somme.

After the first bottle is won, the game is restarted at Hare Pie Bank in the same way. To win the game, a team must win two bottles. Victory achieved, both teams celebrate by climbing the Buttercross and drinking from one of the bottles containing ale, which by now is warm and well shaken.

'So what's the injury rate like, lads? Be honest now.'

There's a lot of umming and aaahing around the table. 'Nothing serious ... oh, a few broken bones ... we're all mates for the rest of the year, but when it comes to the day of the bottle-kicking, it does get a bit vicious on the field of play ...' Sounds about right.

After breakfast I move on to the Bewicke Arms in Hallaton, where Phil Allan, the village's answer to Phil Vickery, is waiting at the bar to fill the bottles with ale. He first started bottle-kicking at thirteen but, regarded as too young to participate, he was dragged out of the scrum by adult players. When he was fifteen, the villagers recognized his determination and allowed him on to the organizing committee. Now the chief barrel-carrier and organizer, Phil's picked up a fair few injuries over the years.

'Broken ribs, a broken collarbone, damaged knuckles, scratches down my arms and legs – but that's all part of the glory of taking part,' he says.

Phil tells me that recent archaeological finds in the village suggest bottle-kicking dates back at least two thousand years, but says he cannot give me any further details as they are being verified by the British Museum. If it's true, then bottle-kicking could be one of the oldest continuing traditions in Britain.

Phil also suggests that bottle-kicking served as the inspiration for the modern game of rugby. Rugby is certainly nearby and there's a suggestion, albeit uncorroborated, that William Webb Ellis often came to stay with his uncle, who was the rector (again uncorroborated) of Hallaton. So maybe Webb Ellis got the idea of picking up the ball and running after watching many games of bottle-kicking. Problem is, we don't know if Webb Ellis really invented rugby. All we know for sure is that he was at the school in Rugby from 1816 until 1825, around the time of the birth of the legendary, but sadly apocryphal, story of the boy 'who with a fine disregard for the rules of football as played in his time, first took the ball in his arms and ran with it'. Yet again it appears I've come up against a bit of local folklore that might be little more than a cock and bull story.

Grinning, Phil starts digging for information on the opposition. 'So how were the Medbourne boys this morning?'

'Oh . . . I'd rather not say. They were telling me all their tactics.'

'What's that? Drink beer?'

'They were making some very rude remarks about you guys. It was very funny.'

'Like what?'

'We met quite early and when I asked whether you lot would already be up and eating breakfast, they said, "They're all still in bed, aren't they? With each other." '

Having helped Phil fill one of the barrels with just over a gallon of All Over A Barrel, an ale produced specially for the event by a local Rutland brewer, I move on to the pub kitchen, where Lynn, Phil's wife, is removing the hare pie from the oven.

With the meat of two locally shot hares, onions and potatoes in it (like a giant Cornish pasty), the pie has taken a day to make and will feed at least one hundred people. It's the third year Lynn's made it and it's a magnificent creation.

'Are you going to taste it later?' asks Lynn.

'Of course. When it's cut up this afternoon.' It would be rude not to.

Later that morning, the village is ready for the bottle-kicking. Brass bands are playing, onlookers with pints of ale in hand are lazing on grassy verges, the beer tent is packed, the sun is shining and there's a lot of bare flesh on display. People are smiling. It's one of those life-affirming good days out.

Just after midday, a gentleman in a green robe appears at the head of a procession, carrying a pole with a green metal hare at the top. Beside him are some women carrying baskets of loaves. They come to a stop at the gates of St Michael's Church, where a crowd of several thousand is waiting. They place Lynn's hare pie on a table in front of the rector, who blesses it and makes the first cut.

'Bless the Lord this pie. God bless this punch as a monster lunch.'

'Amen.'

A few dozen pairs of eyes are on the pie as the crowd jostles around the table and shouts three cheers for the hare pie. Then, according to tradition, Phil gives the rector a shilling and I'm given the honour of being the first to distribute the hare pie, which I toss out over the heads of the people in front of me into the eagerly waiting crowd.

The parade moves off again, now led by men in rugby and football shirts holding the bottles in one hand high above their heads and pursued by a kilted pipe and drum band. By 3 p.m. the procession has reached the top of Hare Pie Bank. With at least ten thousand spectators awaiting kick-off, the sense of anticipation is huge.

First the remains of the hare pie are thrown out into the crowd. Most people duck to avoid it, rather than attempting to grab a morsel for themselves. And then begins one of the most bizarre spectacles I've ever seen.

As the keg hits the ground for the third time, a scrum immediately forms around it. As a newcomer, I find it almost impossible to work out what's happening, who is in each team and which way they're going. But one thing's for sure: if this game didn't serve as inspiration for the game of rugby, it certainly sparked the concept of a riot.

Every now and then someone breaks loose from the scrum and either throws the bottle or tries to run with it. But the bottle rarely moves more than a few feet before falling to the ground, where it's kicked or dragged along by the mass of men. A core of lads gets really stuck in. Around them are lots of other villagers, close enough to see the action but not close enough to risk getting hurt.

Although there's no deliberate kicking or punching, it's very rough, verging on violent. There's no padding or protection, just a generous dose of pain-prevention liquid – ale to you and me – before, during and after the game. Gentlemen's rules say no studs (steel toecaps are fine) and there's meant to be a spirit of fair play, but I detect a few old scores being settled on the battlefield. Maybe someone who stole someone else's girlfriend is getting more knocked about than the game allows. Nevertheless, I'm convinced that if there were more of this kind of event about the place, there'd be fewer wars. It's a safety valve for the latent aggression that courses through so many of us.

To be fair, it's not a great spectator sport, as nothing noticeable happens for long periods. And with some five hundred hardcore players and two thousand sideline players, it's rare to get a clear sight of the bottle. Generally the scrum resembles something between a ruck and a maul with about a hundred people. The heart of it looks quite medieval: a jostling, bellicose mass of men. When the bottle breaks out and the scrum moves on, a few men are usually left lying on the ground. Sometimes someone will manage to throw the bottle over the hedge into the next field, where the action will continue for another hour or so before someone manages to sprint away with it over the fields. Most of the kickers appear to have downed several pints before joining in, but this doesn't stop them periodically leaving the scrum to grab a quick drink from nearby families and friends with rucksacks of beer and water.

While battle continues, I meet some of the non-participants, including sixty-two-year-old Wacka Wainwright, who lived in Hallaton for twenty-four years before buying a business in Medbourne in 1974. Ever since then he's been castigated for 'living in the other camp'. Too old now to get stuck in, in his time Wacka has cracked ribs, severely bruised his knees and cracked a bone in his hand. One year, having grabbed hold of the bottle, he fell backwards into a hedge. That night thirty-five thorns were pulled out of his back.

I also meet George 'Sully' Sullivan from Medbourne, forbidden by his fiancée to play this year, as she wants him to have all his teeth on their wedding day. And in a lane beside the field of battle, I meet the injured. One lad, sitting in an ambulance, has dislocated his shoulder but is refusing to go to hospital. Instead he wants to get back into the maul. Another young man, dressed in a Leicester rugby shirt, popped a rib when the ruck fell on top of him. He counts himself lucky to have picked up only this one injury after many years of playing. The fact that Medbourne are losing pains him more than his injury.

Although ambulances and medics are on hand, refreshingly there's no sign of the dreaded health-and-safety killjoys. As long as there's no prize or money involved, the health-and-safety wonks can't touch it.

Later on, when the game is finished, I meet some lads outside one of the pubs nursing their injuries, including black eyes, split lips, bleeding brows, cricked necks and something they call a 'barbwire wrap'. They cheerfully tell me that there was at least one broken leg this year.

I also meet one of the Burrows lads from Medbourne. He doesn't look happy. 'Bit disappointed. Bit bloody hurt and all.'

A drunk Hallaton lad interrupts with the reason for Burrows' disappointment. 'Robbie! Told you it would be Hallaton. Medbourne lost. Talent won!'

Medbourne lost the first bottle. After that, Burrows concedes, they were overwhelmed and lost the second. 'There's always next year,' he says.

To a big cheer from the crowd, one of the Hallaton players climbs the Buttercross (which looks painfully sharp) and calls out for three cheers for the losers. Then, one by one, the Hallaton lads climb the Buttercross and take a swig from the bottle. Hallaton will get to take the two ale-filled casks back to display in the pub while Medbourne gets the brightly coloured dummy to hide away in a cupboard somewhere.

In parts of the countryside I've passed through on my journey to Hallaton and Medbourne it's very easy to imagine the landscape as it was a thousand years ago. Aside from a few mobile-phone masts, there's often little sign of human inter-vention in the landscape. It's also very easy to imagine the bottle-kicking taking place a thousand years ago or more. It's an event with a life of its own. Those who have grown up here feel it's part of them and they are roped in for life. It's bigger than the place or the people who live there. To outsiders, bottle-kicking may appear to be little more than an organized punch-up, but this strange ritual holds the community together and gives everyone a role to play. Mums get to make pies. Girls get to swoon at the boys. Boys get to beat the living daylights out of each other, then hug each other after the event and tell one another there are no hard feelings and that it's all just a game. And the old men get to drink a lot of beer and say how much better they did it when they were young. Everyone's happy.

It's easy to dismiss events such as the bottle-kicking as local curiosities with little relevance in today's world, but I think that would be to make a big mistake. Even as an onlooker, bottle-kicking and the other events I've seen so far on my journey have been life-enhancing. I'm really pleased to have experienced every one of them.

According to the speedometer, I've done 300 miles since I left London and yet I'm only actually 70 miles away from London. Travelling off the beaten track has led me along a very meandering road and taken a lot of time. But so what? Before the motorways were built, most journeys around the country were made along the wee roads on which I have been travelling and I can tell you it's a much more edifying and enjoyable experience than motorway travel. It's heaven, and sadly most of us miss so much of it on our journeys nowadays.

I've already been to half a dozen extremely eccentric places that you might think were in different countries, yet they are all very British. I've discovered the garden of England is a rich and vibrant stamping ground for an incredibly diverse range of characters. To my surprise, the cosy, comfortable, almost docile façade that dominates so much of the idyllic countryside and quaint little villages of Middle England is a breeding ground for passions and pastimes often done for their own sake. Wherever I look, there seems to be another tradition proudly held on to. And there are just as many new traditions springing up as old ones being celebrated.

I've discovered a state of mind that is proud to be different, that looks danger in the face and stands up to authority. A state of mind that is influenced by all manner of deeply ingrained traditions that affect us in the most unexpected ways.

I'm having such fun.

Chapter Six

Setting off from Hallaton, I continue on my journey north to Glasgow by driving 30 miles east and further away from my ultimate destination, through Rutland, England's smallest county.

Only 17 miles across and 18 miles from north to south, Rutland is so small that you can whoosh right through it if you sneeze and miss it altogether if you blink. But to do that would be a great shame, not least because you'd miss out on two spectacular landmarks. The first of these is the charming village of Harringworth and its most prized treasure, the viaduct. A piece of architectural inspiration, built by the Midland Railway across the Welland Valley in 1877–9, this imposing viaduct, located 2 miles from Gretton at the north-west corner of Harringworth, spans the Welland valley. Three-quarters of a mile in length, it is the longest masonry viaduct across a valley in Britain.

With eighty-two arches, each with a 40-foot span, it dominates the valley, yet, remarkably, it creates an impression of being in tune with its surroundings. Maybe that's because it's constructed entirely out of more than 20 million bricks from the nearby Williamson-Cliffe Quarry, so you could say it's made from the ground beneath its feet. Built to carry the London and Midland Railway between Kettering and Manton, it is part of a line that hasn't been electrified and these days it is generally used for freight trains or steam train outings.

Although my route takes me close enough to catch sight of the viaduct, I'm not stopping to admire it as fully as I would normally have liked. In part this is because I've fallen in love with the Jag. Exactly half a century old, it drives like a dream. And the best thing about an open-top car is that you become part of the scenery. You're part of the road. You're not in some wee quiet box – there'd be no point in listening to the radio, if the Jag had one – but exposed to nature and your journey through it. You feel the weather. And when you drive through forests, you smell the trees. It's a completely different experience.

But the main reason for scooting past the Harrington viaduct with little more than a sideways glance at its fine brickwork and imposing arches is that it's raining, so I'm really feeling part of the weather (the main drawback of a rag top!) as I approach my next destination, where another of those strange British pastimes is about to see its annual enactment.

Mention Stilton to most people and they'll think of that gloriously creamy blue-veined king of cheeses. And if you told those people that there was a village in rural Cambridgeshire called Stilton which is famous for its cheese and which holds an annual cheese-rolling festival, you'd think it would be a safe bet to assume that village was where Stilton is made. And like me, those people would probably assume the festival is a tradition with a heritage as old as the cheese itself.

How wrong we'd all be on every count.

The irony of this famous cheese is that only seven dairies in the world are licensed to make it, and not one of them is in Stilton. By law, the cheese can be made only in the three counties of Derbyshire, Leicestershire and Nottinghamshire – not in Cambridgeshire, where Stilton lies.

So why is the cheese called Stilton? Once again, the stage-coach provides the answer. Situated about 80 miles north of London on the old Great North Road, seventeenth-century Stilton was a major staging post for coaches travelling from London to York and Scotland. Horses would be changed, travellers would often overnight at one of the village's many inns and Dick Turpin (yes, him again) would evade capture by moving between inns through a secret tunnel beneath the road, which is apparently still intact.

At this time, Stilton was already known for the quality of the cheese sold to travellers in several of its inns. Writing in his *Tour through England & Wales*, Daniel Defoe, author of *Robinson Crusoe*, remarked in 1727 that he 'passed through Stilton, a village famous for its cheese', but it's unlikely that the cheese marketed there was the cheese we know as Stilton today.

Exactly how and why Stilton's eponymous cheese came to be produced isn't known. According to one explanation, the recipe for what came to be known as Stilton cheese was passed down through several generations of the Beaumont family of Quenby in Leicestershire. Then, in the early nineteenth century, the daughter of a former housekeeper at Quenby married Cooper Thornhill, landlord of the Bell Inn at Stilton. Thornhill, a larger-than-life entrepreneurial character who apparently won a 500-guinea wager by riding from Stilton to Shoreditch in London twice within fifteen hours, cannily recognized the appeal of the cheese to his captive market of stagecoach passengers. With his sister-in-law Frances Pawlett, a skilled cheesemaker working in one of the nearby villages allowed to produce the blue-veined local cheese, Thornhill established quality and shape standards for the cheese and set about marketing it to passing trade. It didn't take him long to put the village and the soft, creamy cheese that soon took its name on the gourmet's map – and the rest is history.

As for the cheese-rolling festival, its provenance is even more curious. In 1959, the A1 trunk road (a.k.a. the Great North Road and the north–south motorway of its day) was diverted round the village. It's interesting that the word 'bypass' is used to describe both running a road around a town and being ignored, which is what happened to Stilton. Overnight it became a ghost village, in a strange echo of what had happened in the middle of the nineteenth century when the north–east railway line opened nearby, ending the stagecoach trade and depriving the village of traffic until the motorcar and the A1 brought back passing trade. The Bell closed and fell into dereliction. Other businesses disappeared.

Three years after the bypass was built, the landlord of the Talbot and the former landlord of the Bell pubs were desperate to inject some life back into the village, cheer up their drinkers and rally trade, so they devised the first ever Stilton cheese-rolling contest. Aided and abetted by telephone engineer Fred Linstead, who provided a telegraph pole cut into cheese-sized rounds, they set up a course outside what is now the Post Office.

Even in 1961, cheese-rolling was nothing new. There was already a similar event involving a round of Double Gloucester at Cooper's Hill in the Cotswolds; it still takes place every year and is said to date back to Roman times. It may even have its origins in a pagan healing ritual, although that is just as likely to be cock and bull as true. So, in an attempt to give locals the impression that the origins of their newly invented event were lost in the mists of time, on Easter Monday 1961 one of the landlords rolled a Stilton-cheese-sized cylinder of telegraph pole along the course, telling his clientele he was reviving an ancient tradition. The regulars stood and watched – probably open-mouthed. Eventually some of them joined in. And so Stilton-rolling was born.

Since then rules have been established, but in the event's early days a piece of wood in the shape of a Stilton cheese would be produced and teams of inevitably inebriated men would vie to roll it from a starting line somewhere between the Stilton Cheese Inn and the Talbot to the finishing line outside the Bell, with much scrambling and many tussles and spills along the way.

These days, as I discover when I arrive in Stilton, the event is considerably more formalized, not least because it now attracts crowds of several tens of thousands. Teams of four men or women (mixed teams are forbidden) roll cheese-sized chunks of telegraph pole from the starting point outside the Bell Inn and the Angel pub to the finish at the crossroads of Fen Street and Church Street. Each team member has to roll the cheese at least once during its journey. Teams come from far and wide, some in very elaborate costumes and often with somewhat risqué team names (the Four Skins of Edam, Balls of Steel and the Hairy Beavers, a women's team – really, you surprise me – are only some of several slightly dodgy team names this year), and the whole thing has been wrapped into a knock-out competition with quarter-finals, semis and a grand final.

The prizes are the same as ever: a whole Stilton cheese and beer for the men; a whole Stilton cheese and wine for the ladies.

The men compete for the Bell Cup and the women for the WI Cup, but these days there is also a junior event for the Stilton Parish Council Shield, a wheelchair cheese-rolling event and prizes for the best fancy dress and best-dressed baby buggy.

As I arrive, the High Street is lined with stalls, bouncy castles and inflatables, fairground rides, a helter-skelter and a flight simulator, and more food and drink than even a town full of people could possibly consume. Hanging over it all is the wonderfully enticing smell of fried onions, which, combined with the sound of generators and smell of diesel fumes – ah, heaven – always evokes in me the best spirit of a good British day out.

For the locals, cheese-rolling is bigger than Christmas: everyone gets dressed up and uses the event, as if they needed the excuse, to go down the pub. That includes the reigning champions, who have been doing their preparation in the Bell Inn, where I find them indulging in some last-minute training.

'So what do you think your chances are this year, boys? Have you put any money on it?'

Wearing white T-shirts, Native American headdresses and scarves round their necks, the Neckerchiefs are a motley bunch whose bravado appears to be founded more on Dutch courage than rigorous practice.

'I'm extremely confident of success,' one of them says. 'Bet the house on it. I can't see anyone beating us. We're gonna *do it again*.'

This is the team's tenth year together. They've won twice and been losing finalists several times, but in between the joking they reveal they're worried the Poles will beat them this year.

'It means a lot that the cheese stays in Stilton,' says one of the Neckerchiefs. 'It does mean a lot. It's a local event and we'd like to keep it. Yeah.'

It all seems so quintessentially English: a rainy summer's day, fancy dress and an eccentric village tradition. And a team of cheese-rollers from Krakow in Poland. Their team, Lajkonic (it's pronounced 'laconic' and they assure me it isn't a Polish swearword), are wearing Polish national dress and speaking better English than many Englishmen I know. They are also a strikingly good-looking and erudite bunch. One of them tells me their reason for taking part is to recognize the traditions (even if they date back only fifty years) of their new home. 'We like to keep our Polish traditions,' he says in a thick Brummie accent that he must have picked up since moving here. 'And we think it's important to support the traditions of the country we're in as well.'

A short while later I see the noble sport for myself. Stilton is a typical old market town. Like its buildings, its roads are slightly rickety and crooked, not smooth and flat, which makes rolling a heavy slice of telegraph pole along about 50 yards of tarmac all the more difficult. The 'cheeses' are thicker at the middle than at their edges, so making them roll straight is not easy. The secret, I discover from watching the best of the women's teams, is always to have two hands on it. Allowed to roll freely, the cheese veers off at an angle. But keep two hands on it as it rolls and it's obliged to go straight. Like many things, the key to successful cheese-rolling is technique and finesse, rather than brute force.

After a few tumbles and some grazed knuckles, the Neckerchiefs and Lajkonics both lose in their quarter-finals. The Neckerchiefs appear fairly nonplussed about losing their title. 'It's back to the training,' one of them says, heading for the Bell.

The Lajkonics are, well, laconic in defeat. 'One mistake at

the halfway mark and we lost it. But it was fun. It was just great to take part.'

A very English attitude, I think. Honour in defeat is something in which we've become very adept; now it seems our Polish émigrés are so well integrated they're adopting our behaviour patterns. Anglo-Polish relations have never been better.

The Four Skins of Edam, the male winners, are presented with a Stilton and a crate of beer, then face the Hairy Beavers, pink-wigged winners of the women's event, for the Champion of Champions race, in which the men race uphill while the women race downhill towards them. Much to everyone's delight, including mine, the women are crowned Champion of Champions.

Leaving Stilton, I'm impressed by the way in which the village has reinvented itself and put its name back on the map after the A1 bypass diverted its lifeblood. And it's heartening to see Stilton's latest newcomers, the Polish community, embracing the tradition with such gusto.

As I cruise north-west in the delightful Jaguar, I pass the second of Rutland's spectacular sights, another site of reinvention and one of the largest artificial lakes in Europe. Opened in 1976, Rutland Water is England's biggest reservoir by surface area (although Kielder Water in Northumberland is greater in capacity) and supplies 65 million gallons of water a day to the East Midlands, the driest and most densely populated part of England. Set in 3,100 acres of countryside, Rutland Water has become an impressive centrepiece of the county and is now extensively stocked with fish for anglers. It's also home to a water sports centre, a perimeter cycle track, a pleasure cruiser for hire and a nature reserve of international importance that attracts wintering populations of ducks and birds.

But it wasn't always so popular with the locals, who fiercely opposed the flooding of the valley of the river Gwash because the villages of Nether Hambleton and Middle Hambleton had to be submerged to create the lake. The neighbouring village of Upper Hambleton was spared and now sits on an attractive peninsula that juts from the western shore of the lake into the U-shaped reservoir. The most intriguing feature on the lake, however, is opposite the village, on the eastern shore. Normanton Church, formerly St Matthews Church, is a beautiful example of English baroque architecture. With a semicircular portico and a tower, it was designed by Thomas Cundy, then architect to the Grosvenor estate in Westminster, to resemble St John's in Smith Square and was finished in 1829. This lovely church would have been lost beneath the high-water line when the valley was flooded had the locals not come together to save it in a particularly innovative way.

After much consideration, engineers waterproofed the walls and raised the floor of the church 3 metres by filling the lower half of the building to just below window level with limestone and rubble. This was capped with concrete. Outside, a dyke was built around the church and a causeway was laid to provide access from the shore. The church now sits isolated on a spit, surrounded by water. With half of the main body of the building below water level, it looks from a distance as if it has sunk into the lake. It now houses a museum and a collection of fossils and is well worth a visit if you happen, like me, to be passing through this charming corner of the East Midlands on the B-roads.

Chapter Seven

From the largest artificial lake in Europe, my journey continues a few miles further northwards towards the largest hole in Britain. Leaving Rutland, I arrive in the idyllic village of Mountsorrel, smack bang at the heart of Leicestershire. The area around Mountsorrel has been inhabited since prehistoric times but it was put on the map in 1080, when Hugh Lupus built a castle at the top of what is now Castle Hill. Hugh, one of the great magnates of early Norman England, was the son of the Viscount of Avranches in the far south-west of Normandy and a nephew of William the Conqueror, who appointed him the first Earl of Chester. His castle became a key position in political struggles during the reign of King Stephen, when it became a garrison to rebel soldiers who raided local peasants and the surrounding countryside, lending it the reputation as 'a nest of the Devil and den of thieves and robbers'. Unfortunately, all that remains today is an imposing granite crag that stands above the village, which, with its carefully tended parks, rows of cottages and annual front-garden competition, is now a quiet, restful place. Sleepy, even. Except, that is, at lunchtime, when vibrations rise through the floors of every building in the village. These tremors are so regular and so noticeable you could set your watch by them. But where do they come from?

The source is to be found a mile away from Mountsorrel. It's something so vast and so awe-inspiring that you'd think it would be impossible to miss, but, because it's surrounded by woods and hidden by a natural rise in the ground, the only way to see it clearly from any distance is from the air. Take to the skies and the source of Mountsorrel's tremors sticks out like a sore thumb. Ten times the size of Wembley Stadium and set to become even bigger, Mountsorrel Quarry is the biggest hole in Britain. And waiting for me there is a man who is going to teach me how to blast a small part of it to smithereens, something I've dreamt of doing for as long as I can remember.

Mick Stevens is a man who has always known what he wanted to do. Born and bred near Mountsorrel, his dream was to work at the quarry. As a boy he would play there and as a teenager he would study it whenever he could. When he left school he took a job at a hosiery plant, treading water until he was old enough to escape the factory and take up what he now claims is the best job in the world. Officially he's a Phase One Foreman and Explosives Supervisor, which means he's the one who gets to set off the big bang. And what young man wouldn't want to spend all day blowing things up?

Kitted out in a hard hat, protective glasses and a fluorescent orange vest, I'm led by Mick into the quarry to be shown how he manages to blow up 25,000 tons of hard rock without scaring the neighbours or destroying all the windows for miles around.

It's a surreal experience, like being on the set of a science fiction film. With more than ten levels, called benches, the quarry looks like a galleried amphitheatre built for giants.

The sheer scale of the hole seems unreal – it's completely unlike anything I've ever encountered. Standing at the bottom of the quarry I am more than 90 metres below sea level and 300 metres beneath the lip of the excavation, which is almost 1 kilometre in diameter, covering some 135 acres. From this immense hole, 10 million tons of granite (technically, hornblende granodiorite) is excavated every year and there are another 180 million tons in reserve. For those of a geological bent, the stone was formed by an intrusion (essentially a volcano that never burst) that flowed towards the earth's surface some 450 million years ago, when this area was a desert resembling New Mexico. Similar geological events created the granite masses from Dartmoor to the Scilly Isles and in the Lake District.

This extremely hard crystalline rock is used for road building and in the construction industry. Dick Whittington thought otherwise, but according to an eighteenth-century colloquialism, 'The streets are not paved with gold in London. They are paved with Leicestershire granite.' And there's some truth in the saying. Mountsorrel granite was used in the forecourt of Buckingham Palace (although it has now been covered with tarmac) and in numerous pink pathways in royal parks. You can apparently still see it in Windsor Great Park.

Quarrying at Mountsorrel began in the late eighteenth century, and to this day it shapes the character of the village and the lives of its inhabitants. For a time, Mountsorrel was known as Mount Sterile because of the devastating effects of its granite dust. This dust covered a large part of the village, driving many local men to grow bushy moustaches as primitive dust filters and to drown their misery in drink (well, that was their excuse). The current quarry is slightly further away from the village than the quarry used in the eighteenth and nine-teenth centuries, so its effects aren't so profound.

The biggest difference between the original quarry and today's is the use of highly automated technology. Even though it's the largest granite quarry in Europe, far fewer men now work here than at any other time in its history, and most positions available today involve pulling levers and pushing buttons to activate hydraulic tools, rather than the backbone-breaking shovelling of rocks or hauling of wagons that their forebears endured.

Saying that, Mick had to do a fair bit of shovelling as a labourer before he was promoted to setting the charges and designing detonations, the job he'd always wanted. The skill in setting the explosives is to make sure the force of the blast is directed down into the rock rather than into the path of least resistance – up into the air above. Mick and his colleagues have got their pyrotechnics down to such a fine art that they can blow up a section of rock weighing thousands of tons so accurately that they can decide exactly where the pile will land.

'It will actually lift this up,' Mick points at a huge chunk of rock, the top of which is about the area of two tennis courts, 'then take it to one side, smash it up and put it down where we want it.'

Feeding a long length of yellow cable into one of two dozen 6-inch-wide holes drilled deep into the rock, Mick shows me how he is going to fulfil his boast. Liquid explosive pumped from a truck is poured 15 metres into the rock, then a detonator is dropped in at a depth of 4 metres and the rest of the hole is plugged with gravel. Each of the holes has been cut by a 20-ton drilling machine the size of a large digger with a tungsten drill bit, which is the size of a giant fist and lasts only three days. By the time the job is finished, we are standing on nearly 6 tons of explosive. The mind boggles at what this could do in the wrong hands. Well, it would be quick. Wouldn't it?

The charges are timed to go off at eight-millisecond intervals. 'If we blew all this in one go,' Mick gestures with a sweep of his arm at the area they are preparing to blast, 'the vibration would be horrendous. It would rattle straight through to the village.'

A couple of miles away in Mountsorrel, they're used to the vibration, but it's usually no more than a mild tremor. The Horticultural Society members' greenhouses are safe, for now.

As Mick connects together all the detonation wires emerging from the holes, I ask him what happens if he gets it wrong.

'It's not the kind of thing you get wrong more than once,' he says ominously. In fact, he's so confident of his calculations that he tells our cameraman where to position his camera to get the best shot of the blast. 'Put it there,' he says, 'and the rocks will fan out and stop just in front of it.'

Watching Mick reel out the wire to a safe distance, I hope he's right, especially as he now gives me the most important instruction of all: to take cover in a steel bunker a couple of hundred metres away.

Inside the bell-shaped bunker, he hands me two pieces of wire and a charger with a handle. To my immense delight, it's just like in the movies. I connect the two wires to the charger. This is it. I really am going to cause the biggest legal explosion in the country. Big enough to raze Buckingham Palace to the ground – not that I'd want to, Your Majesty.

'Ready when you are.' The instruction comes out of Mick's two-way radio.

I wind the handle until a little light turns orange, then I press a button on the side of the charger.

Nothing happens. Is it really that quiet? I think. Is the explosion that boring?

'Not hard enough?' Maybe I need to put more elbow grease into winding the handle.

Mick nods. 'Give it another go.'

I wind the handle again, then press the button for a second time. There's a moment's silence, like a pause of anticipation, then – *kavoom* – a rumble, a shudder of the ground and a rush of air. It's a fantastic feeling. The noise of the blast isn't as loud as I expected, but I can feel the pressure wave piling into the bunker. What have I done?

Outside, everything is quiet. The only sign of my destructive efforts is a cloud of dust rising slowly to the sky. Where a lump of solid rock once stood – and where Mick and I chatted just a few minutes ago – there's now a very neat pile of smaller rocks lying in front of a new edge.

Just as Mick predicted, the camera we positioned near the rocks before the detonation has survived, thanks to his perfect calculation of the fan of the blast. The spread of 25,000 tons of rocks has stopped just a few feet in front of the camera. Mick's wearing a big smile. 'I think we set it about right.'

'I think we can call it a job well done.' I can't avoid the obvious pun: 'The day went with a bang.'

I tell Mick I'm surprised by how quiet the explosion was.

'You feel the vibration more in the village,' Mick says. 'Even my kids at school two villages away would've felt that more than we did.'

A Terex digger the size of a large house immediately gets to work clearing away the granite rubble, which is loaded into giant Caterpillar dumper trucks. Against the vast scale of the quarry they look like tiny Tonka toys, but these 65-ton trucks have wheels twice my height. Powered by stonking 34.5-litre engines that generate 1,000 horsepower, they carry 100-ton loads of stone out of the quarry. As for the digger, it's the biggest thing I've ever seen moved by an internal combustion engine. It can shovel 25 tons of rocks into a truck in a single scoop. And I am going to drive it.

I climb up a ladder, along a gantry and up a second ladder to the driver's cabin. Settling into the driver's chair, I'm aware that I could make a big fool of myself if I lose control of this beast. It takes two weeks to train someone to drive the digger, and I can see why it takes so long. With the scoop fully loaded with rocks, a small mistake could topple the digger over on its side and there are few cranes capable of lifting this baby back upright.

Despite the potential for disaster, the driver is very cool about a rookie taking charge of his machine. 'Everyone's got to learn sometime,' he says, with twenty-seven years' experience behind him.

All the controls are electronic drive-by-wire. Two pedals control movement of the digger on its caterpillar tracks, one for forwards or backwards, the other for left and right. Two joystick levers are used to direct the powered arm and its bucket. To see to the left, I look out of the window, but my view to the right is obscured by the digger's arm, so I look at a small screen in front of me, which displays the view seen by a camera on the other side of the arm.

With the tip of my tongue poking out of the corner of my mouth in concentration, I gingerly edge the digger's arm forward and around to the right. The engine roars satisfyingly

– and slightly alarmingly – every time I tweak the controls. I move it around some more, and pick up and drop some huge rocks, but after a while I realize I'm slowing things up and hand the controls back to the driver.

'That was wonderful. Thank you so much. Every man in the country is going to be jealous.'

While I've been having a driving lesson, another digger and some trucks have been dispatching the newly blasted rocks. From the floor of the quarry the granite is carried to the quarry's own rail yard, where custom-made rail wagons ferry the stone to destinations throughout Europe. Within two and a half days the mess I created at the push of a button in the blast bunker will have been totally cleared away.

As I leave, I realize what's really impressive about the quarry is the atmosphere. It's full of people who really enjoy their jobs. They know they're doing difficult jobs, but difficult jobs are satisfying and there's never a dull moment here, making it a great place to work. These are proper boys' jobs and the workers' pride in them can be seen all around.

Outside the quarry gates I spot a pile of stones. It's the so-called 'sacrificial pile' from which the locals can take stones for the rockeries in their gardens. Considering the damage this place once inflicted on nearby villages, this is a gesture that shows how much attitudes here have changed, and for the better.

The quarry is one of those places that serves to remind us how small our place in this world is, a characteristic it shares with my next destination, a church in Burton-on-Trent, another 20-odd miles further up the B-roads towards Glasgow.

The poster outside the Elim Pentecostal Church gives some

indication of what awaits me. 'BIKER SERVICE', it says. 'ALL MOTORCYCLE ENTHUSIASTS WELCOME. YOUR FIRST BIKE SERVICE OF THE SUMMER FREE!'

Inside the church, where I'm expecting to find pews, stand two rows of twenty-six gleaming, lovingly polished motorbikes. And in front of them is a crowd of some seventy parishioners. Among the congregation are the Coffin Scratchers, a band of bearded, leather-clad bikers you'd be more likely to find at a Hell's Angels gathering than in a church. With several dozen other bikers in racing leathers, they are awaiting the arrival of the Reverend Paul Sinclair, who likes to call himself the Faster Pastor, although I prefer to refer to him as the revving Reverend.

'Let us pray.' The congregation bows its heads as Reverend Sinclair, a former Glasgow shipyard worker, walks in to lead the prayers. 'We thank you, Lord, that we can have a life of motorcycling. We thank you for the great joy that brings us, the things we see, we feel, we experience, the camaraderie. And we pray for your hand upon this service tonight. Let us all be blessed.'

The service that follows is unconventional, to say the least. But these are not conventional people and it's lovely to see folk with ZZ Top beards and motorcycles being accepted by the Church and the community. After all, the Christian Church was established as a refuge for those who felt themselves to be outcasts from society, so it seems very appropriate that this bunch of bikers, who I'm sure sometimes get the feeling they're not welcome in places, have found a common home. In my opinion, whenever you get a room full of a hundred or so people who feel they don't belong anywhere, well that's the place they belong (not wanting to be too existential about it).

As for the revving Rev. Paul, he does more than tend his flock in this life. When the time comes for them to meet their maker, he guarantees them a uniquely speedy send-off, courtesy of his day job as the founder and managing director of Britain's only motorcycle funeral service.

On an industrial estate in Measham, about 10 miles from Burton-on-Trent, Paul shows me round his nerve centre, where he's working on a new motorcycle hearse to add to his burgeoning fleet.

A coffin on a motorcycle is something to which I think I can relate. Many years ago I had a friend who rode a BSA M20 with a coffin sidecar and I'd take great delight when, pulling up at traffic lights, I'd sit bolt upright in the coffin and scare the occupants of the neighbouring car. Before arriving at Paul's workshops, I was expecting something similar to the motorbike-and-coffin combo from my youth, but his is an altogether classier operation. As soon as Paul pushes up the door to his garage, I'm amazed at how beautifully made, stately and dignified his hearses appear.

'These are unique,' says Paul. 'They're not adapted sidecars or trikes or whatever, they are purpose-built hearses and recognized by the DVLA as a two-wheeled hearse.'

The hearses are hand-built by Paul and a team of specialists, including motorcycle racing team engineers and a Rolls-Royce hearse builder. The fleet includes a Harley hearse for those who want their last journey in this world to be accompanied by that distinctive Harley Davidson blatter. There's also a lovely Triumph Triple hearse with a black leather interior and Rolls-Royce hearse fittings, and, for a more retro effect, a Triumph café racer hearse. And for the ultimate biker's send-off, there's a hearse powered by a Suzuki Hayabusa, the fastest production bike available. It's capable of 247 miles per hour. Finished to Paul's usual high standards, the Hayabusa hearse broke the world record for fastest hearse and won Best Modern Hearse at the Hearse of the Year awards in 2004 (but I expect you knew that).

Those records and awards, I'd guess, mean little to the families of the deceased. But the opportunity for a final burn-up with your motorcycle-loving relative is something many bereaved seldom get. 'You did the ton with my brother,' said one member of a deceased's family as he climbed off Paul's pillion at the crematorium. 'That meant so much.'

Paul's been running Motorcycle Funerals very successfully for five years now. It might be a dying market, but it's clearly a very healthy one. There's obviously a demand, but I wanted to know what made him do it.

'I was a church minister in London and got asked to do a few funerals of bikers who'd died. And it really bothered me we'd put them in the back of a car. You'd never give a Catholic a Protestant funeral or a Protestant a Catholic funeral. So why would you put a motorcyclist through a funeral that was better suited to automobile enthusiasts? It didn't make sense to me.'

And this makes absolute sense to me. After all, no Glaswegian undertaker would place a Rangers fan in a Celtic strip when they died, so why should those who love bikes be last seen in a car?

Paul suspected he wasn't the only person who felt the way he did and after a bit of research he discovered there was a demand for something new and different. But then, Paul has always been a bit of a free-thinker. Over the years his methods of converting sinners have landed him in hot water, most notably when he used images of Clint Eastwood on billboards outside his church. 'COME TO CHURCH, MAKE MY DAY', said one poster beside an image of Clint as Dirty Harry. 'WE WELCOME THE GOOD, THE BAD AND THE UGLY', a second one said. When Paul wrote to Eastwood to tell him about his posters, the reply from Clint's lawyers said he loved the posters but couldn't let his name be used in vain.

So maybe it's no surprise that Paul – a canny Jock if I ever met one – spotted a gap in the market where no one else had thought to look. To date he has conducted more than seven hundred motorcycle funerals all over Britain and demand is growing so much that he recently took on his first full-time member of staff as a funeral arranger, a trendy biker chick who was already working for a firm of undertakers. He's also helped by seventy-one-year-old David Harrison, a former postman, professional undertaker and passionate biker. To celebrate his seventieth birthday, David rode a 1,952-mile round trip from Land's End to John O'Groats on his favourite bike, a 600 c.c. Suzuki Bandit. And, of course, for his own final departure, David has already planned a motorcycle funeral.

As a classic car enthusiast, I can certainly see the appeal of making your last journey in something more appealing than a standard hearse, but it's Paul's attention to detail and dedicated problem-solving that really impress me. For example, because the hearse is a relatively small, enclosed space with windows on four sides, the moisture in the flowers and the vapour in the body can turn to steam on a hot day. The windows steam up and no one can see the coffin, so Paul has built de-misters and ventilation systems into the hearses.

There's also a light to illuminate the inside of the hearse and there's a chrome rail along the top, so that flowers and wreaths can be attached without fear that they'll blow off when Paul cranks up the bike for a final blast-off. He also has a hand-brake on the left wheel for those occasions when he's requested to turn up at some speed and do a handbrake turn to stop. How cool is that?

'I've one other little thing the normal hearses don't have.' Paul points at a wee door that flips up at the front of the hearse. 'If the deceased wants to be buried with his boots, it's not a problem. But because of clean air regulations we're not allowed to cremate the boots, so the deceased can't be wearing them inside the coffin. So we take his boots off, just before he goes, put them in here . . .' He flips open the door to show me where he slips the motorcycle boots into the front of the hearse.

'Just before he goes to the bad fire, then?'

'Just before he goes. And he arrives at the crematorium with his boots in front of the coffin.'

What more could a biker want?

I'd expected it all to be a bit gothic with bikers' boots strung across the petrol tank, but, as Paul pointed out, ultimately a motorcycle funeral involves someone who has died and a lot of grieving friends and relatives, so he makes sure that it's done with great dignity. Paul wears a sombre black motorcycle outfit and a black helmet so that the focus is not on him but on the passenger in the hearse. It's very impressive indeed.

My epic B-road journey continues northwards to Derby, a city that has radically reinvented itself since the days when it was the cradle of the Industrial Revolution. Derby is home to the Silk Mill, thought to be the first factory in Britain, the UK's first purpose-built basketball arena, the world's biggest ever bowl of popcorn and Ellen MacArthur, but it's also home to a swelling

Sikh community, among whom are Britain's most dedicated Sikh Sword Fighters.

Followers of one of the less publicized religions, Sikhs believe in not eating meat, never cutting their hair and worshipping their one god. One of the ways in which they do this is by practising the holy martial art of Gatka.

More than half a million Sikhs call Britain home. Although a minority in India, they form the largest religious group of Indians who have emigrated and settled in Britain. Gatka is more popular in the West Midlands than any other region of Britain, and I have come here to witness two of the best Gatka clubs battle it out for supremacy.

Driving along Grove Street, I come to the grand gates of the first public park in Britain: the Arboretum. Recently cleaned up after many years of neglect, the Arboretum opened in 1840, a time when Derby was gaining a worldwide reputation for its engineering. In the eighteenth century, the town was the site of the first water-powered silk and cotton mills, developing a form of power that was the catalyst for the Industrial Revolution. By the early 1800s, the city was densely packed with textile mills, factories, engineering workshops and railway works. Joseph Strutt, a former mayor of Derby and member of a prominent local family of industrialists, decided that this rapidly expanding and urbanizing city desperately needed a recreational area for the workers amid all the factories and mills. He donated an 11-acre site that had previously served as his summer retreat, and commissioned John Claudius Loudon, a Scottish botanist and garden designer, to create a botanical garden and pleasure grounds. Amid the rickety houses and the dark satanic mills belching smoke there was now a small oasis of tranquillity and nature. The Arboretum was so influential that it led to the creation of dozens of other city public parks and is said to have inspired the design for Central Park in New York. Having seen them both, I can well believe it.

Walking through the Arboretum, I pass the statue of Sir Frederick Henry Royce, the engineering mastermind behind one of the best things to come out of Derby, namely Rolls-Royce. Then, turning a corner, I enter a green space full of men and women in brightly coloured turbans and saris and I know I've arrived at my destination. I'm here to meet the 'Khalsa Panth Gatka Akhara', a group of Sikhs who practise the ancient art of Sikh sword fighting.

I have to confess that I knew nothing about Gatka before arriving at the festival, but once here I am fascinated by it. Passed from generation to generation, the origins of this defensive Indian martial art go back to the founder of Sikhism, Guru Nanak, but it was the sixth Guru, called Guru Hargobind, who formalized Gatka to enable Sikhs to protect themselves against oppressors. Like some Japanese martial arts, Gatka is intended only as a last resort, to be used when all other methods of reconciliation have failed, in common with Guru Hargobind's vision of a global community of warrior-saints working for the good of all society. 'When all other means have failed, it is proper to take the sword in one's hand,' Guru Gobind Singh, the tenth and last of the Sikh prophets, wrote in the *Zafarnama*, a seventeenth-century epistle.

The Sikhs mastered Gatka and perfected its use in combat, winning many battles despite often being heavily outnumbered. Although I'm deeply uncomfortable with any religion that preaches combat and advocates carrying two types of swords to kill enemies, I cannot deny the beauty, elegance and flamboyant athleticism of the sport. Sitting to the side of the main arena, I watch as the warriors, dressed in turbans and long tunics held together with a cummerbund, swirl around one another swinging some very sharp swords round their heads, while their feet perform what looks like an intricate dance. With a hypnotic fighting motion, involving swinging the swords rhythmically in what look like rehearsed moves, Gatka is like an amalgam of kung fu, fencing, t'ai chi and Edward Scissorhands. There are lots of jumps, spins and feints, but when two experienced practitioners fight it's clear that this is serious combat. Although the only battle today is one for supremacy between two West Midlands Gatka clubs, I get an inkling of how formidable and ferocious the Sikh warriors must have been when they appeared on battlefields, their swords swirling around their heads and bodies.

Amar Deep Singh Bedi, who until recently ran the Derby Gatka group, tells me that Gatka is as much about mental attitude as physical skill. Your attitude should be humble, not challenging, he says. Like Japanese martial arts, Gatka is a way of concentrating the mind, but when I remark that it reminds me of Zen, he raises his eyebrows.

The weapons, which range from extremely sharp steel swords to wooden numb chucks, are held in extremely high esteem. Approached with respect and bowed to as if they were a living thing, the weapons are believed to have come directly from God as manifestations of His power on earth. To demonstrate the sharpness of his swords and his Gatka skills, Amar Deep takes three young students and places a banana on each of their necks. Then he blindfolds himself and chops each of the bananas in half with his sword.

Although the stunt sounds amazing, it's curiously unimpressive. Amar Deep lines up his sword with the banana before he puts on his blindfold and can tell how far he has cut through them simply by feeling the resistance to his sword. But as a theatrical demonstration of trust in the master, it's very effective.

Amar Deep's demonstration and the Gatka I've seen look incredibly dangerous and bloodthirsty, but then I notice all the mums and families nearby, watching the festivities and laying out picnics on rugs. And it's fantastic to see this display of multiculturalism in the middle of an English park, not least because as many girls and women are taking part as boys and men. Amar Deep explains that Sikhism believes there are no distinctions between genders, a very enlightened view if you ask me, especially when some religions act as if men and women were born on different planets. Narinder Kaur, who at twenty-four is about to sit her finals to become a fully qualified doctor, says it shows just how equal women and men are in the Sikh religion. She says Gatka is particularly good for women as it raises their levels of confidence and self-defence.

At the edge of the festival area is a group of white teenagers. Dressed in white sports kit, swigging from cans of super lager and dragging on fags, they are shouting mindless abuse at the Sikhs. Suddenly a martial art developed in seventeenth-century India seems strangely relevant in a twenty-first-century Midlands city.

It's a rather depressing sight, not least because I can't help wondering who is going to have the better life: these Sikh kids who are learning to discipline themselves, enjoying a picnic with their families and having fun in the spring sun, or the sad losers in their white sports gear, who can think of nothing better to do than ride their bikes around a park and be abusive to people?

*

By coincidence (okay, I'll be honest, it's less a matter of coincidence and more the product of the itinerary), Amar Deep greets me at my next destination. From a demonstration of Derby's spiritual life, I've travelled a few miles to the epicentre of the city's rational world: the Rolls-Royce aerospace factory.

Now, whenever Boeing or Airbus boast about how their latest aeroplane is more fuel-efficient than any of its predecessors, I invariably want to shout, 'Oh yeah?'

Why? Because the secret of any aircraft's fuel economy relies less on the design of its fuselage or its wings than on its engines. And more often than not, those engines are made by Rolls-Royce.

Rolls-Royce is a wonderful British success story, but I hadn't realized until I visit the highly impressive and sprawling Rolls-Royce factory at Derby that Rolls-Royce cars and Rolls-Royce engines went their separate ways a long time ago.

Henry Royce and Charles Stewart Rolls founded the company in 1906, Royce providing the engineering and technical expertise to complement Rolls's marketing skills and entrepreneurial flair. In 1914 they started making aero engines as well as cars; by the 1920s aircraft engines were the bulk of their business. Royce's swansong, shortly before his death, was the Merlin, the legendary V12 engine that powered the Spitfire, Hawker Hurricane and De Havilland Mosquito fighters, as well as the Lancaster and Wellington bombers. It also transformed the American P-51 Mustang into the most successful (and probably the best) fighter of its time.

Rolls-Royce was a world-beater, but it met its nemesis in the late 1960s when developing the RB211 turbofan jet to power the Tristar passenger jet, an engine so complex and innovative that its development drove the company into bankruptcy. Edward Heath's government bailed out Rolls-Royce, nationalizing the company in 1971. Two years later, amid fears that the aerospace division of Rolls-Royce was endangering the future of the car division, the automobile business was hived off into a separate entity called Rolls-Royce Motors. How ironic now to think Rolls-Royce Motors cut and ran when they thought aerospace was yesterday's technology, particularly as the car company was sold to Volkswagen in 1998. Meanwhile, Rolls-Royce aerospace has become one of Britain's most successful companies, largely thanks to the RB211, variants of which have become one of the most successful engine designs ever built, prized for their reliability, economy and quietness. Built into Boeing 727, 747, 757 and 767 aircraft, among others, an RB211-engined plane takes off every few seconds somewhere in the world.

Nowadays, Rolls-Royce employs thirty-eight thousand people in fifty countries, of which eleven thousand work in Derby, among them Amar Deep. I've come to Rolls-Royce to meet him again and to see the engines on which he has been working – the Trent 900 and Trent 1000. At nearly 10 feet in diameter, the Trent 900 is Rolls-Royce's largest ever engine and bedecked in jaw-dropping statistics. When it's running at full speed, its hollow titanium fan blades suck in more than 1.25 tons of air *every second* – that's more air than in a squash court.

The Trent 900 is intended for the A380, Airbus's new double-decker behemoth. At take-off, the four Trent 900s on the A380 will blast the plane off the runway with a thrust equivalent to the power of more than 3,500 family cars. At the centre of the engine, around the combustor, temperatures are half as hot as the surface of the sun. In fact, it's hotter than the melting point of the metals used to make the components at the centre of the engine, so Rolls-Royce has developed some very clever ways of circulating cooler air through the engine to ensure that it doesn't melt.

Amar Deep's expertise in computer modelling the engine is an essential part of the design process. Modern jet-engine design is so complex that you can't build a rough engine and then tinker with it. You need to know how it's going to act before you build it.

The inner workings of this engine and the Trent 1000, which Boeing will be using in its 787 Skyliner, are considered by Rolls-Royce to be so sensitive to industrial competition that they are highly reluctant to let us in, but in the end I get a whole afternoon to look around the test beds for the engines, which form the largest and most advanced indoor engine-test complex in the world. The engines are run at full power inside the test bed, but anyone standing outside would never know it; the traffic on the road outside is noisier. With typical under-statement, Rolls-Royce says it likes to make sure it won't disturb its neighbours.

The engineers tell me how they use lasers to put microscopic holes in the Trent's scimitar-shaped blades. The holes are so small you can't see them with the naked eye, but they play a part in enabling the Trent to produce more power and less noise with lower fuel consumption – just don't ask me how. I could tell you, but then I'd have to kill you. Although maybe that is a little melodramatic . . .

It's extremely impressive. It's an engine shop, but it's as clean as an operating theatre, with all the parts supplied in vacuum-sealed bags that hang from the ceiling. The overalls and tool boxes are immaculate. Every component is double-checked and every tool is accounted for; they cannot afford to leave anything lying around as it would be sucked into the air intakes when they run the engines.

It's fantastic to see a piece of British industrial heritage that isn't a museum, but a living, world-class operation, and I leave Rolls-Royce a very happy and contented man, ready for a good night's sleep.

Chapter Eight

Clear-headed and well rested the next morning, my first stop off is a venue that many of my predecessors would have first glimpsed through a fog of inebriation and trepidation. About 15 miles from Derby and nestled in the Peak District National Park, the Old Lockup bed and breakfast at Wirksworth was until quite recently open only to those who had ventured on to the wrong side of the law. Built in 1842, it served first as a magistrate's house, then from 1852 to 1952 as a police station. The town drunks sobered up in the cells downstairs, while murder suspects would be incarcerated before being taken to court in Derby.

Nowadays the Old Lockup is a guesthouse much like any other. Where prisoners once slopped out with buckets, today's visitors can take a rejuvenating drink after a day's hiking through the Dales, or they can enjoy a relaxing bath. The drunk tank is now, quite appropriately, a charming bar. A cell has been converted into a bathroom. Upstairs, rooms that once served as offices or quarters for the long arm of the law have been converted into bedrooms. In what used to be the magistrate's room, an antique French bed now dominates.

There's something quite charming about walking into a

building with a large metal sign inscribed 'POLICE' on one side of the main entrance and an English Tourist Board Five Diamond Gold Award sign on the other side of the threshold.

Inside, paraphernalia related to the building's former use, such as handcuffs, shackles, constabulary badges and big bunches of keys, adorn the walls. A row of police helmets sits on the top of a dresser.

Tony Wheeler, an avuncular retired doctor who owns the Old Lockup with his wife Vivien, shows me round.

'I see you've got all the bits and bobs,' I say.

'Well we offer romantic breaks.'

'Okay . . .'

'We get a lot of police officers.'

'Who ask for handcuffs? The picture's emerging now.'

'Well we do get enquiries saying "Do you supply whips and handcuffs?" But my wife always says "You're not handcuffing yourselves to our beds." '

'Exactly. You would have thought they could bring their own.'

Joking aside, I'm intrigued that someone can change something that historically was a place of abject misery into a nice cosy guesthouse. Rooms that used to hold a dozen ruffians overnight now have little tables with doilies and packets of cornflakes on the sideboard.

'Was it only drunks that found themselves incarcerated here?'

'Oh no, not at all.'

'So there were some seriously bad people here as well?'

'It housed a well-known murderer who stabbed his lover through the throat.'

'*Really?*'

'Typical lady – she jilted him.'

'What, after he stabbed her through the throat?'

'No, before.'

'Ah, I was going to say. Although that would sound quite reasonable to me, jilting someone after they'd stabbed you.'

The place is full of fascinating little details, such as that D. H. Lawrence and his German wife Frieda von Richthofen, listed as an alien during the First World War, reported here weekly after being expelled from Cornwall in 1917 on suspicion of spying.

But it's not just the history that's interesting; it's also the physical details of the place. Tony shows me how each chimney flue has a side vent to get rid of excess smoke. In the nineteenth century, when dangerous and serious criminals would be locked up in the cells, their accomplices would try to spring them from jail by climbing on to the roof and dropping a sack down the chimney to smoke out the guards. Hence the vents. I also can't help noticing that the doors are a lot thicker and heavier than would normally be found in a guesthouse. Tony explains how the locks were put into the doors upside down to confuse anyone who somehow managed to get hold of a key.

In the dining room, Tony has a daybook discovered during recent renovations. Written with meticulous care in beautiful copperplate script, it contains reports by the Superintending Officer of the crimes perpetrated by the jail's detainees and charts the life of the lead-mining community of Wirksworth a century ago, from the trivial to the tragic. There's mention of 'Soine Fever at Darley' – foot-and-mouth disease, it's now called – and murder, robbery, burglary, assault and petty crimes appeared to be just as commonplace then as now. There are tales of prisoners being prepared for transportation to

Australia for stealing sheep or filching lead off a neighbour's roof. The details are heartbreaking and intriguing. Reading them has made a welcome alternative to watching *Coronation Street* on the television in my guest room.

Guests travel from all over the world to stay at the Old Lockup. With Tony's medical background, the guesthouse attracts a lot of doctors as well as many solicitors, police officers, members of the judiciary – and what might be grandly called practitioners of the performing arts.

But unfortunately this particular practitioner cannot stop to sample the hospitality and unique atmosphere of the Old Lockup. Instead I must move on: one of the longest and certainly the most spectacular single journeys of the trip lies ahead of me. The next 80-odd miles are just the kind of roads for which the XK150 was built. Winding round some of the craggiest, most furiously wild corners of the Peak District, I'll be travelling through a part of the world in which epic views are two-a-penny. At this point, I'll be breaking my B-road pledge for the first time this journey by venturing on to the Snake Pass section of the A57, simply because it's the only road across one of the highest parts of the Peak District. I'll also have to take a few short sections of other A-roads to link between the B-roads – never more than a couple of miles – but otherwise it's minor roads all the way.

From Wirksworth, which is near Matlock, I drive north along the B5023. Around here are half a dozen limestone quarries with faces as dramatic as natural cliffs, their sides so densely covered in vegetation that it's difficult to know whether they are man-made or natural. And if you know where to look, dotted across the landscape are grassy humps and bumps in the fields, the only remaining evidence of lead mining, which was big around here even in Roman times. Until about a hundred years ago, this valuable underground harvest provided a livelihood for many hard-working families.

After crossing the A5012, I continue northwards on the B5056, which leads me past the Nine Ladies, a Bronze Age stone circle. Regarded as the Peak District's finest megalithic monument, these nine stumpy stones at Stanton Lees are more than three thousand years old. Like half a mouthful of old teeth, they stand in a small circle surrounded by silver birch, ash and beech trees. Legend has it they were formed from women petrified for dancing on a Sunday. The King Stone, which lies about 40 yards away, was apparently their fiddler.

It's an intriguing place, which still carries a spiritual air, not least because it instantly transports visitors back to a Neolithic landscape. Beyond the Nine Ladies stretches the moorland, dotted with further Neolithic remnants and ruins, including cairns, burial mounds and hillforts. Believed to have been built, like Stonehenge, for sun and moon worship, they're a priceless part of our pagan heritage, so you'd have thought they were something worth treasuring.

But oh no, you'd be wrong. Until a couple of years ago, the Nine Ladies were under threat from a mining company that had legal rights to dig a quarry right beside them. In a beauty spot that for millennia had witnessed pagans performing marriages and whirling dervishes dancing, they wanted to excavate a big crater to supply more than 3 million tons of millstone grit for the building trade.

Unsurprisingly, Stanton Moor became the site of an eco-warrior protest in 1999. Led by a character called Wookie, the protestors built more than sixty dwellings on Stanton Moor hillside, including a caravan up a tree and dozens of tree houses linked by walkways and cargo nets. There were clashes with police and an attempted eviction. After five years' occupation, the eco-warriors gained a partial victory when the High Court declared the quarries dormant, although the quarry company then launched an attempt to engineer a land swap that would allow them to expand an existing nearby quarry. The protestors are still living in their camp and intend to do so until plans to quarry anywhere near the site are dropped.

Driving through the Peak District's landscape of limestone crags, gritstone outcrops, heather and peat moorland – Daniel Defoe called it 'a waste and howling wilderness'; Lord Byron wrote of it that 'there are things in Derbyshire as noble as in Greece or Switzerland' – I can't help feeling we should cherish this precious jewel at the heart of England. Ringed by Sheffield, Derby, Nottingham, Birmingham and Greater Manchester, a third of Britain's population lives within an hour's journey of the National Park, yet beyond the tourist hotspots it is possible to find total solitude in this rugged, romantic, remote and barren wilderness.

Created in 1951, the Peak District was Britain's first National Park. Stretching from Derbyshire into Cheshire and Staffordshire, it has a central limestone plateau, the White Peak, ringed by jagged moorland, the sombre Dark Peak. For the next few tens of miles I'm in the grey-and-green landscape of the White Peak, where silvery drystone walls crisscross limestone plateaux. From Stanton in Peak, I head north-west past Haddon Hall, the ancient home of William the Conqueror's illegitimate son Peveril of the Peak, and into traffic-clogged Bakewell, home of that strangely addictive mix of pastry, jam, eggs, almonds, sugar and butter. My doctor advises me to steer clear of sweet things like Bakewell Tarts, and fortunately the journey in the Jag is far too enjoyable to be interrupted by gluttonous thoughts. Consequently, I'm soon veering off the beaten track of the A6 to cross the river Wye at Ashford-in-the-Water via Sheepwash Bridge, where shepherds used to give their sheep a good dunking to clean their fleeces before shearing. Lambs would be placed in a pen on the opposite side of the river to their mothers so that the ewes would swim across to get to them.

From Ashford-in-the-Water, the B6465 leads me towards Little Longstone and Monsal Head, where to my left the stunning beauty of Monsal and Cressbrook Dales, dotted with cowslips and spotted orchids, open beneath me and are bisected by the Headstone Viaduct, an elegant five-arched 40-foot-high crossing built by the Midland Railway over the Wye. Although impressive and now subject to a preservation order, when it was built in 1863 the viaduct was regarded as destroying the beauty of the dale, prompting John Ruskin, at that time Britain's leading writer on culture, to comment scathingly on it in words now displayed on the structure: 'The valley is gone, and the Gods with it; and now, every fool in Buxton can be in Bakewell in half an hour, and every fool in Bakewell at Buxton.'

Nothing remains of Monsal Dale railway station's timber buildings, but with its down line and platform built on a shelf carved in the rock face, while the up platform was built on wooden trestles over the hillside, it must have been an impressive construction. As for the viaduct, it's been reinvented as part of the Monsal Trail, an 8-mile cycle and walking trail from Wye Dale to Bakewell.

Continuing north through a patchwork landscape of green fields bisected by grey stone walls, I spot Gibbet Rock at the top end of Cressbrook Dale. Also known as Peter's Stone, this was the site of the last gibbet in Derbyshire. The bones of hanged criminals would be placed in a metal cage (the gibbet) and suspended for the crows to pick. The last gibbeting in 1815 entails a particularly grisly story.

In the coaching days of the nineteenth century a toll gate crossed the turnpike road at Wardlow Mires, the village nearest Gibbet Rock. On 15 January 1815, Hannah Oliver, a seventy-year-old widow who lived in the toll house, was strangled and her death made to look like suicide. Twenty-one-year-old Anthony Linguard was convicted of her murder and hanged at Derby. His body was brought back on a cart to Wardlow and displayed at Gibbet Rock in front of crowds from far around; stalls were set up selling refreshments and curios. The macabre twist in the tale is that on the same night of 15 January 1815 a foul murder also took place in Yorkshire. Another old lady was murdered at a toll gate, and she was Hannah's sister.

In a further twist, eleven years later Linguard's brother, William, was sentenced at Derby Assizes for highway robbery and assault, having committed the robbery within view of the gibbet on which the bleaching bones of his brother were still hanging. Happy days, eh?

At Wardlow Mires I join the A623, bypassing Tideswell with its magnificent Parish Church of St John the Baptist, known as the Cathedral of the Peak and regarded as the best example of pointed architecture in Derbyshire. Its superb pinnacled tower has dominated the village for more than six hundred years.

Turning right on to the B6061 at the Wanted Inn in Sparrowpit, the scenery changes dramatically as I enter the Peak District's wildest country, where in place of the patchwork of drystone walls found in the White Peak, the Dark Peak hills are dotted with windswept trees. With craggy sandstone outcrops and precipitous edges, the hills here rise to 2,000 feet above sea level, the moors are the domain of shepherds and their collies, and winter snow often closes the roads.

Passing through a cleft beneath the towering limestone crags of the Winnats, I make my slow and winding way down the pass towards Castleton. Winnats Pass, the only westward route out of Hope Valley after the A625, was permanently closed in the 1970s following a landslide and is a narrow road with a very steep, one-in-five, gradient that makes it impassable to buses, coaches and larger trucks, and a challenge to racing cyclists. The 1,696-foot peak of Mam Tor – also known as the Shivering Mountain because of its very loose shale – lies to the north, its summit encircled by a late Bronze Age and early Iron Age hillfort that has been carbon dated to around 1200 BC. Driving down the Pass towards Castleton, I pass the series of show caves, including Blue John Cavern, from which the semi-precious mineral Blue John is mined. The National Park sits on a bigger variety of valuable minerals than any other area of comparable size in this country. Blue John is a kind of fluorspar that locals will tell you is unique to this cave, but that's yet another cock and bull story. Blue John occurs throughout Derbyshire, as well as in many other parts of Britain and beyond. The locals will also tell you that its name is derived from the French *bleu-jaune* (blue-yellow), describing the varied colours of this pretty stone, although there's another, equally plausible explanation for that too, namely that it is derived from bleu john, a name given to the stone by Matthew Boulton, a local craftsman who used it for the base of ornaments that he made. Given that the stone is neither blue nor yellow but more usually purple or white, this seems as likely an explanation as the French derivation. Nevertheless, the price of Blue John pieces in local shops is as steep as the descent into the mine, even if the Blue John sold there is just as likely to come from China as Derbyshire.

Arriving in Castleton, I come face to face with the Devil's Arse. Derbyshire folk have a reputation for not mincing their words, so it's perhaps unsurprising that they named the entrance to Peak Cavern – a large dark hole if ever I saw one – the Devil's Arse. This entirely natural cave has the largest cave entrance in Britain and is part of the most extensive cave system in the Peak District. For four hundred years it was home to Britain's last troglodytes, who until 1915 lived in houses built inside the cave mouth, earning a living from rope-making. The depths of the cave, now popular with cavers, were for many years a haven for bandits and supposedly the place where Cock Lorel, leader of the rogues, and the King of the Gypsies concocted thieves' cant, a secret language used by robbers, beggars and hustlers. Considering the way in which sixteenth-century law dealt with rogues and anyone considered a misfit by the great and the good, it's no wonder they developed their own secret language.

In 1572 the Vagabond Act defined a rogue as a healthy person who had no land, no master and no legitimate trade or source of income – in other words, poor and unemployed. Any rogue apprehended for an offence would be stripped to the waist, whipped until bleeding, and a hole 'about the compass of an inch' would be burnt through the cartilage of their right ear.

A rogue who committed a second offence, unless taken in by

someone who would give work for one year, could face execution as a felon. If they escaped this fate but then became a third-offence perpetrator, they would escape death only if hired for a minimum of two years.

In 1598 a new Vagabond Act took a more lenient line. Instead of execution, rogues could now expect to be banished overseas, while the 1604 Act commanded that rogues have the letter 'R' branded on their bodies. Yikes.

It was about this time that thieves' cant was devised, according to the Elizabethan writer Samuel Rid, 'to the end that their cozenings, knaveries and villainies might not so easily be perceived and known'. Many words from this dialect have entered common use, such as swag or whack for booty, pig for a policeman, fence for a receiver of stolen goods, beak for a judge, hoodwink for con, rat for inform and ginny or jemmy for a crow-bar.

Most of the terms and phrases, however, would mean nothing to most people today. For example, a counterfeiter was a figure dancer or queer bit maker, while a courthouse was a nubbing ken. A death sentence was a cramp word, a dog was called a bufe, and gloves were fams. Victims of crime were known as content or provendors, while a widow was an ace of spades. And it's no surprise that there were a plethora of terms for being hanged, including acorn, artichoked, beilby's ball, cry cockles, cropped, frummagemmed, hearty choked, hempen fever, ironmonger's shop, jammed, leaf, noozed, nubbing, scragged, stretched and swing. Wow. It reminds me why the English language is such a rich and wonderful thing, and so cheery.

Driving parallel to the Great Ridge of Mam Tor, Back Tor and Lose Hill, I continue eastwards through Hope, the village that gives its name to the valley. About a mile after turning left on to the A6013 shortly before Hathersage, where the church overlooks Little John's grave (according to folklore, although it wouldn't be difficult to imagine Robin Hood's exceptionally tall lieutenant leading an ambush on the Sheriff of Nottingham's men round here), the road comes to a massive grass bank stretching to the left. This is the dam of the Ladybower Reservoir, the lowest of three reservoirs in the Upper Derwent Valley. At either end of the dam are two huge and very unusual bellmouth overflows. The locals call them the Plugholes, and that's exactly how they look and act should the water level rise too high. Although man-made, the lake is spectacular and looks totally at home in the landscape.

Driving along the road that snakes along the side of the water, crossing the lake twice on beautifully engineered viaducts, my thoughts drift to 1943, when this beautiful part of the Peak District played a vital role in one of the most dangerous and daring attacks of the Second World War. For weeks, 617 Squadron's Lancaster bomber crews used the reservoirs to practise their raids on the Ruhr dams in Germany. With dummy versions of Barnes Wallis's remarkable bouncing bombs in their bays, RAF pilots rehearsed the approach and release of their explosive cargo at a precise height of 60 feet and exact speed of 232 m.p.h. so that their back-spinning cylindrical weapon would skip over the water, bounce over nets and other defences, strike the dam, sink and detonate at 30 feet.

The rigorous training runs rattled roof tiles off farmhouses and were blamed for a reduction in egg and milk production, enraging many locals who thought the crews were just joyriding. It was, however, all worthwhile. On the night of 16 May 1943, nineteen aircraft of 617 Squadron took off for

Germany. Eleven aircraft returned, the Mohne and Eder masonry dams having been breached and the damage to the Sorpe earth dam sufficient to force the Germans to drain half its lake's contents.

At the end of Ladybower lake, the road starts its long rise to Snake Pass and I enter as empty a stretch of country as can be found anywhere in this kingdom. I pass Doctor's Gate, where according to local legend a Longdendale doctor challenged the Devil to a horse race and, much to the irritation of the Devil, won. Then there's a kink in the road and I'm driving over the apex of Snake Pass, a straight stretch of road 1,679 feet above sea level.

As I descend, the view is clear and spectacular. All of Manchester lies in front of me. With the Jag purring easily down the hill and gripping the twisty turns, I'm soon in Glossop, taking a right-hander on to the B6015 and, a few miles further, passing a succession of reservoirs before beginning a long climb to Holme Moss, from where I can see 50 miles or further into West Yorkshire. This is B-road driving at its best. An open road, clear skies, distant views, sheep grazing, a warm breeze – I couldn't be happier. It's been a great drive with something interesting to see or visit every few miles. The richness and diversity of things to be discovered in Britain if you venture off the dreary old motorways is a never-ending revelation to me. There's so much that I don't have the time to stop at everything that piques my interest; instead, I quite happily enjoy the effortless motoring of the XK150 until, 71 miles after leaving the Old Lockup at Wirksworth, I arrive at the Emley Moor mast.

Chapter Nine

With a height of 330 metres – 10 metres higher than the Eiffel Tower – the tapered, reinforced concrete spike at Emley Moor is Britain's tallest freestanding structure. Reaching the Tower Room, which sits at the top of the concrete part of the tower some 900 feet above the ground and directly beneath the steel mast, requires a seven-minute journey by lift.

I've been told that on a good day like today you can see for 70 miles from the top. But for me this is not a good day. Just looking up at it makes me giddy. The thing is, I'm petrified of heights. And my problem is I've got a television crew standing beside me, expecting me to enter the tiny lift for the long journey to the top. Acrophobic I might be, but unprofessional I'm not, so there's nothing for it but to take a deep breath and head for the concrete eyrie.

As the lift climbs the tower at the eye-watering speed of 40 metres per minute – that's 1.5 m.p.h. for the imperial-minded – no amount of trivial chitchat can distract me from the fact that we are slowly ascending a structure that exists only because the previous tower collapsed.

Built in 1966, the previous mast came crashing down a mere three years later on 19 March 1969. One of the lads who still works at Emley Moor was occupied halfway up the old transmitter the day before it came down. He tells me his colleagues, who were working in the monitoring room next door, didn't even notice that the transmitter had collapsed.

'Two lads – still alive – heard nothing. All the monitors went blank and they thought the generators had gone down. They'd heard nothing more than a little rumble. Then they went outside and the 1,265-foot mast – taller than this one – was gone.'

They found the mast zigzagged down the road that led up to it, fortunately avoiding the nearby cottages. Nobody was hurt in the collapse, but one of the stay cables cut through a local church and wreckage was strewn across the moor. A few days later, some wag who lived nearby crept up to the site and altered a sign, which had read 'TALLEST TOWER IN EUROPE', to 'LONGEST TOWER IN EUROPE'.

The worst effect of the collapse was that several million people in Yorkshire and Lancashire were left without ITV and BBC2 coverage. The BBC restored a diminished temporary service within forty-eight hours; ITV took four weeks to return to normal.

Initially ice was blamed for the tower's collapse. The cylindrical steel mast had regularly become coated in ice during the winter, and ice often formed in large icicles on the guy ropes, placing them under considerable strain. But a committee of inquiry attributed the collapse to a form of oscillation that occurred at a low but steady wind speed. Modifications were made to similar masts, including the hanging of 50 tons of steel chains within each structure. None of the modified masts collapsed, so it seems the committee's finding was correct. However, none of this provides any comfort as I climb the new tower, which took two years to build and opened in 1971.

When I first emerge from the dimly lit lift shaft into the observation room, I'm bowled over by the view. Situated 900 feet above the ground and with windows right round its perimeter, it offers a beautiful view that seems to go on for ever. Thankfully, it's so high that it's like being in an aeroplane and there's little immediate sensation of being suspended high in mid-air. Keeping away from the window, I can just about convince myself I'm standing on a mountain. With the tower's elevated position at the eastern edge of the Pennines, I'm 1,949 feet above sea level, so the analogy is apt. And the trick of convincing myself I'm on terra firma works until I get to the edge and look down. And then it's very scary.

I spend most of my short time at the top repeatedly exclaiming 'Look at that!', wondering who cleans the windows and how they do it (they're self-cleaning), and finding great delight in – and I know it's a cliché – how everyone on the ground looks like a moving dot, just like in *The Third Man* when Harry Lime says: 'Would you feel any pity if one of those dots stopped moving for ever? If I offered you twenty thousand pounds for every dot that stopped – would you really, old man, tell me to keep my money?' I can almost hear the zither strumming.

I'm told the view on a clear day stretches for 70 miles, which means I can see more than 15,400 square miles of England, almost a third of the country by area. Astounding, really. Just don't get too near the edge!

It seems quite appropriate to be in this impressive structure, looking along the backbone of England and over much of the heart of Britain, at this particular stage in the trip north, as I am roughly halfway between London and Glasgow. It's been a very enlightening journey so far, but there's a lot more to be explored, so I'm soon back in the Jag, heading across Lancashire towards Southport on the west coast. On the way I stop briefly in Manchester, but I'll come back to that at a more appropriate point in the story.

Southport is one of those seaside towns that some people find utterly charming and others think is a little too genteel to be real. With its broad promenades, ironwork arcades and immaculate lawns, it appears to have changed very little since Victorian times, which seems totally appropriate because I'm here to visit a temple to British garden-engineering heritage. I speak, of course, of the world-famous British Lawnmower Museum.

At first glance, the lawnmower might seem too trivial – and, dare I say it, nerdy – to warrant its own curator and museum. But that would be to underestimate severely its place at the heart of British suburban life. Most British men (at least most British men with gardens) have a shed. To some men, the shed is their last refuge, a place to escape adult demands and re-acquaint themselves with their inner child. To others, it's simply somewhere to park their tools and assorted bits of garden furniture. However, one thing is certain: nearly every one of those sheds contains a lawnmower, and most of them are in working condition.

Now imagine a Britain without lawnmowers. It would be a kingdom of unkempt lawns and shabby parkland turning to bramble-covered scrub, a country in which only the aristocracy and the super rich could afford the small army of scythe-wielding labourers needed for well-kept lawns. And that's the way the world was before the invention of the lawnmower.

However, thanks to the lateral thinking of the illegitimate

son of a farmer called Budding, millions of people now have lawns that are kept to a higher standard than the aristocrats' labourers could possibly have managed in the early nineteenth century. Examples of Budding Junior's early work are displayed in the Science Museum in London, at Stroud Museum, in several other collections, and of course at the Lawnmower Museum in Southport, which has an example of the first Budding design, a two-man mower which had two handles, so that one person could push it while another pulled.

Housed above and behind Stanley's, an old-fashioned British hardware shop, DIY store and discount lawnmower warehouse in a central side street of Southport, the world's only lawn-mower museum is curated by Brian Radam, a man who collects lawnmowers like Roman Abramovich collects yachts.

With his long hair and beard, Brian looks as though he'd be more comfortable in a rock 'n' roll roadie's uniform of leather and jeans than dressed in his suit and lawnmower-patterned tie. He does, however, have the roadie's fascination for technical detail. It's safe to say Brian is a man who has forgotten more about lawnmowers than most of the rest of us are ever going to know.

'The principle hasn't changed in nearly two hundred years,' says Brian. 'It was invented in 1830 by a gent called Edwin Beard Budding, who was working in a textile mill at Stroud in Gloucestershire when he was asked by the mill owner to build a new machine. The owner had just won an order for guardsmen's uniforms. Wanting the cloth to be perfect, he asked Edwin to make a machine that would cut all the tufts and bobbly bits off the cloth, so Edwin invented a revolving blade.'

A little later it dawned on Edwin that his blades could just as easily trim grass, but when he suggested it to friends and colleagues they looked at him as if he'd lost his mind. Fearing the ring of truth in their verdict, Budding tested his prototype under cover of darkness and discovered it worked a treat. As he was strapped for cash and knew that he lacked entrepreneurial skills, he enlisted the help of John Ferrabee, a local businessman. Working out of a factory in Stroud, they produced their first lawnmower. With 19-inch blades on a cylinder propelled via gears connected to the roller at the back and a front-mounted grass-collection tray, it was little different from the mowers on sale today. Cannily, they licensed their patented design to other companies, which allowed their invention to spread widely while still ensuring Budding and Ferrabee profited from the sales. But just think: if it wasn't for Budding, that uniquely British vista of striped lawns might never have come about.

The first motorized lawnmower arose in 1890 from the Atlas Chain Company's guilt over killing a horse, apparently through overwork, that pulled a mechanical mower around the lawns outside its headquarters. (The horse was fitted with padded leather boots to avoid damaging the sward; if you wanted to raise the cutting height you'd put half-inch higher boots on your horse.) When engineers fitted what was then a newfangled petrol engine to the mower, the company realized it had stumbled on to a winner. They branded their invention with an abbreviation of the company name – Atco – and the rest is history.

The Atco was not the first powered lawnmower per se, but then you wouldn't have wanted to use – or indeed get in the way of – the first steam-powered mower; it weighed 2 tons and cut a metre-wide swathe in each pass.

Brian has more than three hundred precious examples of all the classics: Atcos, Flymos, Ransomes and other well-known makes. And among these brands there are examples of mowers made by companies I would normally associate with other motorized endeavours – Royal Enfield, Rolls-Royce, Daimler, British Leyland (who made a steam model), Perkins Diesel, Dennis, and Hawker Siddeley – and names that have passed into the history books, many of which made ingenious specialist cutters. The Allen Scythe, for example, would cut very long grass in fields, while the Greens Multim in Parvo was designed to mow between gravestones or mark out tennis courts. Made in 1860, it had a gear drive where more modern mowers have chains, for the simple reason that the type of chain used in most modern mowers had not been invented at that time. After all, in 1860 Charles Dickens had only just published the first instalment of his new serial, *Great Expectations*.

Brian shows me a lovely machine from 1926 with a water-cooled engine and a cast aluminium side frame. Made by Jerram & Pearson, a precision engineering company, it has two interlocking cutters designed to send the grass very neatly to the centre of the grass box. Jerram & Pearson set out to make the best lawnmowers money could buy and they seem to have succeeded. It's a beauty.

'We believe this to be the best lawnmower ever made,' says Brian.

I should think it ought to be good; it cost twice as much as a car in 1926.

'Whenever I work abroad, the first things I notice when I return are the neat little gardens and the striped lawns,' I say. 'Are they uniquely British?'

'Yes, totally British. We want our lawns rolled, striped, the edges done and smooth as a carpet.'

'Is that because we invented the lawnmower?'

'You can only get it with a lawnmower, so maybe that's part of the reason. There are a lot of machines out there . . . that . . . er . . .'

I can see that Brian is faltering for words, queasy at the thought of speaking the unmentionable. 'Say Flymo. Go on, say it!'

'. . . well, it would be a rotary type of machine . . .'

'Do you mean a hover mower?'

'That type of machine thrashes the grass off rather than cuts it like a pair of scissors. The rotary mower is fine as a grass-cutter, but if you want a lawn finish, it has to be a lawnmower.'

'So why this uniquely British obsession with stripy lawns?'

'It's to do with our climate. Most people around the world just want to cut the grass, but we want bowling-grade lawns. But unfortunately most people who go out thinking they want a lawnmower now come home with a grass-cutter – that's a rotary – and properly groomed lawns are dying out.'

Brian's enthusiasm for his subject knows no limits. He says the world divides into people who love cutting grass and those who despise it, and he falls very firmly into the former camp. 'All machines have their own character and cutting grass is very therapeutic. It's healthy, you're getting exercise and at the end there's the satisfaction of a job well done.'

Although I rarely mow my lawn myself, I can relate to the Zen of grass-cutting. Walking up and down the garden gives you the perfect opportunity to think things over. Unless the docks, thistles and daisies start to get you down, in which case Brian suggests a robot mower.

Leading me around the museum, he shows off some classic mowers with some beautiful engineering and even a thumb-sized mower with a 2-inch blade for getting into those really awkward corners. He tells me about the Atco car, a boxy body built around a 1939 Atco lawnmower with a 1.5 h.p. lawnmower engine. Looking not dissimilar to Noddy's car, it was built as an economical way to train people to drive during the Second World War.

What interests me is that you can see the history of styling in these lawnmowers. The ones built in the 1930s are all Art Deco and try to look like a streak across the sky. The 1950s models take their cues from Swedish moderne, with teardrop shapes and organic coverings. However, the really serious ones never changed as all they had to do was cut grass very well.

Befitting our celebrity-obsessed times, Brian even has a collection of mowers from famous owners. Next to Hilda Ogden's Qualcast Panther are machines belonging to Brian May, Alan Titchmarsh, Vanessa Feltz, Ainsley Harriott, Brian Sewell and even one owned by Charles and Di, though one wonders if one actually used it oneself.

There's also a pair of secateurs that belonged to Nicholas Parsons (his mower was stolen before he donated it) and Joe Pasquale's strimmer. I ask you, what more do you want from a museum than a chance to see Nicholas Parsons' secateurs and Joe Pasquale's strimmer? And did you know Charles Darwin owned a Samuelson Donkey lawnmower? Probably not.

Moving on, Brian brings up a subject even closer to his heart than lawnmowers: mower racing. As I soon discover, he can talk about it for hours.

'Through here we've got some of the original racing lawnmowers.' He leads me through a door to a secluded corner of his collection. 'It's really good fun. Even people like Stirling Moss are into it.'

'Yes. I've seen film of him racing.'

'And Noel Edmonds.'

'Oh.'

'Oliver Reed ran over someone in a toilet tent on one.'

'That *so* doesn't surprise me.'

'People said he was half cut at the time.'

Ouch. Half cut? Lawnmower? Ollie Reed? That's some pun.

Lawnmower racing can be dated back to a conversation held in 1973 in – unsurprisingly – a pub. A former rally driver and his mates were looking for a cheap and accessible motor sport. Glancing out of the pub window, they saw a groundsman mowing the cricket pitch and had their Eureka moment. Rules were drawn up, classes were decided (run behind; run behind with attached seat; wheel-driven sit-on mowers; and wheel-driven lawn tractors) and a championship devised.

What's particularly appealing is that in this last outpost of non-chequebook racing, anyone can make their own racing vehicle and compete. A budget of a couple of thousand pounds – less than a car racer might spend on tyres in a season – is enough to finance a decade of competition. And Brian should know; he is a legend in the lawnmower-racing world, having won the Northern Championships three times in the past ten years.

'They race under quite strict rules,' says Brian. 'The mowers must once have been used to cut lawns rather than fields.'

'No V8s then?'

Brian points at one of his racing machines made from a Wolseley Webb chassis with a Villiers Mag engine. 'This one will go up to sixty-five miles per hour. It's great fun.'

'Fantastic. But does it not get a bit bouncy racing across grass at that speed?'

'Sometimes you need to slow it down. These machines would originally have been made to go six miles an hour and once you start going more than thirty, they have a mind of their own.'

Lawnmower racing is wonderfully mad. But then so is our desire for a striped lawn. I'm convinced that, like so many British habits and conventions, the origin of our obsession is rooted in class. Before the lawnmower, only aristocrats could afford the manpower to cut lawns with shears. I can imagine the dukes and earls boasting to each other about the quality of their sward. Later, the lawnmower caught on with the aristocracy because it made the job easier and, in the process, it created the striped lawns we know so well today. Then, when a lawnmower no longer cost as much as a house, we class-obsessed Brits copied the practice of striped lawns because of that age-old British thing to do with emulating the aristocracy. The striped lawn is therefore a sycophantic impulse morphed into something creative and healthy. I think it's a good thing.

Chapter Ten

The second stage of the journey – from Stilton through the heart of England to Yorkshire and Lancashire – is, I am coming to realize, loosely concerned with reinvention. Stilton re-invented the cheese-rolling tradition of Gloucestershire to invigorate trade and pull the community together after it was bypassed by the A1. Normanton Church reinvented itself as a museum to the villages lost in the creation of Rutland Water. Reverend Paul Sinclair reinvented funeral procedures with his motorcycle hearses. And now I am staying in a former doctor's home, reinvented as a Brontë Country bed and breakfast run by a couple who have reinvented themselves as guesthouse owners.

Located below the wild moors of *Wuthering Heights* and a short walk from Brontë Parsonage in Haworth, where the Brontë sisters spent most of their lives and wrote their novels, Ashmount Country House is the former home of Dr Amos Ingham, physician to the sisters. I choose to stay in it because it's conveniently close to my next destination – Hebden Bridge – but also because it's a reminder of one of the things that's fantastic about travelling around Britain: stopping off at a simple bed and breakfast, you can find yourself staying in a marvellous Victorian Gothic masterpiece.

With Len Robinson in the Tricker's shoe factory in Northampton. I've been wearing shoes for over fifty years but I never realized how much work was involved in making them ...

...That all changed when Len put me to work. His knowledge of the different leathers and skills used in shoe making was deeply impressive. He did laugh at my efforts either, so he's obviously as kind as he is talented.

Above: *It's an honour to be asked to make the hare pie for the Hallaton and Medbourne bottle-kicking and it was obvious that Lynn Allan had put in a lot of effort. Lovely.*

Right: *In a field full of people it was difficult to separate the teams from the spectators. If I'd been a younger man I'd have been right in there like a daft laddie!*

Below: *The hare is a symbol of spring, fertility and luck.*

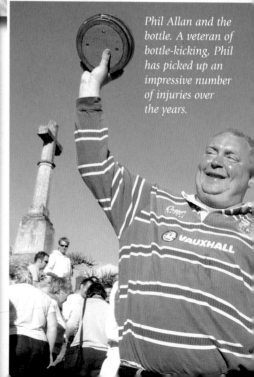

Phil Allan and the bottle. A veteran of bottle-kicking, Phil has picked up an impressive number of injuries over the years.

To the victor, the spoils. Or rather the warm beer and the numb bum!

Jetta Howard in action. The gloves are off! The World Dock Pudding Championship in Mytholmroyd is seriously competitive and even I got caught up in the fervour.

The winner, the 'boss' and the runner-up.

Above: *A fine, modest, solid Protestant building in York. Or is it?*

How did the Ladies of the Bar build this chapel in secret? You could probably smuggle in a cherub inside your bag but a Doric column with gold capitals?

The British Lawnmower Museum in Stockport. A monument to the British obsession with striped lawns. Atco Valhalla. (Don't you think Atco sounds like a scary sci-fi villain?)

A church helmet park – not a sight you see every day!

Below: *The Reverend Paul Sinclair and his bike look right at home in front of the pulpit at the Elim Pentecostal church in Burton on Trent.*

Like many doctors' houses – my father's included – this has been a doctor's house for many generations. Doctors clearly made a few bob in those days and although it's quite small, it's also very grand, with Gothic pillars, impressive archways, and windows and doors fitted with stained glass. In the garden, a former owner has built a Victorian bothy with a panoramic view of Yorkshire to die for.

Waiting for me in the entrance hall when I arrive is Ray, who for two years has owned the guesthouse with his wife, Gill, and filled it with marvellous antiques.

'Every single bed and breakfast in the whole of Yorkshire claims that Charlotte once visited,' I say. 'But in your case it is the truth, isn't it?'

Ray smiles, slightly awkwardly. 'Well, thereabouts. Dr Amos Ingham, who built this house, was physician to Charlotte Brontë and her husband, Patrick. He visited them, as opposed to them visiting here.'

Whoops. Maybe I shouldn't have put him on the spot, but Ray soon distracts me by pointing at two frames above a rather funereal fireplace in the breakfast room. 'We have of course their death certificates displayed here. Charlotte died quite young, at the age of thirty-eight. She was three months pregnant and had complications.'

The death certificate lists phthisis – tuberculosis – as the cause of Charlotte's death on 31 March 1855, although scholars suggest she may have died from dehydration and malnourishment, caused by excessive vomiting from severe morning sickness. Sadly, Charlotte would probably have survived if she'd been born a few years later.

Located 800 feet high in the Pennines, Haworth was a crowded industrial township during the Brontë period, the population having more than doubled in the first half of the nineteenth century. However, there were no sewers and the water supply was polluted and inadequate. Unsurprisingly, the mortality rate was high. Between 1840 and 1850 there were 1,344 burials in the churchyard; and this in a town of only 3,365 people in 1851. The average age at death was twenty-five years and nearly half the population died before reaching its sixth birthday. With raw sewage flowing down the gutters and no awareness of the link between diseases such as cholera and bacterial infections, the Brontë deaths, though tragic, were unremarkable at the time.

When I ask Ray how many people come to his bed and breakfast to see the death certificates, I detect a slight frisson. And it's not a frisson of excitement. More like a *froideur* at my suggestion that his establishment is a bed and breakfast. 'Is this not a B and B?' I ask. 'Or would you say it was a guesthouse?'

'Everyone from America thinks we're a hotel because the building is so magnificent. They'll phone asking for our best bed and breakfast rates, but I like to say we're a guesthouse because to me it means the next step up. When you say bed and breakfast I think of Blackpool.' Well, excuse me!

Encapsulated in that assertion is everything that I love about being British: those subtle nuances of status and class that to some people mean so much.

'On our travels we've discovered castles that you can stay in overnight,' I say. 'On paper they're a bed and breakfast, but they've got turrets and a view of stunning valleys.'

Ray seems to be satisfied with my answer, so I ask him from where most of his guests come. A lot are walkers, but just as many are Brontë Society members, some from as far afield as Japan and America. The Brontës are big business, attracting millions of visitors to Haworth every year. When the Reverend Patrick Brontë arrived as minister at Haworth Parish Church, the village was little more than a collection of stone-built weavers' cottages huddled together for protection from the harsh, cold winds. But thanks to a series of books written by his daughters, Charlotte, Emily and Anne, this obscure Yorkshire village had within a few decades become a major centre for literary pilgrimage. Nowadays it even has a curry house called Brontë Balti.

Ray tells me he'd always wondered why young Japanese women made up one of his largest groups of visitors and recently he found out why. Among certain circles in Japan, young women apparently need to show they are widely travelled and cultured to attract the best husbands.

'A visit to the Brontë Parsonage in Haworth is highly prized for getting a very well-to-do suitor.'

'You're joking?'

'It's absolutely true. We discovered it very recently. We do get a disproportionate number of young Japanese women staying with us, and the majority of them are very wealthy.'

'Do you give them a stamp on their passport or CV: "I've been to Haworth and seen the Parsonage, therefore I am a cultured sort of person"?'

'Absolutely . . .'

Whether it's true or not, it's a great story. 'I suppose boasting of a visit to Haworth is better than having the Japanese equivalent of an Asbo or a huge unattractive tattoo that looked better after a few sakes,' I say. 'It's an extraordinary idea.'

I'm very interested that Ray and his wife have given up other lives and occupations to become the owners of a bed and breakfast – sorry, *guesthouse* – not least because there are endless television programmes about people giving up their jobs in search of a different lifestyle. And more often than not in these programmes it all goes horribly wrong. The wannabe escapees often work twice as hard as they did before they changed their lives and consequently are plagued with doubts over whether they made the right decision.

But Ray has no regrets. Maybe it's because he's helped by a really very charming wife and two friends who have me fascinated because their day jobs were as private detectives specializing in identity-theft cases and tracing absconded suspects and criminals. We had a lot to talk about . . .

'There are mornings when I don't feel like getting up at half past six to cook breakfast,' says Ray. 'But equally there are days when the guests leave by ten o'clock and I have the day to myself. I go into town and chat with the butcher or just do whatever. The really great thing is no one tells me what to do from the moment I get up to the moment I go to bed. That is worth all the hard work.' I hear you there, Ray.

Driving away from Haworth, I'm heartened by what I've just seen. Ray and Gill are proof that anyone can do what they want and get away with it, provided they are prepared to work very hard. With no guarantee of success, they paid a lot of money for Ashmount Country House, then poured a lot more money into it to renovate and maintain it. The result is a beautiful place to stay – I can heartily recommend it – in a town that is well worth a visit. With their passion, dedication and vision, it's no surprise Ray and Gill have built up a loyal clientele who return frequently to their B and B – sorry, guesthouse!

I follow a succession of minor roads on to the Brontës' magnificent moors and across the 1,300-foot-high fell, the road twisting, the views changing every few hundred yards, as I pass a few stone houses that appear to have risen out of the ground, before descending through some steep wooded valleys to Mytholmroyd. This small village is joined on to neighbouring Hebden Bridge – the centres of the two places are only a mile apart and, although technically they are separate, many inhabitants regard them as one and the same place.

Pronounced to rhyme with haemorrhoid and sounding like an associated cream – 'Ooh, I couldn't have got through the day without my Mytholmroyd' – this was the birthplace of Ted Hughes, who said of it that 'my first six years shaped everything'. It was also the childhood home of Bernard Ingham, former press secretary to Margaret Thatcher, who once said that next-door Hebden Bridge's supposed status as the lesbian capital of Great Britain didn't say much for its men . . . Sir Bernard's comment backfired, bringing good business into the area in the form of young, isolated lesbian couples alerted to a safe haven. You can tell from these comments which of the two men was universally regarded as the finest poet of his generation and which was widely thought of as a cantankerous so-and-so.

But so much for Mytholmroyd's alumni; I'm here to pick some weeds. 'Why?' you might well ask. Well, someone thought it would be hilarious if I entered something called the World Dock Pudding Championship. You can guess what I thought of that.

I start my culinary quest on the bank of the river Calder, where I meet Jetta Howard. This lovely woman, with an easy, relaxed laugh, won the World Dock Pudding Championship in 2004, but caused quite a controversy because her recipe was entirely vegetarian. A flurry of outraged letters to the editor of the *Hebden Bridge Times*, the local newspaper, called for poor Jetta to be stripped of her title because it lacked the essential ingredient of bacon fat. Jetta wrote back, saying '40% of the population of Hebden Bridge is vegetarian. We must move with the times or the tradition will die' and has vowed this year to regain her title with her olive-oil-based recipe.

In most local families, recipes for dock puddings have been passed down through generations. But Jetta is different. She's a Dane who married a local lad, so she was freed from the constraints of heritage. 'I did it my own way. I made up my own recipe and applied my own cooking methods.'

I don't want to fall foul of the judges, who I am told can be quite formidable, so I'm going to stick to a traditional recipe.

Believed to have been invented several centuries ago, dock pudding was resuscitated during the war, when the country was in the grip of rationing and food shortages prompted people to use wild produce to get their vitamins, leading the German wartime propagandist Lord Haw-Haw to say that things had got so bad in Britain 'they're even eating grass'.

The pudding's primary ingredient is fresh young dock, but it also contains nettles, onions and oatmeal, plus an optional secret ingredient at the discretion of each participant. The taste of dock is said to be a cross between spinach and rhubarb, only sloppier, and the pudding is made only in this part of the country.

Yorkshire has a long and proud tradition of local specialities. As England's largest county, it occupies a prominent place in the food consciousness of the nation, no more so than for its Yorkshire Puddings, the essential accompaniment to roast beef. However, in Yorkshire large puddings are often served as a starter before the meat, filled with gravy. These throwbacks to more privative times were measures to make the meat go further. Savory Ducks, the northern version of the faggot, are another example of ingenuity in the face of limited ingredients, as is the Yorkshire Parkin, a dark, spicy, sweet gingercake, and the teatime treat of Yorkshire Fat Rascals, a currant teacake similar to rock buns. Most of these Yorkshire specialities can be bought ready made, but dock pudding can't be found on supermarket shelves, which, in a way, is what makes it special.

The dock pudding isn't unique, however. It has long been a tradition in many different cultures to go into the countryside in springtime to collect fresh herbs and greens to revive the health of communities weakened by the restricted diet of a hard, hungry winter. In China, wild herbs and spring greens were traditionally cooked in a communal pot and shared with every family to purify the blood and refresh the spirits. Barefoot doctors still perform this service in rural areas. In pre-medieval England, hedge-witches collected and sold spring greens, a mixture of chickweed, cleavers, dandelions, daisy, strawberry and nettle leaves, primroses, Star of Bethlehem, buds and flowers of hawthorn and bark of birch, pine and willow. Again, they provided a welcome vitamin and nutrient boost at the end of a winter of spuds and turnips (despite this, the nonconformist hedge-witches were later persecuted by religious reformers as evildoers, mischief-makers and heretics!).

For centuries – and up until as recently as fifty years ago – many Yorkshire and Lancashire housewives collected wild greens, mainly nettles, dandelions and burdock, and added a few leaves of bitter dock in a pudding that accompanied the first meats after Easter fasting. In many cases, the original purpose of detoxification and replenishment had been forgotten and it was seen as a form of penance, so when more recently the grip of Protestant asceticism loosened its hold on the hearts of modern families, the merits of eating bitter dock pudding were relinquished with relief. These days, wild-food foraging has become a very trendy pastime, so much so that the more pretentious London restaurants highlight it on their menus.

To aid my journey into foraging and Yorkshire's culinary traditions, Jetta has volunteered to be my mentor and is waiting for me on the riverbank with a plastic bag containing some prime dock leaves picked at a location that only she and her family know.

'They look very good. Very clean and very green,' I say.

'Yes, not too big and not too small.'

'So there's a right size?'

'Yes.'

'Could I eat them now?'

'You could, but I wouldn't eat a whole lot of them. They're full of cellulose.'

'Oh right . . . say no more. You might be self-propelled for the rest of the day.'

'Exactly.'

Jetta tells me I need two carrier bags of dock leaves and a bag of nettles. There are plenty of dock patches all along the riverbank, although I'm slightly concerned about their provenance. 'I have to say, this is the kind of path where a lot of people take their dogs for a walk. You have to wash them particularly well.'

Jetta laughs. 'You *always* wash them well.'

Is it true, I ask Jetta, that the docks are an antidote to nettle stings.

'No. That's the cow dock, a much bigger, thicker, coarser leaf.'

It turns out that the dock leaves we're collecting don't come from the common cow dock but from a special type of dock called Bistort, which looks like a soft art nouveau privet leaf. Sometimes called gentle dock, sweet dock or passion dock, its Latin name *Persicaria bistorta* refers to the twisted appearance of the root.

Jetta takes me over to some cow dock to show me the difference. 'The cow dock tends to grow like a bouquet.' She steps towards the river and points at the ground. 'And these, the sweet dock, grow in a nice pillow.'

She's right. They're much more attractive to look at and – I hope – much more pleasant to eat, so I fill my plastic bags with the small, soft leaves, then move on to a patch of nettles, for which there are just two rules concerning picking technique: wear gloves and pick only the tips.

Standing in Jetta's kitchen a short while later, I'm led through the cooking method. It's a straightforward recipe: remove the stalks and spines from the dock leaves, then put them in a pot of water; add raw onions, a couple of spoons of oats and chopped nettle leaves. Cook until soft, drain and put aside for reheating in a frying pan with bacon fat (or olive oil, if you're Jetta) and your secret ingredient.

While I'm cooking, Jetta gets out her folder of newspaper cuttings to show me what happened when she challenged the dock-pudding orthodoxy with her bacon-free recipe.

'This is what you'll come up against,' she warns. 'When I won the World Championship, there really was an ill feeling. Not everyone hated me, but there definitely were people who were quite upset. And I think the media played a part in it.'

' "Burn the witch" I think was the headline, wasn't it?'

'No, no, no. Do you want to see the headline? I'll show it to you.' She holds up a photocopy. Beside a picture of Jetta, emblazoned in large type across the top of the page is the head-line: 'WHATEVER HAPPENED TO THE BACON?' And beneath that: 'Veggie recipe takes the dock pud crown'.

'That's hilarious.'

There's more: another article headlined: 'FRYING PANS AT DAWN. PUDDING JUDGES IN THE DOCK'. And a letter to the editor: 'Bacon fat is an essential ingredient'.

'Hang the bitch! Drag her through the town naked. They didn't like it, did they?'

'No. So I had to write my own letter.'

'Oh brilliant. What did you say?'

'"Why don't you all go and . . ."' Jetta laughs; she didn't really write that. Her letter is actually very reasonable and she defended herself well.

Back to the cooking. I follow Jetta's instructions to the letter, then when she leaves the kitchen, I shoot outside to get my secret ingredient from the boot of the Jag: a large round of Stilton, bought a few days earlier after the cheese-rolling competition.

Returning to the kitchen, I drain the dock and nettle mixture, then throw it in the frying pan. There's no bacon fat around – what's a guy to do? – so I compromise with a knob of margarine. I hope it doesn't kill the village.

Now for my secret ingredient. The Stilton is huge, so a thin wedge is more than enough. I crumble it into the dock pudding and give it a good stir to ensure Jetta cannot visually identify it. Within seconds, I can tell the dock pudding has been trans-formed from something rather dull and worthy into something that's going to taste fantastic. *Ding dong!*

Although thrilled, I'm now starting to worry that I might win the competition. And that would be embarrassing. I don't want to end my noble journey to Glasgow in Mytholmroyd, having been dragged naked through the streets, then hanged, drawn and quartered. When I think of what might happen if I win, my imagination runs away with me. 'Scottish bloke off the telly? Take him round the back and sort him out.' However, this isn't the time for worrying about the consequences of my creation. The smell is mouthwatering, so I call Jetta for a tasting, first making sure I've hidden the huge Stilton.

'What do you think of that then?' I hold a teaspoon up to Jetta's mouth.

'Mmmm . . . ah . . . you've added a secret ingredient.'

'I may have done.'

'You've done a cheffy thing, haven't you?'

'Not too cheffy.'

'I like it, but I'm a rebel when it comes to this stuff. When it comes to food, I do my own thing.'

'Well I think it's delicious. And I don't care if they say "stone him".'

'You put in fancy Italian cheese.'

'Nearly, but not quite. It's Stilton.'

'Stilton?'

'It really goes with the flavour of the greens, doesn't it?'

'It does. I like it.'

'Not a word to the others.' It seems I've got the master's approval. And it's still vegetarian.

My dock pudding really is delicious. To my great surprise, I've stumbled on to a winner. And even better: we have dock leaves all over the place where I live – tons of them – so when I'm having one of my poncy showbiz dinners I can enthral the guests: 'Guess what this is? I found it on the estate.' Not that I live on an estate, but you get my drift.

In the meantime, it's off to the World Championships at Mytholmroyd Community Centre, a whitewashed breeze-block, brick and corrugated-roof construction that is very much the hub of the community. It's packed and buzzing when I arrive and I'm introduced to or told about many of the other competitors – present or not – as well as the judges and spectators.

There's Cecilia Mansfield, who has been running the championship for most of the years since it was revived in 1971, despite thinking dock pudding 'looks slimy and disgusting' and is only made palatable if 'they pretty it up a bit with bacon and eggs'. Then there's Doris Hurst, the defending champion, now in her early seventies and one of the few competitors who used to eat dock pudding as a child. I'm warned that Claire and Kate Morrison, fifteen-year-old twins who won two years ago, might be entering, but they are in their GCSE year at school and might not be present. Like Jetta's win, Claire and Kate's victory was controversial because they used to help a local lady, a renowned dock-pudding cook, gather dock leaves and nettles. The lady in question died and the twins, using her unique recipe (which included bacon), won it. Inevitably there were murmurings of a sympathy vote and a lot of people weren't happy – another indicator of how seriously the locals take this competition and how careful I need to be when I submit my entry.

By far the most vocal participant in the proceedings is a flamboyant and formidable woman in a blue suit, blue hat and gold chain. She's Betty Ward, mayoress of Hebden Royd town council, championship judge and, quite clearly, someone with whom it would be very unwise to mess.

'Pleased to meet you.' I flash my best smile. 'How do you do?'

'I am very well, thank you. And you may call me Betty.'

'Betty it is then.' I turn to her husband. 'And can I call you Betty too? No?'

'I'm Harry.'

There's no stopping Betty as she holds forth in a voice that could strip paint. 'We've been married fifty-one years.'

'Good for you. Fifty-one years? By jove.'

Betty leans over conspiratorially. 'And he doesn't get any time off for good behaviour.'

Betty personifies that saying about Yorkshire folk – you can always tell a Yorkshireman, but you can't tell him much – and I can see I'm going to have to tread very carefully around the mayoress. Time to laugh pleasantly, I think. She'll be all right when she gets over her shyness.

'Would you like to come through, sir?' Betty starts leading the way. 'And be our honoured guest? But on one condition: you behave yourself.'

The hall is rammed to its gunnels. Tables with freshly baked cakes, buns and cups of tea, raffle prizes and a tombola are arranged around the sides. Hebden Bridge brass band is playing beautifully. There are old boys in blazers and young lads in fleeces. The bar is open and the place is buzzing with conversation and laughter. It's great; a proper community event.

In the kitchen I meet Jetta, who looks very nervous.

'I'll see you later.' She leaves the room, carrying a basket with her ingredients and looking determined. 'I'd like to get that trophy back.'

'I've bribed all the judges,' I shout after her. 'And slept with most of them too.'

'Good luck,' she laughs.

Waiting backstage while Jetta cooks against two rivals, I'm really quite nervous, as if I'm about to step on stage for a show. As long as I don't burn the sausages, I tell myself, everything will be all right.

Meanwhile, Jetta is on stage with the first group of contestants, cooking her dock pudding. After ten minutes she returns to the waiting room. It's not gone well for her, she says, and she warns me that the gas burners on the stage are extremely ferocious. My sausages could burst. I realize then that if I cook my bacon, sausages and black pudding from scratch while heating up my dock pudding, the pudding will be an overcooked mushy mess by the time the bangers are cooked through. This calls for some forward planning: I decide to pre-cook the meat products and bustle into a kitchen at the back of the hall to get them sizzling before the on-stage cook-off.

Suddenly it's my turn and I'm carrying my pans up on to the stage. This is nerve-wracking. Once on stage, I am overcome with the smell of gas. An official tells me not to worry and that I've got ten minutes to prepare my plate. Feeling like a contestant on *Celebrity Making an Arse of Himself*, I get cooking in front of an array of cameraphones and digital cameras, all pointing at me. Next to me, two other contestants are frying away on burners like the flames of hell, but mine looks cooked already, so I decide to put the bacon, black pudding and sausages on a plate with my Stilton-infused dock pudding, which has now reached a nice claggy consistency.

As the plate is labelled with a number to maintain anonymity and taken away ceremoniously for judging, I'm confident about my pudding; in fact I'm now very concerned that I might win. They'll probably say it's a fix and lynch me. 'Fatty only won because the cameras were here.' Then there'll be a punch-up with the mayoress. And she'll win – trust me.

At this juncture I have a slight advantage over the other competitors. The camera crew follows my plate, with those of three other competitors, into the kitchen, so I can see afterwards exactly what the four judges thought of each pudding and how they allocated their marks for taste, texture and presentation.

Betty, of course, dominates proceedings and is on fine form. 'Those sausages look a bit suggestive to me . . . sorry, I do beg your pudding . . . look at that bit dangling . . .' It comes in a steady stream '. . . I'm a traditionalist, so no cheating . . . that black pudding's lovely, but the sausage is a bit mean . . . hey, do you mind . . . I'll make my own mind up in my own time . . . more momentum . . . that presentation is a bit of a laugh, but I won't tell you why . . . bit soggy oggy . . . I'm missing the colour that me mother's was . . . that's tasteless . . . *that* was never cooked in a farmhouse kitchen . . . is it heck . . . you don't have *raw* tomatoes with your breakfast . . . that just doesn't look right, trust me, I'm an artist . . . for goodness' sake, relax, you're in Yorkshire, the centre of the universe . . .'

At the end, I realize that Betty is biting her tongue because of the cameras. I wonder what she's like when she's not on best behaviour. She's some woman.

As for me, I am in the waiting room attempting to recover from the heat of the burners and, for the first time in my life, hoping that I'm not going to win a competition that I've entered. If it all goes wrong and I win, then I'll need to get out of Mytholmroyd fast. Apparently there's a big tree with some rope burns that they use for special occasions. And it's got nothing to do with a child's swing. Maybe I should check if someone's keeping the engine going outside?

Inside the hall, the band is playing 'A Whiter Shade of Pale'. When it finishes, Betty and the judges appear on the stage and one of the officials makes an announcement.

'Ladies and gentlemen, we have a result.'

'At last,' chips in Betty, standing beside the official.

'I'd like to call third, second and first in that order.'

Jane Kennedy, in third place, is called up first. She was beside me when we were cooking on the stage.

'In second place – and I don't know if you are going to believe this or not – I would like to call Mr Robbie Coltrane.'

There's a big cheer as I punch the air, but I can also hear some jeering at the back and a few shouts of 'fix'. You can't please all of the people all of the time. Betty greets me on stage, kisses me – 'I give everyone one of those' (just in case I thought I'd got lucky) – and hands me a small brown envelope. Inside it is a crisp £20 note, which I show to the crowd. But it's not about the money, it's the honour of taking part, so I donate my prize to the young kids in the brass band. Altogether now – aaaah.

'And the title of 2007 Dock Pudding World Champion is going to go to someone who has never entered before – Mr Darren Kay.'

There's a massive cheer. He's obviously a very popular winner, but I feel sorry for Jetta, who looks upset not to have won. The band plays 'Congratulations' as Darren comes to the stage and collects his trophy. As for me, I'm chuffed beyond my wildest expectations.

It's been a hugely enjoyable day. Before arriving at Mytholmroyd, I'd wondered what could be so interesting about boiling up some wild leaves, but the competition is another one of those magical things that's more than the sum of its parts. It's not about winning or even competing, but about everyone getting together to have a good time. It's also a rather brave and interesting thing to do, to call something a world championship when almost no one in the world is aware that it's going on, but there's something rather sweet about it. Not only because I came second.

And there's one other thing that really surprised me. That dock pudding is really rather tasty. Well, mine is.

Chapter Eleven

Flushed with success, I head east, counting my blessings that I wasn't crowned World Champion Dock Pudding-Maker. It could have been very ugly. Leaving Mytholmroyd, the weather turns a wee bit nasty, but it's not roof-up weather yet, and I start to think about the next destination.

There's an old saying in Yorkshire that has become a bit of a cliché, which is: where there's muck, there's brass. That was true until a few years ago, when all the money came from making smoke and digging holes and getting coal out of the ground. Sadly, it's not true any more.

However, there's another expression that's still apt, you might say, which is: where there's brass, there's music. And to investigate it I'm heading east towards Grimethorpe, the colliery town where they used to have huge winding engines and slag heaps and almost everyone either worked down a mine or did something associated with it.

Those of us who remember the 1980s remember coalmining going horribly, sadly wrong. When I was a lad, you'd see many pitheads as you travelled between London and Glasgow. Now they've all gone. The winding engines are now museum pieces and in their place are high-tech sheds making electronics equipment. A whole industrial heritage has vanished.

Deep in the heart of South Yorkshire's coalmining belt lies Grimethorpe, a village as unromantic as black pudding. Since the pits closed, one-industry towns like Grimethorpe have been through some very tough times. Nevertheless I'm always amazed how places like this survive. It's not as if they haven't got the scars to show for it, the suicides and the kids on drugs – no thanks to the government of the day – but most of them have come through it. Driving into Grimethorpe, there's a sense of a place on the up and up. And part of that is that one of the greatest traditions of the whole mining era has remained with us: the brass band. From the dreariest of landscapes, for years the glint and gleam of the brass band lit up the lives of men who worked in darkness. Emerging from the pit, they'd make for the band room where, with a discipline that was second nature to men working in an industry where self-control meant the difference between life and death, they rehearsed to the impeccable standards that won them recognition as masters of their art. Now, twenty years after the pits closed, they're still going strong and a lot of people think their art has improved in the interim. I cannot wait to find out for myself.

Pulling into an industrial estate on the edge of Grimethorpe, I can hear the glorious sound of a very good brass band wafting out of some windows. Following the call of the music, I find twelve lads inside the building, playing 'The Bandwagon' on gleaming brass instruments and a thirteenth lad on percussion standing behind two huge kettle drums. They're playing what I'd call holding-hands-and-watching-the-sun-go-down music and it's quite beautiful.

It's joy itself just to hear them rehearsing and while they

move effortlessly through their repertoire, I survey the room. Dozens of posters and photographs of the Grimethorpe Colliery Band line the walls, including a poster for the film that made them famous, *Brassed Off*, starring Pete Postlethwaite and Ewan McGregor.

This is the rehearsal room of arguably the best-known brass band in Britain, if not the world. '1970 CHAMPION BAND OF GREAT BRITAIN' it says on one banner, but their illustrious history goes far further back than that, to 1917, when several Grimethorpe miners formed the band. Their first run of local successes was in the 1930s, but national and international success did not come until the 1970s, since when they have frequently toured the world, won major championships, recorded bestselling albums and featured in dozens of television broadcasts.

Looking round the room, the most impressive item is a fantastically ornate silver cup, about 2 feet high and nearly as wide, displayed directly behind the conductor, Roger Webster. Acclaimed as one of the world's greatest ever cornetists, Roger usually plays with the band, but today is leading the practice. He tells me that the large cup was awarded at the National Brass Band Championships, which the band won in 2006 and 2007. I ask him how the connection between brass bands and collieries came about.

'They wanted to give the miners something that took them out of the mundanity of their lives; their jobs were hard and pretty boring. And brass instruments at that time were modern, accessible, easy for rough colliery workers to maintain and quick to learn.

'When I started with the junior band at Grimethorpe in 1970, it was taken for granted that wherever there was a mine, a steelworks, a mill or a car factory, there would be a brass band. They had no trouble recruiting young players from music colleges, youth bands and village bands, and very little trouble gaining the support of the local industry.'

It seems remarkable that such horny-handed toilers produced such beautiful music. After all, music wasn't their profession and the classical boys were always a bit snotty about them. But the number of former brass band players who are now principals in the London Philharmonic, the BBC Symphony Orchestra and other leading ensembles is testament to the depth of talent and dedication that was to be found in colliery and other industrial brass bands.

The biggest threat to this rich industrial heritage came when the axe fell on the mining industry: it spelt the end of quite a few bands simply because the players had to move to find work. I ask Roger if it's more difficult to keep a band together and organize rehearsals now than in the days of the pit.

'It's a nightmare. When I first played with Grimethorpe everyone worked at Grimethorpe pit, so you'd see each other every day and you could easily arrange things.'

These days, the band's members include teachers, doctors and other local workers who have to find time after work to meet for rehearsals. It was very different in the mining days, says Roger. 'It was great. They were allowed time off to rehearse twice a week in the daytime when they were supposed to be at the pit. Most of the pits allowed that, and if they didn't allow it, you'd come out early, get a bath, go to rehearsal and still be home before the rest of your shift.'

'At Grimethorpe when it was band practice day, they'd clock on in the morning, go to the canteen, have breakfast nice and leisurely, then off to band practice for a couple of hours, before going home early. And they did that twice a week. And if they got home from a concert past midnight, they didn't have to go to work the next morning.'

'Really? So they were the aristocracy of the pits?'

'It was resented by some of the miners, but generally they accepted it. Especially when the band brought a trophy home.'

And also, I assume, when they heard the band playing. If I'd been a miner, just a snatch of the glorious sound of the brass would have been enough to justify its existence to me. In their own way, these lads would put in just as much hard labour as their colleagues at the coalface. Few of the band members would have access to sheet music, a gramophone or a radio, so their only exposure to new music would come from the musical director, who would listen to the radio and note down scores by ear. Consequently many bands played mainly orchestral transcriptions – Berlioz and Tchaikovsky were favourites – and it was seen as quite revolutionary when Grimethorpe pioneered the playing of original brass band compositions in the 1970s – a decision that propelled the band to its greatest success.

Roger tells me the band has a formidable itinerary ahead of it. Between concert performances there are several major competitions: the English National Championship at Manchester in June, the British Open in September, then it's heads down for rehearsals to retain the big one, the National Brass Band Championship at the Royal Albert Hall in October.

'The last time we won it before this was in 1992, the year before the pit closures,' says Roger. 'It surprised a lot of people, who thought our spirits would be down with all the bad news in the village. The closures took the heart out of the village; the pit *was* Grimethorpe. But the area has regenerated and people are coming back now. Things are looking up.'

So, with such a tight schedule ahead of them, the big question is: have they got a short-term vacancy for a trumpet player at their next gig? I'd love to play just one number with them. After all, I've got previous form. As a boy I played first trumpet in the school orchestra, although I hesitate to mention to Roger that I haven't played since.

Roger agrees to an immediate audition. I squeeze out a few decent notes on a cornet and even manage to play it like a bugle, although my lips don't have the strength they once possessed. Too much kissing and not enough playing, I believe they used to say in the orchestra. In fact it's all coming back now. I can hear the musical director of the school band, a formidable man with a crisp upper-class accent, issuing his frequent admonishment: 'Less kissing and a bit more *embouchure*, boys, and we'll get a better tone.'

I turn to Roger: 'I'm afraid the lip's gone, so it's back to the kissing.'

I try some other instruments and get some good notes – even some tunes – out of them. After my feeble attempts on the cornet, Roger gives me an alto horn. 'If you hang these out of car windows, they play themselves. They're that easy to blow.'

The alto horn has the same fingering as a trumpet, though the horn points upwards and it has a different pitch, but I find it difficult to play. 'That's lovely. In about six years' time I'll be able to get a nice noise out of it.' I play a few more bars, but run out of puff.

'Something bigger?' Roger is a very modest, nice man, who isn't the sort to be judgemental, but I suspect that secretly he's maybe not that impressed.

'Yup. I think so. I'm not getting anywhere, but it's got a lovely tone.'

'Yes. In the right hands it's a beautiful thing.'

I try a euphonium, a much larger instrument with a horn that ends worryingly close to my ear. It has three top-action valves, played with the first three fingers of the right hand, plus a compensating valve played with the left index finger. It's not an easy instrument. Maybe I could try my hand at conducting the band instead? After all, that doesn't require mastery of any instrument, just an innate ability to boss people around while your hair flails romantically and your arms wave dramatically. Surely I'm just the man for the job?

Like many people listening to their favourite pieces of music, I've imagined myself in front of a band or orchestra, conducting the musicians, but I'm also aware that you need to know what you're doing. This is no time to attempt to busk it. No, really. It's not. So does Roger think I could pull it off?

'Most of the time the bands play automatically. They just get on with it. But there are occasions when you do need some help and you need someone who's fairly strict in the middle who will give you some direction.'

'And who might that be? Do you think I could give it a shot?'

'Absolutely. The band are kind-*ish*.'

'They might be kinder to me than they are to you because you're a pro. Maybe I should watch you.'

'Okay,' says Roger, looking down at his score.

I can read music, but I've a friend who's a conductor and I've seen his scores. Your mind has to be all over the place at once. 'Can you shut your eyes and see all those notes?' I ask Roger.

'It does help.' Roger says the band have a gig in a few days and that they're not unfamiliar with guest conductors.

'Maybe it would be good for them to get used to a bad conductor?'

'We haven't got a lot of time. But how about taking away one of the pieces, having a look at it and seeing if you're up to it.'

'We'd get a rehearsal or two, would we?'

'Well . . .' Roger ums and ahs. It looks like I'm not going to get any face time with the band before my big night.

'I couldn't . . . it's a very generous offer, but I wouldn't want to bugger it up,' I tell him.

'The worst that could happen is that we would stop playing and the audience would have a jeer or throw things.'

'Right.'

'But they've never thrown things before. I think we should give it a go.'

Roger suggests that we have a look through the repertoire before the gig at Wakefield Opera House. And he tells me a few stories about the mistakes that professional and experienced conductors have made. I don't know if they're meant to reassure me that everyone makes mistakes and it's nothing to worry about, or that conducting is so difficult that even the pros sometimes get it wrong. Whatever the purpose, we press on and decide on 'Nimrod', one of Elgar's *Enigma Variations*. Fortunately it's one of my favourite pieces of music. And fortunately I already know – although I use the term loosely – how to conduct 'Nimrod'. Or at least in my mind I do . . .

I mentioned in the previous chapter that I stopped off briefly in Manchester. The time has now come to divulge the reason for my detour. Knowing I was going to be visiting Grimethorpe, and worrying – justifiably as it turned out – that my trumpet playing may not be quite concert class, I have already taken instruction with an expert in the noble art of conductorship at Chetham's School of Music, the largest music school in Britain.

Let me take you back to that afternoon when, over the course of a few hours, I was given a crash course in baton-waving by Simon Threlfall. He's conducted the BBC Philharmonic and various other orchestras, so he should know his stuff.

Chetham's is based in a handsome red-brick building of 1421 in the heart of Manchester, from which I remember hearing wonderful music drifting when I was passing during the making of *Cracker*. I never thought I'd be inside it learning how to conduct. Lucky old me.

Simon, tall, slim and grey-haired, lays out a score on a table in his office. 'This is your simple task.'

The score has eighteen staves, all of which the conductor has to read simultaneously. 'Can you really read all of that at once?'

'Yup.'

I'm speechless. Then Simon explains that there is a shape to a score and that's what he looks at, plus the rules of music are such that no member of the orchestra or band is likely to play a completely unexpected note.

Fortunately for a mere mortal such as me, Simon has a piano reduction, which distils the score into a more manageable form. I can use it to learn the beats and basic structure and melody of the piece while Simon accompanies me on his grand piano.

'Do you feel happy about using a stick?' he says.

'Yeah . . . well . . . I . . . ah . . .' I feel at a bit of a loss.

'Try it.'

'Like most people, when I conduct at home, I hold a baton.' I wave my arms around to show Simon how I stand in the middle of my living room, conducting an imaginary orchestra. I guess we've all done that. No?

Simon smiles. 'Just by doing that, you've shown me two or three things you do very naturally. You're not stiff. You've started well.'

There are three things I need to grasp, says Simon. 'Nimrod' has three beats in the bar, which freaks me somewhat, but Simon says not to worry about the maths. Second, it carries an instruction of *noblimente* at the top, which means it's very slow, with a degree of pomp. Third, I need to concentrate on using my right hand to keep the beat and save my left hand for emphasis. A common mistake is to mirror the right hand's movement with the left.

There are a lot of other things to remember – irregular or excessive baton movements can get very wearing for the band; use both hands like chest expanders to grow the volume towards the end of the piece; think of walking a slow, funereal march to get the correct pace – but if I concentrate on the basics, the rest should come with a bit of practice. At least that's what Simon promises me.

'What's the most common mistake made by first-time conductors?' I say.

'They're so impressed by the sound coming at them when they start, they go out of time on the second beat.'

Maybe there's a way to avoid slipping out of time: 'Can I tap my feet?'

'Don't do that. Oh no. Not ever. Banishment.'

'Absolutely *verboten*?'

'Yes.'

Help ma boab.

We spend about half an hour practising the motion of the right hand, first without music, then with Simon's piano accompaniment. Like anything worthwhile, you can't master it immediately, but there's not time to get it absolutely right. A student brass band is waiting in a nearby rehearsal room for me to conduct them. Yikes.

'The trick is getting it started,' says Simon as we prepare to leave for the rehearsal room. 'They need to know you're ready to go.'

'Because they're building up breath?'

'Exactly. So if you do a quiet one, two up to the top . . .' He shows me a hand motion involving a stroke to the side before starting the piece. '. . . two and three and . . . then you should be fine.'

Apparently the trick is to take a big breath as I build up to the first beat. If I do that, the band should follow me and be ready to start when I give the signal. I give it a go and get it right first time, but then Simon tells me I'm too fast. There's so much to master in such a short time and before I feel I've had enough practice, Simon's secretary is interrupting us to say the band will go home soon if we don't join them.

In the rehearsal room, a dozen or so young musicians are waiting. Some members of the band have already departed, but there's a wonderful sound coming from the room, even without my guiding contribution.

'And your guest conductor for the day . . . is me.'

There are a few titters as Simon and I make our way to the conductor's stand.

'Mr Coltrane.' Simon gestures into the room. 'The band.'

'Hi. How are you?'

My greeting is met with silence. Let's hope it's shyness, not disbelief.

Simon points at a lad sitting close to me. 'This is Sam. He'll look after you.'

'Ah, a cornet man. They're always trouble.'

Sam smiles shyly at my attempt to break the ice.

'Robbie's been thrown in at the deep end to do "Nimrod" with the Grimethorpe Colliery Band. We've been doing a quick conducting lesson. Far too much in far too little time, but you just follow Robbie at whatever time he does.' Simon turns to me. 'No pressure.'

'So we're all on the same side, aren't we?' I look at the faces all staring at me and tap the music stand. 'Forgive me, it's my first day.' I take a deep breath. 'So . . . are we all happy?'

I take another deep breath, raise my baton and with Simon's instructions to keep it slow and steady running through my mind, I start.

Nothing.

'Okay . . . let me rephrase that,' I say. The students laugh – the first noise I've elicited from them. 'I raise my baton and you start on the first downbeat. Isn't that what you do?'

Simon comes to my aid. I forgot the preparatory beats.

I start again. Two beats to the side before lifting my baton to the top while taking a deep breath, then down. I reach the bottom of the stroke and stop just as the band starts playing.

It worked! Only problem: I should have kept going.

'Trust me.' I grin nervously at the band. 'It'll be fantastic on the night.'

Another attempt. This time I get beyond the first beat, but Simon stops me because I'm conducting in two-four time, which is easier to do than you might think.

Simon holds my right hand, directing my baton movements as the band plays on. Then he leaves me to it and after a while I realize that they're really following me. Actually they know what they're doing and to some degree it doesn't matter if I don't get it quite right – they'll make it sound good. If only I could have Simon holding my hand when I do it for real at Wakefield Opera House.

Fast forward to several days later. Having met the band at their rehearsal room, I'm now outside the Wakefield Theatre Royal and Opera House. This is where it's all meant to happen: my auspicious debut conducting the world-famous Grimethorpe Colliery Brass Band. This is my 'poster's up' moment. That moment when you walk past the theatre and the poster's up, and you think: oh God, it's going to happen, no matter what. There's nothing for it but to go inside and get on with the job.

It's a beautiful theatre, instantly recognizable as designed by Frank Matcham, the famous theatre architect whose work includes the London Coliseum and Hackney Empire. In fact, it's the smallest theatre he designed in England. Walking down the side aisle towards the front row and orchestra pit, I spot some engineering bricks, the type they put steam engines on because they're unbreakable. There's some stunning plaster-work along the front of the balconies and on the ceiling. To think this nineteenth-century beauty was no more than a bingo hall in the 1970s. As in all Matcham theatres, the acoustics are fantastic and I'm very pleased it's been so lovingly restored – a magnificent arena in which to make my debut as a conductor.

A short while later, I am sitting to the side of the band on the Theatre Royal's stage, contemplating the task ahead. Of all the things I could have been asked to undertake, telling a bunch of Yorkshiremen what to do is probably the worst. But I've accepted the task and there's no going back. First a rehearsal, then I'll be making a right royal arse of myself in front of an audience of five hundred.

'How do you feel?' says one of the band members.

'Nervous just about covers it.'

They're one of the best brass bands in the world and I really don't want to let these very talented, dedicated fellows down. To me it feels a wee bit like going into the pits at Ferrari to give Schumacher some encouraging words before a Grand Prix. But I put my hand up, so now I've got to do it.

I watch as the lads, some of them already in dinner suits and dickie bows, others still in their work clothes, set up their music stands and arrange their chairs. They do it all themselves. No room for roadies, aides or prima donnas in this outfit.

'Can we just get ourselves sorted out, lads,' says the band's proper conductor, the man I'll be trying my best to emulate. 'Let's do a couple of minutes to check the sound; then give Robbie eight bars of "Nimrod", please.'

In the rehearsal I ask them to let me know if I'm going too fast or too slow, but I suspect most of them are too polite to say anything. No probs. As long as they're not thinking: why is that man waving the stick and ruining the time while I'm trying to play?

The rehearsal passes without great incident but with utter admiration of and delight in the band on my part. Standing in front of all that talent is a real privilege. There's not much I need to remember: slow march; triangle; one-and-two-and-three-and . . . After all, I don't have to remember how to play the notes.

Afterwards, in my dressing room, I put on my lucky

tangerine G-string, and my lucky cufflinks. Outside in the corridor, the band is milling about, instruments in hand, tuning up and shooting the breeze until curtain-up.

Roger arrives. 'You ready?'

'Just about, mate.'

'Want to go through it all one more time? Remember all you've been taught?'

'So much to remember.'

'Once you're out there, just enjoy yourself and go with what you know.'

'It's so hot in here.'

'We're all right. Must be you.'

I laugh. 'You bugger.'

'You'll be fine. Don't worry.'

'I just want to get it right.'

'It's a difficult one to conduct.'

'Thank you! Is it really?'

'Yeah. Slow music always is.'

'Great. No pressure then.'

He leaves me to go and play in front of a full house of brass band aficionados. When I hear the band strike up their first number, a chilling thought runs through me: there's no turning back now.

Sat in my dressing room, kitted out in my dinner suit, braces and dickie bow, wearing the shoes I made at Tricker's in Northampton, I grease back my hair so that I look like Paul Sorvino in *The Godfather*. With the sublime sounds of the band wafting up from the stage, I consider my predicament. I'm not looking for any sympathy, because I did decide to do this, but I am scared.

Conducting the band during rehearsals, I realized for the first time that all those times I thought I was hammering out the beat when I was pretending to conduct a band in my living room, I wasn't making the beat at all. I was following it. I was a millisecond behind. And it's only when I have an entire band in front of me, following my lead, that I realize I am making the beat. For this to work, I have to be the drummer. It takes me back to when I was making *Tutti Frutti*, when I realized all my power and energy had to be in the first note, or else I was fucked. It's particularly true with rock 'n' roll. There's no holding back. You have to be convinced you're the sexiest man in the world for that first note, or the game is up. And like acting or leading a rock 'n' roll band or directing a film, conducting is a performance. I have to play the part of being a conductor. And to do it successfully, I have to walk on to the stage looking like I know exactly what I'm doing. Whatever's thrown at me, I must give the impression I know exactly how to react. It's all an act.

There's a knock at the door. It opens. Benedict, one of the backstage staff, sticks his head in. 'It's your ten-minute call. We're waiting for you. Good luck.'

Yikes.

A few minutes later there's another knock. Benedict again. 'Come to the stage, please.'

One last check in the mirror. Dickie bow straight. No food on my teeth. 'A-wop-bama-loobap a-wham-bam-boo.' Talking to my reflection, I grease my hair back a final time. 'Here we go, big boy.'

I wait in the wings, listening to the band playing a fast march, the last tune before I go on. Then the music stops and the conductor turns to the audience to explain why there are so many television cameras around the building. 'Tonight we have a special guest. He's travelling around Britain, stopping off in lots of different places. Tonight he's in Wakefield. And he's here to conduct one of the best-known tunes we're going to play tonight. He's the star of the television programme *Cracker*, and if anyone has seen *Harry Potter*, he's Hagrid. You know who I'm going to introduce: Mr Robbie Coltrane is going to conduct Elgar's "Nimrad" . . .'

The audience bursts into laughter.

'. . . er, Elgar's "Nimrod". Please give a very warm Wakefield welcome to Robbie Coltrane.'

It really is time to face the music.

Walking on, I rehearse my mantra: three, three, three, three. I try to remember: no more than a 12-inch baton movement until I get to the louder bits towards the end. Then, turning to the audience, I take a bow and mutter under my breath to the conductor, 'Can I borrow your baton?'

'You certainly can.'

Thank the lord he didn't say no. I turn to face the band. 'I'll do a big breath in and then the first stroke. Okay? Are you ready?'

Are *they* ready? What am I thinking?

Inhaling deeply through my nose, I lift the baton to the top of the stroke and start. As I reach the bottom, the band starts perfectly on cue. The sublime sound almost makes me stop, but I remember Simon's and Roger's warnings and keep going. We're away. The big engine is running.

Standing with the band fanned around me is unbelievably exciting. It is so much better than being in the audience. I can hear every little subtle nuance. It's a privilege. After about eight bars I allow myself a quick eyebrow raise at Roger, who is sitting directly to my left, playing his cornet with all the beauty and subtlety that earned him his reputation as the best in the world. He said he'd give me a kick if I slipped out of three-four time – he's certainly close enough to reach me with his foot – but so far, so good: no need yet for a prod.

By the middle of the piece I am less anxious in front of the Grimethorpe band and an audience of five hundred than I was with the pupils at Chetham's. The kids were very nervous and needed strong guidance. If I made a mistake, it was likely to show. However, the Grimethorpe band is like the best crew and a stellar cast on a movie – provided there's a shot list, it will direct itself – so I can relax and enjoy it.

Whenever I've thought of 'Nimrod' in the past, I've thought of those beautiful cello lines: haunting, mellow, heartbreaking stuff. But conducting the band I think it sounds more unified in brass. The band is playing instruments of which I don't even know the names, but what I do know is that they perfectly complement the tones and pitches of the string instruments specified by Elgar. The trumpets play the violin parts, the tubas are playing long, resonant notes like a bass fiddle and it all sounds wonderful.

Getting carried away towards the end, I even allow my left hand into the action, using it to bring the band to a crescendo, a massive smile creasing my face. And then, far too soon for me, it's over and I'm bowing in front of the audience, calling the band to stand up to acknowledge the applause.

I leave the stage a very happy man and with a presentation photograph of the band under my arm. What a moment.

Back in my dressing room, the door's open as the band troop past.

'Well done, mate!' one of them shouts.

'Shit hot, Robbie!' shouts another.

'Shit hot?' I say. 'Is that the musical expression?'

'Oh yeah. We're going for a pint now. Are you coming for a quick one?'

'In the interval?'

'Oh yes.'

The band manager doesn't allow it, but this is Yorkshire after all.

When I stop to think what most of these Yorkshire men – and most of the audience and most of the inhabitants of every town in a 20-mile radius – have been through in the last twenty-five years, it's an astounding tale of reinvention. Their lives and their communities were torn apart by the policies of Margaret Thatcher, who, to my mind, acted as if anyone working class and articulate was a threat. A lot has changed around here, but the band has remained a constant, going from strength to strength. Maybe it's because when times were at their toughest, the band provided a much-needed escape. Or maybe it's because when the mining was over, they realized that playing in the band wasn't so much a part of working at the pit as being part of something much more inspiring. Every one of the lads I spoke to said the same thing: there was a time in their mid-teens when admitting to playing an instrument such as the tuba was the most uncool statement any of them could make, particularly as everyone else was playing electric guitars or keyboards. But now, twenty or thirty years later, their friends who gave up playing brass instruments are kicking themselves. At thirty-five, playing the tuba suddenly seems like a very cool thing. And it brings with it a feeling of unity and companionship that many of us spend half our lives trying to find.

Chapter Twelve

There's only so much you can pack into one day, so it's time to bed down for the night. And as I'm up in Yorkshire I've booked into a little place in York that I've read about. It's a bed and breakfast like no other: the oldest surviving Roman Catholic convent in England.

Drawing up outside an extremely handsome, eighteenth-century, four-storey, double-fronted, red-brick building in a side street in the centre of York, I never would have guessed I was about to enter a living, breathing convent, complete with its own Renaissance chapel.

In 1686 Frances Bedingfield, a member of Mary Ward's Institute (a religious order for women modelled on the Jesuits) came to York with a small group of nuns to purchase a modest seventeenth-century house standing outside the city walls, on the site of which their eighteenth-century building now stands. Catholics at that time faced widespread persecution – they were forbidden from holding public office, from meeting in groups larger than five people, from attending Catholic Mass, and from giving their children a Catholic education or educating them abroad. Consequently, the nuns established a secret community, known as the Ladies of the Bar. Under this title they set up a boarding school and a free day school for Catholic girls, with a chapel built secretly at the centre of their complex of buildings. The nuns kept their existence secret until the early nineteenth century, when Parliament passed the Catholic Emancipation Act in 1829. For the first time Catholics were granted almost equal civil rights, including the right to vote and to hold most public offices, although some older anti-Catholic legislation, such as the Act of Settlement of 1701, which excludes any Catholic or anyone who marries a Catholic from the throne, remains in operation today. Throughout this time, the school and convent continued their work. More recently, when the intake of nuns started to dwindle, they decided to open their doors to paying guests, such as yours truly. Divine inspiration, I suppose you'd call it.

When I arrive, I find Sister Agatha waiting in the Grand Hall, a strikingly ornate glass-covered courtyard with an intricately tiled floor that stretches between the Georgian buildings that make up the convent.

Very well spoken and very spirited considering her seventy-five years, Sister Agatha has been a nun for fifty-five years. For much of that time she worked as a teacher in the school attached to the convent, but since the school became independent from the convent, she has spent most of her time working with sisters who have dementia.

'I think this must be Mr Coltrane.' Sister Agatha extends a hand as I walk in. 'Good journey?'

'A wonderful journey. It's been incredibly sunny and beautiful really. Yorkshire at its best.'

'Marvellous.' Sister Agatha has that very pleasant, slightly old-fashioned way of talking that involves issuing firm instructions with great charm. 'I'm not going to tell you how to get in and out of the house, Mr Coltrane, because I don't want the whole of England knowing. But I'll show you in secret later.' She leads me into the great parlour. 'This is where we meet guests and interview them.'

Sister Gregory, the convent's archivist and historian, and its oldest member, is standing in the middle of the Great Parlour, a room lined with portraits of the convent's mothers superior. Although frail, Sister Gregory is as sharp as a pin, explaining to me with obvious delight how Frances Bedingfield established the convent. 'She was the first of the unenclosed nuns and she was a great educator.'

'Unenclosed means it's not an enclosed community?' I say.

Sister Gregory nods conspiratorially. 'All nuns were behind bars and she had the idea that they could do more good if they were unenclosed. So we were called galloping girls and chattering hussies.' She appears tickled pink by the idea of being called a chattering hussy. 'Yes, and wandering gossips.'

'So they had a *Sun* even then, did they?'

Moving on, Sister Agatha points out how the seats of the Chippendale chairs in the room are all at different levels because the nuns cut the chairs' legs to suit their own heights.

'You really touch history in this room,' says Sister Gregory. 'It's the first post-Reformation convent in England and the oldest living convent in all of the British Isles.'

Sister Agatha chips in: 'It was incredibly brave of us. Our foundress was imprisoned four times.'

'In a prison cell that was under water when the tide rose,' adds Sister Gregory. 'In those days we pretended we weren't nuns. We were the Ladies of the Bar, which comes from the entrance into York, called Micklegate Bar.'

'Have we told Mr Coltrane enough, Sister Gregory?' Sister

Agatha is moving towards the door. 'We must show him his room. And he's going to send us *Nuns on the Run*. Our favourite viewing.'

I'm very surprised that they like the film, which I made in 1990 with Eric Idle. It's quite disrespectful of nuns and religion, but Sister Gregory looks very pleased at the idea of receiving their very own copy.

'On DVD,' I say. 'With the good sound quality.'

'I can't tell you the enjoyment that film gave us,' says Sister Agatha.

'But we were quite rude about Catholicism.'

'No you weren't.' Sister Agatha sounds very definite.

'Oh, we were.'

'No, no. What was so wonderful is that you had it checked out by the Jesuits. It was absolutely correct in everything. And the nuns were portrayed in the most down-to-earth way and I loved it when the Superior said "God works in mysterious ways" when she saw a great bundle of money.'

Well I never. I didn't ever think I'd have fans among the sisterhood.

My convent tour continues through the Great Hall, which has a roundel design on its tiled floor found only here and in the House of Representatives in Washington DC, then past the loos to a very plush lift with hand-painted stencils by 'the girls', says Sister Agatha.

'This is the poshest lift I've been in since Claridge's. In fact, it's much posher than the Claridge's lift. It's the nicest lift I've ever been in.' With chairs in the corners and beige walls with paintings of trees, it really is extremely pleasant.

Sister Agatha presses a button. The doors close and a few seconds later we arrive outside the chapel, the heart of the house and a miniature Palladian masterpiece. Looking as if it could have been built by Robert Adam, it has columns and a glass cupola.

'It was built in 1767 and finished in two years.' Sister Agatha's commentary is non-stop. She is an excellent guide.

'Lovely.' I look around the chapel. 'It's post-rococo, isn't it? Not too overblown.'

'I'd say it's neo-classical and I love it because it is so domestic. And because it was built in penal times, a number of exits were made.' Sister Agatha is referring to eight escape routes for the congregation in the event of a raid by magistrates and a priest hole that offered further safety.

To hide its existence, the chapel was built with plain lunette windows that reveal nothing of its religious use to the outside world and its beautiful dome is hidden from outside view by a pitched roof. I am bedazzled by the idea that someone could have built the chapel in secret. It's something I find hard to understand. 'You build something as huge and beautiful as this, then keep it secret?' I point to some of the carvings on the wall. 'So what happened to the guy who carved this?'

'I've often wondered about that. In 1829 it was all right to be a Catholic, so maybe it was done then.'

Maybe there was a secret clique of Catholic craftsmen who helped create the chapel. Who knows? It's like one of those escape movies in which the prisoners build a complex underground network of tunnels under the noses of the guards. It's very intriguing, especially as there's nothing covert about it. It isn't a Catholic chapel disguised as something else, such as a Masons' hall. It's unashamedly a chapel, with statues and the Stations of the Cross and an altar, pews and all the paraphernalia of Catholicism. Maybe it just goes to show you can never suppress religion.

Wanting to move on, Sister Agatha shows me to my room, called St Ignatius. Presumably that's Ignatius Loyola, I think to myself, the principal founder of the Society of Jesus, or Jesuits. The room, which used to be part of the school washrooms, is simple and plain, but comfortable in a Shaker kind of way.

'I'm so glad that you've got a proper big bed,' says Agatha. 'Here's the key, which means you can get in and out of the house as much as you like. You could have a rave-up and I wouldn't have any idea.'

She's quite a card is Sister Agatha. 'Is this unique?' I say. 'Do any other convents open to the public?'

'It's the only one. In 1985 the school went to more modern buildings and we were left with this historic site. We had to reinvent. And we had to do something we were able to do, so we decided on a museum, café, shop, pastoral centre and bed and breakfast. Sir Paul Getty helped us with money to set it up. It has been a wonderful thing.'

Ah – reinvention, the recurrent theme of this portion of my trip. 'It's extraordinary how people reinvent themselves or the situations in which they find themselves,' I say. 'On my journey, one of the really remarkable aspects has been seeing how extraordinary things happen to communities and completely change them. You wonder how they are ever going to cope with it, but they do, they reinvent themselves. And always with the same spirit with which they invented the original thing that they lost.'

'Out of failure something always better comes,' says Sister Agatha. 'Something of which you would never have thought.'

'That's a bit Nietzsche.'

'I can't help that. I think he was a god as well. But now you must be very tired. I am going to leave you to go to sleep. Good night, Mr Coltrane.'

The door clicks closed and I'm left with my thoughts.

My next destination is York Harness Racing Club, the scene of the world's most popular and Britain's least-known form of horse racing. This modern-day version of chariot racing is extremely popular in North America and continental Europe, but harness racing is almost unknown here.

York, one of thirty-six tracks available to British harness racers, is the country's fastest all-weather half-mile track. When I arrive, two horses are pulling a couple of two-wheeled buggies at great speed around a track, leaving a faint whistling noise and click-clack in their wake. Seated on each buggy – or sulky, to give it its proper name – is a jockey, legs stretched wide apart along the arms of the buggy that lead to the horse. On a sunny day, with a light breeze kicking up a dust, the speed they reach is quite astonishing, but what's particularly appealing about harness racing, or sulky racing as it's sometimes known, is the fact that it has none of the elitist connotations of flat or steeplechase racing. It's for people who love horses and love racing but don't necessarily have the money or connections to get into the thoroughbred racing world.

Whereas a decent thoroughbred costs at least £100,000, a good standardbred (the type of horse bred for harness racing) can be had for as little as £4,000. As closely bred as thoroughbreds but with refined, solid legs and powerful shoulders and hindquarters, standardbreds are generally more muscled, longer-bodied and a bit heavier than their thoroughbred cousins. Tougher, friendlier and easier to train than thoroughbreds, they are also considered more placid, which suits racehorses employed in a sport that involves more strategy and more changes of speed than thoroughbred races. Mostly bay or brown in colour, standardbreds fall into two camps: trotters and pacers. A trotter's racing gait involves the horse's legs moving in diagonal pairs, right foreleg and left hind leg simultaneously, and vice versa. By contrast, the pacer has a two-beat lateral gait: its forelegs move in unison with its hind legs on the same side, but like the trotter it can pace almost as fast as a thoroughbred can gallop.

A particularly appealing aspect of harness racing is that it is a very family-orientated sport. The racing teams are often a genuine family unit and I am about to meet one of them when the two racing horses and their sulkies pull over to where two men are standing at the side of the track.

John Gill and Michael Lord have been training and racing since they were eight. They grew up together and both now breed standardbreds.

'We were rivals then and we're rivals now,' says Michael, the smaller and more easygoing of the two men.

'Although my hair has lasted longer,' says John, a ruddy-faced man with a few strands of blond hair covering the top of his head.

John's family team is one of the top harness racing teams in the country. He is a horse trainer and his wife, Mary, breeds horses, while their twenty-seven-year-old daughter Vicki is one of the best drivers in the country. John has been riding since he could walk, and with twenty-three horses in his charge he's got his work cut out for him, although as a professional trainer, not all of them are his.

As for Michael, he is one of only seventy-six professional

drivers in Britain, a former British champion who has made numerous appearances at the Harness Racing World Championships. Like John, he has a farm and is a professional trainer. His wife, Sheila, is also a trainer, while his daughters, Kelly and Katherine, assist the team. The two families have grown up side by side in the harness racing world and are incredibly competitive, although it's largely good-natured. John was best man at Michael's wedding and Michael is godfather to John's daughter Vicki.

For all the friendliness, I can see there's still a fierce rivalry between these two lads. John is much more of an archetypal Yorkshireman than Michael, with no hesitation in speaking his mind.

'He didn't beat me in the race yesterday,' says Michael by way of example, 'so he's a bit touchy now.'

They explain the sport to me. The majority of races are one mile and there's a maximum of ten in a race, in two lines of five, handicapped through distance behind the starting car. As far as I can make out, the sulkies came about by the usual transport-engineering route: two bold boys took what was a standard two-wheeled sulky and removed as much from it as they could without impinging on its overall strength. Now made of aluminium, they can be as light as 28 lb.

'Here's the question that every man wants to know,' I say. 'What's it like sitting with your legs wide open and your vitals just a few inches from the kick of the horse's clumping hooves?'

'Can you see the tears in my eyes?' says John.

It might be great to look at, but it's certainly not my idea of a relaxing time.

'It's very safe,' says Michael.

'Is it?'

'Absolutely,' says Michael. 'Do you fancy a go?'

'I'm not sure I could do the open-legged thing.' Fortunately I've got a good excuse. 'I've just had an operation on my knee.'

'We've got a cart down there especially for you.'

'Really?' Surely I'm too heavy for one of those flimsy sulkies. They're little more than two large wheels and a pole for sitting on. 'Is it an old Mini with the roof off?'

'More or less.'

Before I commit myself to the track, I want to know a little more about this fascinating and very elegant sport. In North America and continental Europe the sport is shown on television, but in Britain high-street bookies don't take bets on it, so it's rarely seen on our screens. Why that is, I don't know, so I ask the lads if it's because the prize money is less than for flat racing and steeplechases.

'Don't know,' says John. 'There's nine races in America and Canada that if you win them you're a millionaire.'

'Blimey. So when are you going?'

So far, the lads' foreign excursions have been limited to racing for the British team at events such as the World Driving Championships in America, which doesn't require competitors to bring their own horses and sulkies. However, they've both exported horses to the big bucks world of American harness racing and imported mares to improve the bloodlines of their standardbreds.

Eventually there's no avoiding the purpose for which I am here: I have to hoist myself on to one of the buggies.

'Let's go hot-rodding,' says Michael.

Consoling myself that it can't be as scary as my ascent to the top of Emley Moor tower, I walk over towards the track. 'Who is it who's going to take me round the track?'

'A nice young girl. One of the nation's leading lady drivers.'

'Lovely. That sounds fantastic. Take me to it.'

John's daughter Vicki emerges from a horsebox trailing a standardbred in a blanket. She removes the blanket and attaches the buggy, which I am pleased to say looks less like the large-wheeled flimsy racing sulkies I saw tearing round the track earlier and more like something the milkman might have used to collect urns of freshly drawn milk from farms a hundred years ago. It's called a custom dobble.

Vicki has been driving competitively for twelve years and risen to the top of her field. She squeezes a helmet on to my head – it only just fits, which makes her giggle – and gives me a pair of protective spectacles. 'Not very sexy, I'm afraid.'

The strap under the helmet is so tight I can hardly breathe. 'How long have you been doing this – sitting on one of these, I mean?'

'Since I was five. I started on my dad's lap.'

'What a wonderful way to grow up! I'm quite jealous.' I look at the sulky. 'This is a lovely piece of kit.'

We move off. 'You okay?' asks Vicki.

'I'm fine.'

'The seat's quite wobbly.'

'It wouldn't be if it was just you on here.'

We're led by John to the track and then let loose. The horse immediately speeds up. 'She's an old racehorse.' Vicki is loosening the reins. 'She knows everything that's going on.'

'How old is she?'

'About ten years.'

Despite the old girl's age, she is impressively powerful. We complete several laps, the cinders on the track sandblasting my face and teeth.

'This is very pleasant,' I say.

'This is just the Surrey-with-a-fringe-on-top speed. You want to see it go.' Vicki cracks the whip and the buggy takes off like the proverbial off a shovel.

Because we're so close to the ground and so close to the animal, we get a wonderful sense of speed. It seems a lot faster than the 30 m.p.h. or so we're making. Only a foot behind the horse's backside, I can see her muscles straining and hear the thunder of her breath. Now I know how the boy racers of the nineteenth century got their thrills.

Buggy racing is so wonderful and so exciting that I'm amazed it's not the national sport. In Wales it's more popular than traditional horseracing. And in Ireland gypsies take over motorways early on Sunday mornings without permission to race and crowds of spectators drive slowly behind the racing field to block normal traffic. Bets of up to £10,000 are made. However, in England harness racing is seen as little more than an eccentric variation on horseracing. I really can't quite understand why.

By the time we finish at the racetrack, the wind has picked up and the shadows have grown long. It's been a delightful day, but I have many more miles to drive before I reach my next destination, Wray in Leicestershire, about 80 miles west of York Harness Racetrack. About halfway there I come to Pateley Bridge, a pleasant market town with a particular claim to fame that I'm going to investigate. Having been on the road for a long while, and with the last leg of my journey coming into sight, inevitably my thoughts have turned to home and more specifically to my children waiting there. It's been a while since I've seen them and, like any good father, I know I'm expected to return home with a wee something from my travels. Fortunately Pateley Bridge has just what I need: the oldest sweet shop in the whole of England.

Nestling up in the Dales, Pateley Bridge is an attractive little market town. On its charming, steeply winding High Street lies the sweet shop, apparently still selling the same sugary delights it did when it opened back in 1827.

Shopkeepers Keith and Gloria Tordoff have been serving for ten years, priding themselves on keeping everything as it always has been. A bell tinkles over the gingerbread door as I stoop to walk into the oak-beamed, low-ceilinged shop with its delicious aroma of chocolate and sugar. Inside, it really does look as though nothing has changed in nearly two hundred years. There's an open fireplace with a kettle and cooking pans for boiling sugar suspended over the fire grate. On the counter there's an authentic nineteenth-century till with large paddle keys and a wooden drawer. Beside the till is a traditional Avery scale pan. However, the centrepiece (if you can call it that, because it stretches around three walls of the shop) is the array of antique pine shelves groaning under the weight of more than two hundred jars of the sweets of yesteryear. It's a retro delight for those with a sweet tooth.

Humbugs, butterscotch gums, liquorice allsorts, midget gems, liquorice sticks, aniseed balls, wine gums, sugared almonds, mints, jelly beans, truffles, Belgian chocolate, fudge, caramel, Turkish delight, nougat, sherbet crystals, lemonade powder, fruit salads, blackjacks, lollipops, dolly mixture, bubblegum, millions and bonbons are just some of the delights that would have most children's eyes out on stalks. There are marzipan teacakes, Spanish gold that looks like sweet tobacco, pink and yellow peardrops, rhubarb and custard, multicoloured and multishaped Yorkshire mixture, floral gums, the black discs of Pontefract cake, lilac blackcurrant and liquorice, pink and white alphabet letters, the brown-striped cushioned triangles of mint humbugs and multicoloured rainbow crystals. The selection on offer is mindboggling, but it begs the question: why?

'Sweets are a passion of ours,' says Keith. 'And the shop is a passion. I can honestly say I've eaten most of the sweets on sale in here.' It doesn't seem to have done him much harm, although he insists it's given him 'a bit of a belly'.

'I only have to look at a jar and I put on a pound,' I say. But before Keith answers, my eye is drawn to the delicacies on the shelves. 'What's this? I've not seen these before. Marry Me Quick? I suppose they're also known as Unwanted Pregnancy in some parts?'

Keith and his wife laugh. 'It's a mint rock with a hint of bonfire toffee running through it, so it gives you a combination.'

'A *hint* of bonfire toffee?'

'It's a very old sweet and it's been called Marry Me Quick for many years.'

I wonder why. There's also a type of mint humbug called a Julie Barrett. 'Who was she, then?'

'In the past local sweetmakers might name their creations after their daughters. Somehow that particular sweet has lasted when others have died away. We get people coming in asking for Jap Desserts but they simply aren't available anywhere in the country.'

Jap Desserts? I remember them. Little square striped things. 'What happened to them?'

'Maybe it needed a special mould that broke,' suggests Keith, 'and it isn't viable now to get a new part made.'

Many of the sweets originate from the old chemist's shops or apothecaries, where they were once used to treat all sorts of ailments, from gout and scurvy to headaches and diarrhoea. Or as Yorkshire folk call it, the skitters.

'Certain things have a medicinal purpose,' says Keith, 'such as mints for digestion, liquorice for the bowel.'

'Do you think that's how they started off? They added some sugar to make them more palatable and people thought they'd have some anyway because they were delicious?'

Keith tells me that archaeologists have found evidence of sweets going back thousands of years. 'On archaeological digs they've found honey that's been boiled into the form of a sweet.'

Back in those days, sweets were only for the wealthy. Sugar was an extremely expensive luxury that only the very richest people could afford, so it wouldn't be surprising if they justified their extravagance by saying it had medicinal value.

'Even now doctors send people to us for throat and chest sweets because our sweets are cheaper than medicine.' Keith looks at me conspiratorially. 'It's rumoured that Sarsaparilla drops have the effect of a poor man's Viagra.'

Well, I couldn't possibly comment on that. But, as for another of the shop's little treats, I've just spotted a blast from my past. 'Oh Pontefract cakes. I haven't seen them since I was a child – oh God.' My doctor says I'm absolutely not allowed anything sweet any more – being here is a bit like being in a whorehouse with my vitals cut off – but call me weak-willed, I just can't resist. 'God, that's good. I feel like I'm seven years old again.'

Who would have thought that in a little shop in the Yorkshire Dales I'd find my Proustian moment? It's blissful, but it also prompts another thought: sweets completely define your age. When I was a lad, the sweet shops did sweetie tobacco. This brown-coloured shredded coconut came with a smoking set of a pipe, cigar and cigarettes – it's remarkable when you think about it now – and I'd fill the pipe with the smoking tobacco. Of course, the Pateley Bridge shop stocks sweetie tobacco and dozens of other sweets I've not seen for forty or fifty years. It is quite extraordinary and maybe explains why Keith and Gloria joke that they don't want children in the place: they've recognized that nostalgic adults will be the big buyers. And it beggars the question: how do Keith and Gloria themselves work here without rotting all their teeth and clogging all their arteries?

'It is difficult,' says Keith. 'My favourites are the jelly beans and when I'm stocking the jars I will have one or two myself.'

It reminds me again of that Greek expression: He who deals in honey cannot help but lick his fingers. Keith and Gloria laugh loudly when I mention it to them.

Now it's time to get a wee poke of sweeties to sort out that sugar fix for my daughter. As we go round the shop, filling the bag, I realize I'm living vicariously through my daughter's sweet tooth.

'What do you want?' says Gloria.

'Oh anything, really. Well, everything.' Pointing at a jar on the shelves, I start getting a sugar rush just looking at them. I'll be talking loudly and showing off next. 'She would love those. Definitely. And alphabet letters. And strawberry candy sticks. Ooh, violets. A few of those . . . a sherbet fountain, obviously . . . dip dabs, oh yes . . . chocolate saturns . . . blackjacks, my God . . . mini marshmallows . . .'

Suddenly it's 1955, I can almost see the trolley buses and I'm in shorts, standing in a sweet shop, saying, 'Mister, do you have cinnamon balls?' and when the owner answers 'Yes', running out of the shop, shouting 'They do a cream now.' Happy times.

'You seem to know your sweets, Robbie,' says Keith.

'Well . . . there's a visual clue here.'

My selection has turned into a large plastic bag instead of the wee paper poke I'd intended. But no matter, they'll bring a smile to a wee girl in Glasgow. And that, I realize, is what's remarkable about this shop. Anyone who enters it is immediately happier. Kids are amazed by it and adults reminisce. In fact, I'd go so far as to say that sweets are like music: they send you on a trip down memory lane.

'Well, that's me,' I say. It's time to leave. 'Four thousand, three hundred and ninety-five pounds later.'

Keith points at his till. 'We only go up to £3.99 on that.' But every penny of change that comes out of it they still count out into your hand in this delightful place. If only they had caps for my Lone Ranger 6-gun.

Chapter Thirteen

My journey through Yorkshire completed, I arrive in Lancashire at the village of Wray. For many years Wray was best known for its flood of 1967, when houses, bridges, livestock, vehicles and personal possessions were swept away by a flash flood of incredible speed and ferocity. Remarkably, despite the trail of destruction left by the river Roeburn, no one in the village was seriously injured.

All very interesting, but I'm here to see something for which Wray has recently become better known. A clue to it can be found in the front gardens of almost every house in the village. The village is overpopulated with what I can only describe as elaborately constructed stuffed superheroes. Behind these large puppets is an intriguing story that began fifteen years ago when Wray was a place with no folklore of its own. Whilst other villages had cheese-rolling, well-dressing and dwile-flonking (I kid you not: it's a drinking game of dubious parentage that's popular in Sussex), poor little Wray had only the Wray Fair. This annual extravaganza (I use the term loosely) had been going on for many years, not loved by the Church but, with the exception of during the two World Wars, a simple but permanent fixture on the calendar. However, by the 1980s the fair was in the doldrums, attracting few people from outside the village and raising just £300 a year for the village's community hall, a 1920s jerrybuilt construction that required constant upkeep. As a way of uniting the community and raising money, the Wray Fair was underperforming on all counts.

This all changed when local resident David Hartnup, a tall, ruddy-faced, disgustingly healthy-looking man of about sixty, went on holiday. Standing with me in the High Street, he explains what happened next.

'I was on holiday with my wife in the French Pyrenees and I happened to see a chap hanging from a tree.'

As you do, of course. David shows me a photograph and, lo and behold, there's a man hanging from a tree by a noose around his neck, looking entirely real, as if he's been the victim of a Pyrenean lynch mob. 'That must have been a bit scary?'

'I thought it was a real man. It wasn't until I got fairly close that I realized it was a scarecrow.' As if that wasn't strange enough, things became weirder still when David got to the nearest village. Dozens of scarecrows were hanging from trees. 'It suddenly struck me that if we did this in England, we'd pack our village.'

Strange as it might sound, David was absolutely right. Looking down the High Street, it's thronging with people and it's still early in the day. The festival hasn't officially started yet.

'How many scarecrows do you reckon have been made for this day?'

'About two hundred.'

'Two hundred? Are they all that big?' I point at a 14-foot-high scarecrow of a whiskered man in a brocade waistcoat directly behind David.

'There's half a dozen of those. We did them to make our scarecrows better than anyone else's.'

And therein lies the paradox of the Wray Scarecrow Festival. Since it started fifteen years ago, the festival has become a monster, attracting tens of thousands of visitors, which has prompted other villages to attempt to copy its success. Britain now has more than twenty scarecrow festivals, stretching from the Isle of Wight to Langwathby in Cumbria, so Wray has had to up its game to keep ahead of the pack. Having seen giant figures worn by people in Barcelona, the Wray festival organizers decided to make six 14-foot scarecrows every year, some of which have since been displayed at museums in Britain and abroad, including Tate Modern.

The festival has also become a huge financial success. When Dave started it in 1992, the festival committee was worried they were about to waste £300 on prizes for the best scarecrows. They soon realized their concerns were unfounded when thousands of people turned up on the first day. They had nowhere for the visitors to park and no refreshments or toilets for them, but they managed to get through the day and raised more than £3,000.

On that first day, only ten scarecrows were on display. But spurred on by the immediate success of their festival, the inhabitants of Wray kept working. The next day, more than fifty scarecrows were standing in the village streets and, another day later, more than one hundred were up.

Nowadays the festival raises a lot of money for charity, the village institute, the chapel and the village school. Although the scarecrow displays are free – they're in every front garden – the village uses them to advertise the Wray Fair, which has an entrance fee. Through it, the festival brings in about £14,000 a year.

'It surprises me that you can invent a tradition,' I say, 'but I suppose all traditions were once invented.'

'You've got to start somewhere,' says Dave. 'All the surrounding villages now join in, as well as local pubs and garages. And the bed and breakfasts from Morecambe to Ingleton, they're all full. The tourist board says it brings two million pounds into the area.' Blimey.

The festival now lasts for ten days. On the first day the scarecrows go up and there's a 10-kilometre road race. A car boot sale occupies the second day and on day four a committee of half a dozen people from outside the village judges the scarecrows in several categories, including Best Traditional Scarecrow, Best Moving Scarecrow and Best Theme Scarecrow – this year's theme is Hollywood blockbusters and cartoons. On day four of the festival, a torchlight procession of the giant scarecrows winds through the village, accompanied by a samba band and culminating in a hog roast, prize presentation and firework display. The festival reaches its climax on day ten with the Wray Fair, which has stalls, woodcarving, goose-herding and other entertainment. I really like the idea that the whole village is involved – nearly every home and shop has a scarecrow outside it – and it is a wonderfully imaginative activity.

David, who has made a scarecrow out of Jacob's crackers to symbolize a criminal psychologist in a popular ITV series – *Cracker*, geddit? – takes me on a walking tour of the village. Some of the scarecrows I see are fascinating. Others are quite frightening. And some are simply amusing, such as one of an old boy, arse in the air and head under a bonnet as he repairs his car, or a scarecrow of a woman in a robe and crown labelled: 'Her Maj the Queen. Ho-hum Katie's gawn. Is one bovvered?' Then, among the Rocky Balboas and the

Spongebob Squarepants, is a magnificent Vegas-era Elvis Presley scarecrow that has been tied to the corner of a stone cottage; nearby a Basil Fawlty scarecrow is goose-stepping from the doorway of another cottage. Someone has even made 101 little black and white scarecrows to depict *101 Dalmatians*, and there's a giant Gulliver scarecrow pinned to a grassy patch by a horde of Lilliputian scarecrows. There's also a small tree covered in scraps of paper and small objects. It's a wishing tree, derived from a medieval tradition that involved pinning items to a tree to symbolize a wish.

'What kind of wishes?' I say. 'You mean wishes such as having a baby or hoping someone you are in love with falls in love with you?'

'Exactly that kind of thing. Every little sign on it is a wish.'

There are little dolls (fertility symbols maybe?), a lot of handwritten notes and what looks like a dog's bone on a string. No idea what that represents, but the sweetest of all the wishes is touchingly simple. No, it's not 'I wish I had an iPod.' It's a note saying, 'I wish I had some frogspawn.'

Leaving Dave behind, I arrive at the home of Stella Kenyon, a marvellously eccentric straw-hat-wearing oak and willow weaver who has made a giant wicker scarecrow of the Queen of the May, a task that has taken her six weeks. Stella has lived in Wray since before the first Scarecrow Festival and has seen how it has changed the village.

'Wray Fair was just a cattle fair, but it got very drunken and disorderly, so much so that the villagers would refer to it as "that day". It was one of the most drunken and disorderly fairs around.'

According to Stella, in those days the village had seven pubs that would be open twenty-four hours a day, but eventually the villagers became fed up with the bacchanalian excesses and a temperance movement emerged in the village. The Wee Frees – the Presbyterian Church of Scotland – arrived with the aim of building seven churches, one for every pub. Only one of the churches was in fact built, but the village became a less sociable place and the fair suffered financially; the advent of the Scarecrow Festival was therefore a very welcome shot in the arm for village life. 'It's the one day the whole village gets together, pulls together and nobody worries about their own lives,' says Stella. 'It's great and the children look forward to it all year.'

Having lived in Wray for so long, was Stella surprised, I wondered, at the invention of the festival?

'What was really wonderful about it is that it was a spontaneous creative thing. One scarecrow was put outside the institute and immediately everyone else joined in, putting them outside their homes. I couldn't believe it. I walked down the hill three days later and there was a chimneysweep scarecrow on a chimney and there were burglar scarecrows climbing into windows. And yet nobody had been told to make scarecrows. They just saw one and thought: "Let's make one." That first year, people started coming to see them. They'd stop their cars and ask: "What are these goblins all over the place?" So we told them it was to advertise the fair. A few days later, ten thousand people came to the fair and a few thousand people came each day before the fair to see the scarecrows. We just couldn't believe it.'

It's an amazing story, and to me it's about a community looking for something to focus on. Yet again I've found an example of a community united by adherence to an old custom or reinvigorated by the invention of a new tradition. It doesn't seem to matter if it's bottle-kicking or Stilton-rolling or dock-pudding cooking or scarecrow-building: it gives everyone a common focus – something that has largely disappeared in modern secular life. Strictly speaking, the Scarecrow Festival is entirely bogus – it belongs in the Pyrenees, not Lancashire – but that doesn't matter because it's a focus for everybody in the village and for everyone who visits and throws wads of cash at charity. How perfect is that?

Moving on, I enter the Lake District and can hardly keep my eyes on the road. It is truly stunning here; around every bend and over each hill lies yet another breathtaking view. There are twelve of the largest lakes in England in this spectacular National Park, and it was on one of them – Coniston – that a childhood hero of mine met his end. In January 1967, Sir Donald Campbell was on Coniston Water, attempting to break his own world water speed record, but as he hit an estimated 328 m.p.h. his boat, *Bluebird*, lifted out of the lake. It somersaulted into the air, then hit the water again, killing Sir Donald on impact.

The Lake District was associated with power boating and water speed record attempts for most of the twentieth century. But that association has recently come to a sudden end. To find out why, I'm heading for a particularly beautiful part of the region. When I reach my destination the clouds racing across the sky are reflected in the water of Lake Windermere, in front of which Ted Walsh is waiting. Ted is a local councillor and chairman of the Windermere Motor Boat Club, the club to which Donald Campbell and his father Malcolm belonged.

We walk up to the clubhouse and what a nice wee gaff they have here. Built in the nineteenth century as a country house retreat and used as a location in the film of *The French Lieutenant's Woman*, Broad Leys was bought in the 1950s by the club. It's an absolute doozie. With roughcast walls and massive rendered stacks on sweeping slate roofs, it's regarded as the masterpiece of Charles Voysey, an architect who bridged the gap between the Arts and Crafts movement, Art Nouveau and the Modern movement. The building is in excellent condition, but sadly it's no longer where the club races.

'We're not allowed to race here any more – a bit sad really,' says Ted, his long, grey-streaked hair blowing in the wind.

'Is that because you misbehaved?'

'Far from it. We have an impeccable record of good behaviour, but the government and the National Park Authority decided the Lake District should not be used by power sports any more. Consequently there's a ten-mile-an-hour speed limit on the lake.' This means water-skiers and other power sports aficionados are also banned.

'What sort of speeds did you get up to?'

'A hundred and twenty to a hundred and thirty miles an hour.'

'Blimey.'

A powerboat enthusiast for twelve years, Ted has the fastest boat in the club, a £25,000 1997 world championship Formula One boat capable of 140 m.p.h. Painted bright red with a skull and crossbones across the side, the 350 h.p. boat can go from 30 m.p.h. to 120 m.p.h. in six seconds. *Ding dong!*

Thirteen miles long, narrow and deep, Windermere was ideal for powerboat racing and, although it's quite understandable that the authority wanted to preserve the tranquillity and ecology of England's largest lake, it had the unfortunate effect of ending the sport's longstanding and symbolic association with the Lake District. You could say that the deafening sound of engines resonating on the lake was part of the traditional fabric of the place in the twentieth century, so it seems a shame that it has come to an end.

Playing devil's advocate, I ask Ted why he should be allowed to drive noisy, big things at 100 m.p.h. up and down a place where people come to have a quiet escape from city life.

'The National Park is a very big place. It's got more than a dozen large stretches of water and plenty are very quiet. Windermere, however, has never been tranquil. There are lots of tourist steamers. And as for provenance: we've been racing here for eighty-five years.'

But isn't that like wife-beating, cockfighting or foxhunting? People have been doing it for a long time, but that doesn't necessarily make it a good or correct thing to do. Ted, however, would argue that racing doesn't necessarily detract from the National Park and that it's as much a part of the Lake District as Beatrix Potter. And as he tells me, the club allowed its members to race on only twelve afternoons a year. I don't point out to him that that's the time when thousands of other people want to fish or take their families on a picnic or do something that might be spoilt by screeching powerboat engines.

'In other National Parks, the authority manages and restricts the use of the facilities between different groups,' says Ted. 'But here, the authority has the view that the only way to manage it is to impose a blanket ban.'

Instead of seeing the lakes as a resource, it appears the authority wants to see them as passive pieces of scenery. As someone who lives near Loch Lomond and likes to cast a line out for a fish, or go swimming, or have a wee barbecue beneath a tree, I can sympathize with that view. In my opinion, if people want to show off on their jet-skis or make a lot of noise, they should go to Showy-offy-land or to somewhere where no one is disturbed by the noise.

'Is it genuinely a National Park if you exclude a fifth of the users?' argues Ted. He thinks the ban has taken away from the character of the place and that its prime motivation was to restrict use of the park.

'So what have you done now?'

'We've been very fortunate in finding a venue about thirty miles up the road in the docks at Barrow-in-Furness. We have an agreement not to race when ships are moving about, but apart from that we get the water to ourselves.'

The view might not be quite as idyllic as at Windermere and they miss having a beautiful clubhouse on the water's edge, but at least they can now race to their hearts' content. The social aspect of the club is struggling, but the sporting side is doing very well, thank you.

I've never taken much interest in powerboat racing, but I suspect much of that lack of interest is because it's filmed as poorly as Formula One racing – all long telephoto shots that compress distances and rob the viewer of any impression of the speeds and skills involved. I've never actually seen a powerboat race, but I've always been impressed with how insanely brave it looks. On the road there are tyres and brakes and things with which you're familiar. But when you see these skiffs going so fast, it does appear phenomenally dangerous. To the untrained eye, it looks like an aero-engine bolted to the arse of a shovel.

'That's pretty much the level of it,' says Ted. 'It's like anything else to do with motorsport: the biggest engine you can possibly put on the tiniest lightest platform is the way you want to do it.'

Powerboats fall into two categories: V-shaped hulls and catamarans, of which the latter is essentially a boat flying above the water. As Ted explains to me, 'Water is a horrible sticky thing and if you want to go fast, you cannot be in it. You have to be in the air above it.'

All this sounds very scary, but also very exciting – particularly when Ted says the club keeps a boat specially for novices to experience the sport.

'Has it got room for a big chap?'

'We could probably do something.'

'Really? What kind of engine has it got?'

'A V6 two and a half litre two-stroke.'

'My favourite kind of engine. Has it really? An outboard?'

'Yes. Knocking on 250 horsepower.'

'That's enough.'

'It'll get shifting, even with a big lad like you.'

'You'll have to tell me how to turn. Does it automatically turn into the corner?'

'No. It goes the other way.'

'Logically it would. So how do you stop it doing that?'

'It's called skill of the driver.'

'Ah . . . so no pressure then?'

Ted laughs.

'I either get it right or go over?'

More laughter. 'Possibly.'

'Got any crash helmets down there?'

'We could sort something out.'

'Actually I've brought my own.'

'It's got to be orange.'

'Why's that?'

Dacre Castle – in the background, an example of something built for safety and function, in the foreground, an example of something that was built to be loved.

Below: *Trevor and Tracy Hodgson. Both farming and wrestling run in the blood in this family.*

Below right: *It looks very simple but there is much more to Cumberland and Westmorland wrestling than brute strength.*

Victorian wrestlers originally embroidered their costumes to identify their farms. I wouldn't advise making cracks about the pansy patterns – you are likely to need the paramedics!

Sir Humphry Wakefield believes we have enough Victorian castles and, since he bought Chillingham Castle in 1982, he has spent years restoring it to its original medieval glory. A sight to see.

Below left: *Dedicated to explaining the inexplicable, our technical ghost hunters stayed up all night in the creepiest part of the castle whilst I slept off a lovely trout and a glass or two of malt whisky!*

Right: *Sir Humphry. Great company and a generous host. Just don't get him talking about the marauding Scots! (Actually, do, he's very entertaining.)*

British
Nuclear
Group

Management Services

Chapelcross

Main Gate

It was very exciting to watch the towers topple, but it was so much more than a bit of industrial history for Bill and Mary Thompson.

Above: *Just as a smithy should be. You could have made a bicycle from the stuff he had impaling his head, and you just knew the local punters made a lot of room for him as he made his way to the bar, but underneath, Ross Berry is one of nature's gentlemen. (It's never the big guys that cause the bother.)*

Below: *Rik Allsop at Drumlanrig Castle. Living proof that you can know an astonishing amount about a subject without being a bore.*

Bruce Williams' brewery in Alloa.
I thought heather beer was a modern
fancy for tourists but, in fact, we
didn't have hops in Scotland until the
eighteenth century so the Scots have
been brewing heather, pine and herb
beers for centuries. The ginger and lime
was spectacular.

'So that when you fall out of the boat, we can use you as a turn buoy.'

Now it's my turn to laugh. 'Waste not, want not? He's dead, but it'll give us an extra lap?'

'It's all good, clean fun.'

I've always loved the throwaway madness of the speedheads and decide to have a go. You only live once and all that, although I suspect my children would want me to live a little bit longer.

Before leaving for the club's new racecourse at Barrow docks, I head into the clubhouse to meet Gina Campbell, daughter of Sir Donald. Gina was just seventeen when she lost her father and wasn't present when his jet-powered boat disintegrated. In spite of the crash, she has fond memories of growing up around boats and of record-breaking. The danger of the sport never dawned on her and Donald's achievements and activities were as normal to her as those of her friends' dads who went to the office.

Gina certainly has something of which to be proud. Her father held seven world water-speed records. And it seems Sir Donald really was that suave James Bond-like character most of us men would secretly like to be.

'He always said that he wanted to die making love to a beautiful woman,' says Gina. 'I'd say he died at the hands of a beautiful bird.'

'Nice one,' I say. 'Well, my ambition is to be shot by a jealous husband when I'm ninety-four.'

'Why do you want to wait till then?'

With that kind of spirit, it's little surprise that Gina followed in her late father's (and her grandfather, Sir Malcolm Campbell's) thrill-seeking footsteps. She began racing in 1984 and has won the British, European and World Offshore Championships. She held the women's World Water Speed Record twice (186 m.p.h. on the second occasion) and won her class at the most recent Round Britain Powerboat Race, which she told me was the most frightening experience of her life.

'Going round Land's End in a thirty-foot sea, I thought: What am I doing here? I leant over to my co-driver and shouted: "I want to go home!" As I did so, I looked behind us and realized it was safer to go forward. There was no going back.'

It's hard to associate the delicate, elegant lady relaxed on a plumped-up sofa in a comfortable, wood-panelled lounge with a sport such as offshore powerboat racing, but clearly there's something special in those Campbell genes and heritage. Maybe it's simply a sense of responsibility and honour – Gina talks of not wanting to let down the other people in the team and the organizers of the race – but I suspect it's mostly love of the adrenalin rush of speeding at 180 m.p.h. She says the buzz comes from putting your 'life on the line', and although she has already had one accident similar to her father's, Gina remains undaunted.

A passionate objector to the speed ban, Gina thinks the park authority members are spineless idiots and wonders what on earth has happened to what she calls the 'great British spirit'. Now in her fifties, she's very bright, fit, and very calm and measured as she describes the risks I am about to experience.

'What you are going to do today is classed as one of the most dangerous sports in the world. The water is extremely hard. Above sixty miles an hour, it's exactly the same as being on a road.'

'Is that so?'

'Jump out of a boat at that speed, you will do the same damage as if you jumped out of a motorcar.'

Sitting in a lounge in the clubhouse we are surrounded by photographs, trophies and mementoes from the club's past, and her father's and grandfather's record-breaking achievements. There are beautiful pieces of aluminium 1930s kit, all rivets and discreet union flags, beside fabulous photographs of mechanics and racers wearing collars and ties beneath their spotless overalls. They're exactly the kind of things that I could spend all day looking at, but sadly these artefacts are now becoming memorabilia of a bygone age of adventure as far as the Lake District is concerned.

'It's a travesty of justice,' Gina says of the power sports ban on Windermere. 'We are breeding a nation of prissies who aren't given the spirit to win. If a bank of water doesn't get you, the number seven bus will. You know, it's dangerous to live. You can die from it.'

What a lady.

'The legacy of Windermere is fantastic. Witness it on a beautiful day, see the wonderful clubhouse and its surroundings, meet the people – it's wonderful up here and if it were to disappear altogether it would be a disgrace. A gravel pit in Milton Keynes doesn't have the same ring to it.'

I discover the truth of Gina's words when I arrive at the racecourse at Barrow. In contrast to the masterpiece at Windermere, the clubhouse is a one-roomed mobile home into which about twenty participants have crammed, most of them leaning uncomfortably against walls and chipboard furniture. Outside it's a starkly industrial landscape, but within that is a nice, long stretch of water, and that is clearly what matters most.

We start with a marshal's briefing covering the race programme and safety procedures, then I go outside to meet Chris Loney, who will take me round the course in a two-man powerboat, and his wife Helen. Clad in a black, flame-retardant suit, crash helmet and flotation vest, I make my way over to the boat, *Sumo 2*, which to me looks like the classic powerboat: a long V-shaped hull with a cockpit large enough for three people to stand, about two-thirds of the way back from the bow. Chris explains the controls to me.

'That's the steering wheel. Detachable, so you don't want to pull too hard on it during a race.'

'I can see that.' Obvious really.

'Foot throttle down here.' Chris points at the floor of the boat.

The wheel has two buttons to trim the boat so that it rises out of the water for speed on the straights and settles into the water to get more grip when going round corners. Then Jim Noone, the club commodore, comes over to scrutinize *Sumo 2*, checking that all the safety systems are working and the mechanical components are ship-shape.

'You're ready to go,' he says. We haul the boat to the water and I climb in. A few more safety checks and we're away, bouncing over the water at 65 m.p.h., trailing a long plume of water spray. By powerboat racers' standards, it's quite slow. However, by my standards it's bloody fast. This close to the water, it feels twice as fast and every time we go into a corner I think the boat is going to drop or flip over, but Chris expertly skids it round the buoy, water pouring into the boat. Even more surprising than the speed is the braking. Take your foot off the throttle and the boat immediately comes off the plane and dips into the water. It's a more effective method of cutting speed than any carbon-fibre disc brake. And as for the catamaran powerboats, Chris tells me the G-forces when coming off the plane or cornering in a catamaran are more extreme than in Formula One racing cars.

It doesn't take long for my body to feel like it's done ten rounds with Tyson. The constant banging on the floor and the shuddering leave me shattered. And as for the boat, all those forces must put it under a lot of stress, I suggest to Chris.

'It's a lot of work to keep it mechanically sound,' he says. 'But it's a hobby so you put in the work.'

How many times have I heard that on this journey? The dedication of so many people to their pastimes and traditions has been a revelation. Ted, for example, told me his powerboat engine has a lifespan of only two hundred minutes, then he rebuilds it.

Meanwhile, powerboats are screaming around the dock. It's extremely exciting. There's a lot of overtaking, under-taking and action. With about a dozen boats in each race, a handicap system is run, with the slower monohulls setting off first, the faster catamarans following at intervals and the fastest boat setting off last, which gives everyone a fair chance of winning and makes for an interesting race. The lap is an L-shape and about a mile long. Winning isn't just about who is the fastest, but also takes overall 'consistency' into consideration.

As for me, obviously I'm not here to win any races but for the thrill of taking part and for the simple pleasures of the smell of the petrol and the fabulous sense of speed as we skim across the water. Because of the handicap system, I can't tell where we come; suffice to say we aren't first.

Afterwards I watch a few of the other races, then bump into

Ted as he winches his boat out of the water. 'So are you pleased with yourself today?' I ask.

'I think we've done all right. It's in one piece, which is always a good thing. It lives to fight another day.'

It's a perfect evening, the sun is glinting on the water and I can see there's a lot that's appealing about powerboat racing. It's more exciting than many types of motor racing and it's the most affordable high-speed sport. Ted's boat is the pinnacle of the sport, yet cost him only £25,000. 'If you look around the pits,' he says, 'there are far more affordable outfits and people have just as much fun.'

'I have to say, for all your regrets about Windermere, this is a tip-top place for racing.'

Ted agrees. 'This is a proper venue, as good as anywhere in the country. It's just a shame it's not right beside our clubhouse door. Instead we have a couple of caravans and it's salt water, which requires more maintenance on the boats.'

I've had a great day. Put me beside some big rusty cranes in an industrial marinescape and I'm in heaven; it goes back to a childhood spent hoiking around the Clyde shipyards. And I've also had a revelation: I've realized I haven't been a fan of powerboating simply because I haven't been exposed to it. Now initiated, I fully appreciate its appeal. Yes, the old clubhouse was an absolute peach and a privilege to visit, but in my opinion the Barrow docks are a much better venue: the sound bounces off the quay wall, making it even more exciting to spectators, but also keeping the noise contained at the venue. And because it's long and flat with no obstacles, you can see every bit of the race. Even Gina Campbell admitted it was a better venue than Windermere, despite not having the history. It also seems much more egalitarian to me. There's a burger van at Barrow, which never would have happened at Windermere because it feels so much like a rich man's club. Here, no one has to be a member of an exclusive club to take part; they just need to turn up and know how to tune a marine engine. Even ten-year-olds can take part in the junior races. And if the old club members still want to gaze out at Windermere from their beautiful clubhouse, they can still do so without disturbing everyone else. I think it's a very reasonable compromise.

Driving out of the Lake District to my next destination, I climb over the Kirkstone Pass, the highest road through the Lakes' mountains. A few miles further north, having skirted Ullswater, I pass Dacre Castle, a peel tower. Built in the fifteenth century and looking like miniature castles, there are a lot of peel towers dotted along the border with Scotland in what used to be Cumberland, Westmorland and Northumberland. They were built to stop the Scots nipping over the border on fast horses, beating up people and nicking everything that was bright and shiny. Apart from their primary purpose as a warning system, these towers were the homes of the lairds and landlords of the area, who dwelt in them with their families and retainers while their followers lived in simple huts outside the walls. The towers also provided a refuge. When cross-border raiding parties arrived, the whole population of a village could take to the tower and wait for the Jock marauders to depart. If you're English, sorry about what we Jocks did, but that's the way things were in these parts.

Throughout its history, this whole neighbourhood has been invaded by just about everybody, the consequences of which are seen in a lot of the local traditions and practices, including the activity I'll be witnessing next – Cumberland and

Westmorland wrestling. Its history goes back centuries, but that's not the only reason it's interesting: it involves legalized violence, so naturally I'm on the case.

My first stop is a cowshed at the edge of the Lake District, where Trevor Hodgson is feeding his herd of Friesians, helped by his daughter Tracy. With his cows chomping silage and pissing noisily behind us, Trevor explains that he and his daughter are preparing for a crucial round in the Westmorland Wrestling Championship later in the day at an agricultural show being held at a nearby stately home, Dalemain House.

'This is obviously good training for it, then?' I point at the piles of silage and straw that Popeye-armed Trevor and Tracy have been hefting around the shed. 'It is a farming sport, isn't it?'

'You'd be right,' says Trevor. 'They're all farming connections somewhere along the line.'

As for the training regime of silage shovelling and straw lifting, Trevor leaves me to draw my own conclusions.

Cumberland and Westmorland wrestling is an age-old Cumbrian tradition. Followed by generations of northern agricultural families, it attracts crowds of up to twenty thousand at major agricultural shows. Although the Cumberland and Westmorland Wrestling Association was formed relatively recently – about a hundred years ago to purge wrestling of the 'virus of dishonesty and gambling' – the sport is thought to have been brought to Britain by the Vikings, though it may be a variant of Cornish or Gouren styles of wrestling, which go back as far as the fourth century.

In the eighteenth and nineteenth centuries, men competed for substantial cash prizes and local status. In those days match fixing was a problem – it was known as barneying – hence the establishment of the Association to formalize rules and clean up the sport.

To start a match, the wrestlers 'tekk hod' of each other, gripping their fingers together behind the back of their opponent and putting their chin on their opponent's right shoulder. The referee sets the contest in motion with the simple command to 'wrestle'. Except for kicking, anything is allowed; the first wrestler to break their hold or touch any part of their body on the ground – except the soles of their feet – loses the round. The contest is the best of three rounds. If both competitors hit the ground at the same time, it's a 'dog fall', which makes the round null and void, so it has to be repeated.

Until recently girls and women competed with the boys and men, most likely because of an oversight when the rules were redrawn in 1906 and no one could imagine that women would do anything so unladylike. Tracy, a strong-looking lass and an absolute charmer, is one of the sport's young leading lights.

'How many bouts will you have today?'

'Dunno.' Tracy is quite shy.

'How many girls take part?'

'When it's a big competition, there's quite a few.'

'Is there someone called Donna?' Aged seventeen, Donna Thompson doesn't come from a family of wrestlers. She was intrigued at a local show two years ago and had a shot. Now hooked, her ultimate ambition is to beat Tracy once and for all.

'Yeah.'

'And is she your main rival?'

'Yeah.' A nervous grin.

'Are you hoping to get to battle with her or not?'

'Half and half.'

Wrestling is very much a family thing in Cumberland.

Trevor's mum took him to watch wrestling when he was five years old and he took up the sport when he was eleven, then Tracy took it up after watching her father wrestling.

'I'm having visions of you two keeping each other fighting fit by wrestling around the kitchen, trying not to break cups.'

'We do manage to tekk hod in the kitchen,' says Trevor. 'And we can land anywhere.'

'Really? So there's a lot of broken furniture in your house?'

'We have to try to avoid that, else we'd be kicked out for good.'

'So who's your big rival?'

'There's a lot of big rivals. The Harrington family. The Brocklebank family.'

'So it is a big family thing. Sons and fathers. And now the daughters.'

'The girls used to wrestle with the lads,' says Tracy. 'But now they've stopped it.'

'Really? EU regulations, was it?'

'A bit like that,' snorts Trevor.

'Health and safety? No, I know what it was. You were worried about the humiliation of being beaten by a girl. I don't think the boys would like that much, would they?'

'Toughens them up,' says Trevor.

'Exactly,' I say. 'Good practice for marriage.'

'Learns them to get on.'

'A family that wrestles together stays together,' I suggest. 'So, Trevor, has Tracy ever beaten you?'

'At times.'

'Has she got the speed, then?'

'You can't beat youth. Youth and speed go a long way.'

Nimbleness, suppleness, balance and strength make a good

wrestler, Trevor says. Then he gives me a demonstration in the shed.

'Well you shake and then you tekk hod.' He reaches behind me. 'Then it's right arm under.' He puts his right arm under my left and makes me put my right arm over his left arm. I'm starting to get nervous.

'Then you get hold of him like that.' Trevor starts a move.

'Right . . . I'd rather not wrestle with you, sonny.' Stepping back, I look at Trevor's hands. I'm thought of as being a man with big hands, but they're like toys compared to his.

Later, sitting in the farmhouse kitchen, the Aga burbling behind us, Tracy talks me through her many wins and her injuries. Pain, it seems, is no barrier for this young lady.

'Do people get injured?'

'Oh yes.'

'Like what?'

'Ankles mainly.'

'Are you allowed to kick?'

Tracy looks away as she smiles. 'In a way. Not directly, but you can sweep their feet away.'

'Have you ever been hurt?'

'In Grasmere last year, my knee went pop.' Having just had knee surgery, I wince as I listen. 'I don't know what happened, but stupidly I carried on because I knew that Donna was ahead of me on points. I needed to win both Grasmere titles to catch up with her. It was the under-eighteen final. I slipped and my knee gave way. I couldn't put any weight on it. Everyone wanted me to pull out of the all-weights final, but being me, I refused and then I won it.

'The day after, I thought I was going to be okay. I'd milked that morning and I felt all right. But I ended up being taken off in an ambulance.' Tracy giggles as she tells the story, as if she'd done something very naughty. 'They couldn't work out what I'd done. I limped a bit and kept going on it. Dad told me to keep bending it and in the end I was all right.'

'You're a very competitive person, aren't you?'

'Er . . . yes.'

Behind us a trophy cabinet is groaning under the weight of Tracy's cups, shields and awards. She could win another trophy today. I tag along to the agricultural show in the hope that while I'm there I'll get to the bottom of who introduced the locals to such savagery. Wrestling historian Roger Robson, an ex-wrestler and farmer from Carlisle who is president of the Cumberland and Westmorland Wrestling Association and the fount of all knowledge on the sport, will be there. Wrestling runs through Roger's family. His grandfather, born in 1890, wrestled; Roger has won Grasmere three times; his son was champion in 1990; and these days his grandson competes.

'Are you certain about the origins of Cumberland wrestling?' I ask him. 'No one seems to know if it's Celtic or Pictish, or whatever.'

'People always say it is a Viking sport and there are all sorts of things that support that in a way. A lot of Cumbrian place names are Viking in origin; there are artefacts that are derived from the Vikings and the genotype of people in West Cumbria is closer to the Faroese than people living in Kendal, twenty miles away.'

So it seems there is a strong connection between the Vikings and this part of Cumbria. Added to that is a tradition of wrestling in Iceland, so it's entirely possible that the Vikings brought wrestling to the area more than a thousand years ago.

'What I come down to in the end is that wrestling is such a

natural activity. Boys do it all the time,' says Roger. 'The place with the nearest style of wrestling to ours is in Sardinia. In the mountains of Sardinia they have back-hold wrestling with exactly the same rules.'

It seems too much of a coincidence. Surely there must be a direct connection between Sardinian and Cumberland wrestling?

While we're talking, the strangest aspect of this fascinating sport suddenly confronts me when a bunch of wrestlers walk past us towards the ring. Now, there's no doubting that wrestling is a tough old sport, one in which man is pitted against man, but if a Martian landed in this field they'd have good reason to wonder at all the jessies in girly costumes who just minced past me, each of them dressed in socks, longjohns, vest and a centrepiece made of velvet. I mean, we're talking floral pants and vests with roses on them.

Incongruous as the outfits might seem to us today, Roger has established from research in nineteenth-century journals such as the *Illustrated London News* that these weird and wonderful Cumberland wrestling strips were perfectly normal in Victorian times.

'It's standard Victorian athletic dress. There are photographs of Grasmere Sports from 1872 onwards in which you can see the big men in their wrestling gear, but behind them you also see pole-vaulters and fell-runners wearing exactly the same thing.'

What's changed since Victorian days, however, is the attention paid to the decoration on the wrestling strip. Roger takes me to meet Audrey Malloy, veteran chief expert in pant sewing and now a judge of wrestlers' costumes.

When Audrey's three sons used to wrestle they were

renowned for their immaculately embroidered flowery pants and won many best-dressed competitions. In her old age Audrey continues to be an active supporter of Cumberland and Westmorland wrestling, frequently attending events in Cumbria even though she now lives in Preston. Although she thinks girls' wrestling is 'inappropriate', Audrey believes that flowery pants are extremely masculine 'as long as you don't put pansies on them'.

When I meet her, she is standing at the edge of the wrestling ring, taking very close notice of the wrestlers' smalls.

'They form up in front of us in a straight line,' says Audrey. 'And we're the ones who move around, having a look at the backs of the costumes. They're decorated back and front, you see.'

'Standing around watching men's pants is what you do really?'

'You could say so. We don't feel them for the quality of material. We're looking for the overall view.'

As we watch, seven lads, including Trevor, line up in the middle of the ring, looking faintly ridiculous to me in their longjohns and flowery pants. 'Chests out, lads,' says the announcer over the PA system as Audrey and her fellow judge, handbags over their shoulders, head out into the ring. You don't often see two middle-aged women standing in a field looking at young lads' underpants. I don't know why not – it seems such fun.

I think this is what the rag trade would call 'individually accessorized dress'. One of the youngest lads appears to have the album cover of *Tubular Bells* sewn on his arse, for which I think he deserves some kind of prize. Another has a dragon embroidered on his chest, while Trevor has a red tractor, in common with others whose pants and vests are embroidered with farming symbols indicating the family to which they belong. Wearing a shirt or pants embroidered with a cockerel or kingfisher would make more sense than having your competitor number safety-pinned to your back, particularly in the days when few people could read.

It's all beautifully handmade, without a whiff of the corporate sponsorship that often homogenizes this kind of event. The strange thing is that looking at these lads dressed in white longjohns and velvet pants embroidered with flowers, I don't for a minute think it's silly. Somehow it looks quite butch. Maybe that's because I know instinctively that it wouldn't be a good idea to laugh at these lads because something might get broken, like your arm.

'Have we got a result?' says the announcer as the competitors stand with hands on hips, not showing the least embarrassment at the slightly ridiculous nature of their display.

After much head-nodding and whispering, Audrey and her fellow judge award first, second and two equal third prizes. Richard Dixon, a tall lad wearing a particularly ornate pair of black velvet pants, wins first place. Trevor comes third.

The costume display over, the first round of the under-12s wrestling begins, with some of the boys in traditional dress and others in simple tracksuit trousers and jumpers. Next the ladies get under way and I get a chance to see Tracy in action. Most of her bouts last less than ten seconds and are very exciting. There are a few tussles and twists before she unbalances her opponent, sending her to the floor. After a series of scrambling wrestles, Tracy reaches the final.

'Who are you fighting in the final?'

'Donna.'

'Surprise, surprise. Go for it, girl. Show no mercy.'

The girls don't wear the fancy costumes of the male wrestlers. For once, they don't bother getting dressed up. They're only here for the battle.

Tracy wins the first fall, tripping her arch rival easily and quickly. They shake hands and prepare for the second fall. This time they're on their feet for longer. Donna appears to get the upper hand, toppling Tracy off her feet, but Tracy shifts her weight so that Donna falls beneath her, touching the ground first. It's a straight win for Tracy, who returns to the edge of the ring wearing a big smile.

'That was very close, Tracy,' says Trevor. 'You did well to get two clean falls. You controlled it. Brilliant.'

'You're very well matched,' I say.

'Both determined to win,' says Trevor. 'That's when you get a good contest.'

He's right about his daughter's determination, but what makes it charming is that she combines great competitiveness with a very kind and pleasant nature.

'What's it like to beat Donna again?'

Tracy beams. 'All right, actually.'

'Did you think you were going to win?'

'No. I wrestled her in France as part of the English team – it was really close and she's fairly come along since then.'

'Is she younger than you?'

'No, older. Doing her A-levels now.'

'You've got youth on your side.'

A giggle.

'Getting on a bit is Donna. Seventeen.'

More giggles.

The men's competition follows in weight divisions. In

contrast to the women's and boys' competitions, some of the bouts take a long time. It's a serious business. In the past, as much training was done in the beer tent as on the field, but these days the real wrestlers take their sport very seriously, performing warm-ups and watching their diets carefully. As for the wrestling, it appears to be much more tactical and more a matter of carefully controlled aggression than brute force. It's more athletic than I'd anticipated and very subtle.

Eventually Trevor reaches the final, but loses in straight falls.

'Well done, Trevor,' I say as he returns to the edge of the ring. 'It's been a good day for the family.'

It's been a delightful day. Trevor and Tracy are so understated about their achievements, with none of that grandstanding and talk of fulfilling dreams that's so often trotted out for the television cameras. And having watched it all day, I'd love to have had a wrestle. But what's really interesting about people doing something of which nobody quite knows the origins, or what it's really about, is that if you do it for long enough the habit becomes who you are – which is quite an intriguing idea, I think.

Chapter Fourteen

I still haven't got over the joy of cruising around in a darling like the XK150, particularly on the beautiful roads I take from the rural north-west over the Pennines to the industrial north-east. These are the kind of winding lanes and remote countryside for which she was built. The only problem is getting something to eat. On motorways you're spoilt for choice, but sadly it all tastes the same. In many cases the food's been warming up since seven in the morning, when I'm sure it tastes great. But at four in the afternoon? Not such a good idea.

Fortunately I'm not on a motorway. Oh no, you wouldn't get me anywhere near one for all the tea in China – although right now I'd settle for just a couple of teaspoons of that tea in a teapot with a nice slice of toast or pie on a plate beside it. When you're travelling off-motorway, satisfying thirst and hunger can be – pardon the unintentional pun – a matter of feast or famine. Most villages will have a bakery, pub, café or shop. And the larger roads will have truckers' caffs or a bacon butty wagon in a layby. But veer more than slightly off the beaten track – such as at the top of the Pennine pass, where I find myself today – and refuelling stops become as scarce for body as they are for car.

Or so you'd think. Right now I'm on the roof of England, at the top of the Hartside Pass, 1,904 feet above sea level (the snow poles either side of the road are here for good reason). On a good day you can see both coasts, the Lake District mountains Helvellyn, Great Gable and Skiddaw, as well as a magnificent view across the Solway Firth to Criffel in southern Scotland. I say on a good day because today it's overcast and blowing a stormer, so I'll have to take the locals' word for the extent of the vista. To be honest, I haven't stopped here for the spectacular view; I'm here for a welcome cup of something warm and some scran at the highest café in England, called Hartside Top.

Somehow a cup of tea always tastes better when you feel you've earned it. And having coaxed the Jag along 15 twisting miles of road from Penrith, the last 5 miles of which have dozens of bends and twisties – including two 180-degree hairpin bends in quick succession – I think it's fair to say I deserve it. Sitting in the café I'm surrounded by dozens of bikers, for whom the Hartside Pass is a motorcycling Mecca, all of whom recognize the virtues of the back road over the motorway.

Physically refuelled, it's back in the car for the descent across Alston Moor – officially an Area of Outstanding Natural Beauty, although Area of Raw Desolation would be more accurate – to Alston, England's highest market town, and on to Ryhope in Sunderland, where I'm going to visit arguably the strangest listed building in Britain.

On this journey I've seen many listed buildings: old churches, stately homes and historic village high streets. But this is something different and unique because – wait for it – it's a pigeon cree.

235

Like me, you're probably asking yourself why on earth anyone would seek to list something that is little more than a glorified shed. The answer is to be found in a fascinating parable of a working-class community fighting to preserve its culture in the face of corporate indifference and capitalist greed.

The venue is an unprepossessing scrap of land on a local allotment in a former colliery village. Next to nine gardeners, seven retired miners breed and race pigeons in a collection of crees that have been the nerve centre of their collective hobby for almost sixty years. Painted in the colours of the union flag and looking a little raggedy round the edges is a cree belonging to Maurice Surtees, a seventy-five-year-old former pitman. Maurice, a classic northern character in a flat cap, has been racing pigeons since 1955, when he and his brother completed their National Service. They built their cree from materials purloined from the local pit and other sources, then proudly painted it red, white and blue to celebrate their return to Britain. After the death of his brother, Maurice teamed up with fellow allotment pigeon fancier Lewis Llewellyn, a retired fitter who is now his racing partner and whom he refers to as 'the boy' because he's only sixty-five. With Lewis – who speaks the language of a sports manager, believing that 'fitness and motivation and confidence' are the key to training his 'athletes of the sky' (he calls them his 'little Kelly Holmes') – Maurice is the proud owner of forty pigeons and believes a cree should be a man's second home, so much so that he will do anything to protect it – including getting it legally preserved.

'Is it true that this is a listed building?'

'It's the only listed cree in the world,' says Maurice in a thick Mackem accent. He and Lewis are a formidable double act –

even their names sound like a 1930s music hall act: *Maurice and Lewis, a laff and a dance and a bit of chat chat* – and they're bursting with spirit and bonhomie.

'That's fantastic!' I say.

'Aye, it is.'

'So it should be,' I say. 'It's really bonny.'

'Wants painting again, like. We paint it every couple of year.'

'How long did it take you to build it?'

'Took us about a month.'

'That's not bad.'

'But I donna tell you where I got the wood from, mind.'

'Why? Does it say British Rail on it?'

'There's a bit of that in there.' Maurice roars with laughter.

'British Coal, more like,' says Lewis.

Whatever the provenance of its building materials, the cree has a beautiful view out to sea and, less than a minute after meeting Maurice and Lewis, I can tell that this little spot means everything to them. Lewis says pigeon-keeping is a 365-days a year job and that he got so happy during race season last year that his wife thought he was 'seeing another woman' – part of the reason Lewis and Maurice teamed up was so that the workload could be split, as Lewis's wife was feeling neglected.

Unfortunately this Sunderland Shangri-La has recently come under threat again from developers, who want the land to build a block of flats, a saga that goes back to 1997, when it was bought by a Newcastle businessman.

'Our families have been on these gardens for over a hundred year,' says Maurice. 'Same families have always paid rent to the co-op. They always said they were looking after the members from the cradle to the grave, but they sold it to developers. We didn't even know the land had come up for sale until we read about the auction in the local paper and then they wouldn't even sell it to us.'

The pigeon boys and allotmenteers travelled to Glasgow to bid for the land that had been their second home for generations, but when they arrived at the auction, they found it had already been sold.

'We've been paying rent a hundred years, our families,' says Maurice. 'The co-op is meant to be for the working man, but they sold it under our noses. We were really disappointed.'

Undaunted, Maurice and his fellow pigeon fanciers fought a long battle to save their crees, enlisting the help of their local MP, Fraser Kemp, and Tony Banks, Minister of Sport at the time, to back their case. Their campaign struck victory when English Heritage granted a Grade II listing to the cree on the grounds that it was a structure of national historical importance. The landowners backed down from instant eviction and, under considerable public pressure, granted a ten-year extension to the pensioners' leases.

When I visit, the end of that ten-year extension is only months away. Again, the landowner is determined to move the old boys off the land. Maurice and his fellow pigeon fanciers have turned down compensation payments of £2,000 each. Moving the crees, if it were physically possible, would cost around £10,000 each and there's another factor: with sixty-five-year-old Lewis the youngest of the bunch, for many of the cree-holders a move is out of the question.

'They've given us notice, but it don't make any difference. We're not coming off,' says Maurice. 'There'll be a hell of a fight on and we've got the backing of a lot of local people – a *lot* of local people.'

Maurice and Lewis have led long and, at times, hard lives –

wartime childhood, National Service and mining – and I can see they're real fighters. They're not going to give up just because someone tells them.

'These huts have been here for a hundred and fifty years,' says Lewis. 'It's a part of Ryhope. Just for the simple reason of someone making some money out of it they want us away, where money doesn't come into it for us. It's just the enjoyment of coming up here every day.'

'We canna give in, man,' says Maurice. 'This is a way of life for us.'

'So why do you really have these huts?' It's time to get a bit mischievous with the lads. After all, I've got a hut of my own, albeit a rather large one, big enough for my beloved jalopies. 'Is it for the same reason that every man needs a hut: to get away on his own and maybe even to get away from the wife?'

'No . . .' says Maurice.

But Lewis immediately interrupts: 'That sounds like a good idea . . .'

'. . . I'll tell you the truth, Robbie . . .' Maurice again. 'If you have a wife that doesn't like pigeons, you're wasting your time keeping them.'

'Do you mean the pigeon or the wife?'

Maurice guffaws as Lewis interjects: 'The wife!' Then Lewis thinks better of it: 'Donna put that on the telly or I'll never get home again.'

But Maurice has a serious point. 'If you fall out with the wife and come to the cree bad-tempered, the pigeons'll tell ya. The pigeons know.'

'Do they?' I can't quite believe this. 'They can tell if you're in a bad mood?'

'Oh yes,' says Maurice.

'How can you tell?'

'They're frightened. They can sense it.'

Maybe it's like with dogs: they can tell from the tone in your voice.

'When the question comes up, the wife or the pigeons,' says Maurice, 'then the wife comes first. Definitely.'

'Good man,' I say. 'It's the right answer.'

To help me understand their passion for their crees and pigeons, Maurice offers to let me choose a bird for myself for tomorrow's big race.

'They go away tonight,' says Maurice. 'It's only a short race, mind. Only a hundred and fifty mile.'

'One hundred and fifty miles?' It seems a long way to me.

'That's not far.'

'So what's long for a pigeon race?'

'Five hundred or six hundred mile.'

I find it quite amazing. 'So how the hell do the pigeons get home?'

'Ah . . . we dinna wonna know. That would spoil the sport. There's fellas with more degrees than a thermometer and they don't know how it works.'

I suppose Maurice and Lewis are right. After all, pigeons have brains the size of peas so it can't be a process of rational thought that leads them back to the cree.

Lewis beckons me to the end of the cree and points at a chimney in the distance. 'That's Rye waterworks chimney. That's our landmark. You can see them coming past it and turning this way.'

Maurice says that when the A19 led directly from London past Ryhope, the pigeons used to follow it north, but since the M1 was built to the west, they follow the motorway route.

They'd do the journey in four or five hours from London, which is about as long as it would take by car.

I wonder if the pigeons fly home so quickly because they're hungry. 'Do you feed them before they fly?'

'We feed them before they leave in the lorries. But after that nothing unless they're delayed by bad weather.'

'So why don't they stop on the way for a snack?'

The lads laugh.

'Are they racing home to get fed?'

Lewis grins. 'Pigeon racing is mainly done for the same reason as the best part of us will go all day for: sex.'

Maurice agrees. 'They've got to love their home. And if they've got a bonny lass waiting, they'll be home all the quicker.'

'You've got to have an incentive,' says Lewis. 'And the incentive for everything in life is sex.'

'So do you keep the females behind, waving at the window – "Bye, boys" – to bring them home?'

'Oh yes,' says Lewis. 'When they come home you want the females waiting there so they know why they've come back and they do it even faster next time.'

'Fantastic. Does that mean you race only males?'

'No. Females too. There's some queer lasses about,' says Maurice.

'Then you get the females racing each other to get back to the males,' says Lewis.

It seems like clever stuff to me. 'Just the same as with us.'

'Aye.'

Only the young birds ever get lost on the way home. Birds older than two years old always make it back to the cree unless they collide with wiring or are picked off by peregrines or falcons, but I wonder how the other pigeons regard the homing pigeons. Maybe like Ferraris speeding past them.

The time has come for me to pick a bird. 'Can I see ya doos, as we say in Scotland?'

'Aye,' says Maurice. 'Ya can see the boards.'

'The *boards*? Right.'

The lads lead me into a section of their cree in which the pigeons that will race tomorrow are being kept. A couple of dozen birds are standing on the floor, pecking at feed, or sitting in wee open-fronted boxes mounted on the walls. 'They're bonny.'

'Take a pick and if it wins we keep the money,' says Maurice. 'Ha!'

Lewis leans past me to point at a bird on the floor. 'That one there looks like it's going to be good. See that one coming towards us?'

'Yes.' I try to pick it up. 'I don't want to hurt him.'

Lewis gently scoops up the pigeon and shows me how to hold it. 'Put your fingers between its legs and hold them still.'

'It's a beautiful creature, not at all like the pigeons we city boys are used to.'

'We'll call him Robbie's Boy,' says Lewis.

An old pal of mine used to keep pigeons and would look them directly in the eye. I ask Lewis if it might help.

'Oh yes. Some have eye sign, some don't.'

'You're keeping it mysterious . . .'

'It's something you can only see if you know what you're looking for.'

'Is it to do with seeing if they're in good health?'

Lewis smiles. 'It's to see if they're good breeders, good racers, good all round.'

No better informed, I step outside with Robbie's Boy in hand to where Maurice is waiting. 'Do you fancy that one?' he says.

'Surely do. Can I kiss it good luck?'

'Why aye.'

I kiss the bird, then Maurice packs it into a basket. 'That'll do. That's yours and we'll hope for the best for tomorrow. Keep your fingers crossed.'

After picking my bird, it's off to the smoke-filled clubhouse to register him and pay my 50p entry fee. He's tagged with all the rest, so we can tell he's my birdie, then he'll be loaded on to a truck tonight with the other birds, including Maurice's and Lewis's twelve hens and five cocks, for the 150-mile journey south to the start line.

'It's really exciting, isn't it?' I point at all the other pigeon fanciers putting their birds in the club baskets. 'You think all these birds – and tomorrow they've got to fly all that way.'

'You'll get butterflies in your belly tomorrow, mind,' says Maurice.

'I bet you do.'

'Just before they're due.'

With registration completed and the birds tagged, it's time to join the other club members to synchronize and seal all our clocks. Invented by miners, these clocks are very sophisticated, costing up to £300 each. When each bird arrives back, the tag on its leg will be put through a slot in the top of the sealed clock, recording the time the bird landed, so no one can cheat, but now it's time to make sure all our clocks are in sync.

One of the committee members counts down from ten as about a dozen pigeon fanciers stand around two tables, their clocks in front of them. It's like a scene from a commando-raid war movie. When he reaches zero, everyone pushes a button on their clocks in unison and – kerching! – the clocks are ready and running.

Then it's a weather forecast – sunshine, showers and a light wind from the south-west, which means they'll be fast, maybe averaging 40 m.p.h. – and outside to watch 425 pigeons being loaded on to a truck that looks like something out of *Wallace and Gromit*. This week the race is only for the 'Fed' – the federation – and there's only one truck, but next week the whole combine is racing and there'll be fourteen trucks driving in convoy to the starting line. That must be something worth seeing – maybe ten thousand pigeons being simultaneously freed.

Late the next morning I arrive at Maurice's and Lewis's cree, my clock dangling on my shoulder in a very smart black leather case and a packet of biscuits in my hand to go with the cups of tea I'm confident the lads will be making. It's a beautiful day with a clear blue sky and Maurice is staring into the distance, whistling to call his pigeons home.

'You all right?' he shouts as I approach.

'I'm very well, and you'll laugh: I dreamt about pigeons all last night. As I was going off to sleep I had this thought: if they come out of the baskets this morning and fly north, surely that means yesterday they know they went south.'

'No.' Maurice has his arms firmly crossed against his chest. 'I get what you mean, but it makes no difference. They can't see where they're going and you could take them anywhere, they'd still come home.'

Maurice and Lewis tell me it takes seconds for the birds to get their bearings after being set free. It's all very intriguing, but the lads are reluctant to delve too deep into the mechanism by which homing pigeons find their way back, so I research it myself later. It turns out that no one knows for sure how they do it, but the general scientific consensus is that the homing ability is a combination of an internal compass, sensitivity to the Earth's magnetic field, smell and mapping. The internal compass appears to be based on the sun and sets the birds in the correct general direction. Several scientific studies have identified the bird's trigeminal nerve (which runs to the jaw and is responsible for sensation in its face) as sensitive to magnetic fields and found that disrupting the magnetic field around the home loft disrupts the bird's homing ability. Pigeons are also thought to orientate themselves using atmospheric odours and, finally, when they approach home, they probably use visual landmarks. The lads say they take longer to land when it's darker.

'Somebody told me,' I say, 'that you use something called a tumbler to get the birds down.'

'Why aye.' Maurice leads me over to a basket containing some white pigeons. 'We have them walking about. When the pigeon comes home, he sees them and he goes in better.'

Tumblers are a special breed, of which there are more than a hundred varieties, so called because they tumble through the sky when they're flying. The wings on these, however, have been clipped to keep them on the ground. 'When the pigeons are coming down, I throw them in.' Maurice shows me how he tosses the tumbler towards the open door of the cree. 'And the tumbler makes the pigeon go in.'

'I thought someone was winding me up when they told me about tumblers.'

'Oh no – we just call them droppers.'

Lewis then tells me that to attract the pigeons they need some peace and quiet around the cree, with as few people as possible.

'Is this a nice way of telling me to bugger off?' I say.

'Will you just bloody listen for a minute?' says Lewis. 'When they come back they're on edge. They're not used to lots of people and we're faster than you at clocking. We're talking about seconds making a difference today over the first six back. With a strong south wind, they could be doing seventy miles an hour.'

Maurice adds: 'So you've got to be nippy on your pins when they come.'

Half an hour later Maurice has a chance to show how nippy he is on his seventy-five-year-old pins. For several minutes now, pigeons have been passing closely overhead, darting in all directions. Suddenly Lewis is leaping around and I'm being beckoned to sit down out of the way.

'Come on, lads. Come on in!' Lewis is shouting at the sky and scattering pigeon feed in front of the cree. 'Come on here. Come on, lads. Where the friggin' hell's he went? Come on, boy. Come on here.'

All around I can hear other pigeon fanciers coaxing their birds out of the sky. It's a great atmosphere, quite fevered as they bid to be the first to clock their bird back.

'It's not ours,' says Maurice, shaking his head and holding a tumbler so that its wings flap freely.

Then a bird lands. Maurice tosses a tumbler towards the door of the cree. 'It's one of Jones's birds,' he says before shouting across the fence to Jones, his neighbour.

It's very exciting and there's something quite special about taking part in an activity that goes back to the Romans, although I suspect we're having more fun doing it than the Romans did. I'd always struggled to understand the appeal of pigeon racing, but now that the birds are coming back and the lads are leaping about, calling them in, I can totally understand the attraction. It's a very simple interaction between man and nature and utterly wonderful. I used to rent a room in a house belonging to a Professor Mulligan, who kept pigeons. He would say that when you let the pigeons out, a bit of you went with them. Of course in communities where most of the men spent eight to ten hours a day on their bellies hacking out coal, or on their feet forging steel and building ships, the thought of a few hours' vicarious liberty gained through your pigeons is even more appealing.

We wait another five minutes, then the first of Maurice's and Lewis's pigeons arrives. 'It's too late to clock,' says Maurice. We're not in the medals, so they let me clock it. My bird arrives another ten minutes later. Although he's taken only two and a half hours to fly home, Robbie's Boy is clearly not a winner, although I notice he reckons he fancies a little reward when I see him sidling up to one of the hens. The dirty bugger.

It's good to know that Robbie's Boy is safely landed and clearly enjoying himself, but outside we're still nervously waiting for the stragglers. I keep thinking of Second World War movies when they're waiting for the Spitfires to come back: 'No sign of Ginger . . .'

Much to my surprise, I'm completely taken with pigeon fancying. Maurice and Lewis have turned me on to its charms and I tell them if I didn't travel so much for my work I'd be tempted to build myself a wee cree at home. 'Go on,' says Maurice. 'We could bring yer pigeons down here and let them off for you. It'll be grand.'

It's been a great day in the wonderful company of two old boys who have been pals for decades, with a shared activity that bonds them and gets them out of the house every day. The thing about keeping pigeons is that in the media it's always been portrayed as a rather coarse, flat-cap kind of northern thing, but that could not be further from the truth. The whole idea of taking wee birds 150 miles away and watching them come home is a wildly romantic one and – like fireworks and wing-walking – completely unnecessary; but therein lies its magic. And you think of those guys hacking away at coalfaces and battering in rivets – they bloody needed something to lift their spirits. If your bird doesn't come home first, well, there's always next week and a pint down the pub in the meantime. Long may it continue.

As for their cree, at the time of writing its fate has still not been sealed, but the boys' bid to save it has reached the House of Commons, where their local MP tabled a motion calling for the crees to be protected indefinitely as an important historic site. Andy Burnham, secretary of state for Culture, Media and Sport, visited the cree two months after Maurice and his mates were served with their eviction order. Although he wouldn't completely rule out removing the cree's listed status, he acknowledged that it was a 'crucial part of heritage in the North East' and said it should be protected for future generations.

It seems the lads' cree saga is not over yet. The fight goes on!

When many people think of the north-east of England, it's precisely places such as Ryhope that come to mind: old mining and shipbuilding communities, an industrial heartland. However, the north-east also contains some of Britain's best scenery. Back on the road as the day draws to a close, I'm heading into Northumbria, a part of Britain that has been fought over for centuries. In the distant past, Northumberland marked the northernmost frontier of the mighty Roman Empire. To prevent military raids by the Pictish tribes (as ancient Jocks were known), Emperor Hadrian had a wall built to protect the Roman province of Britannia to the south and to mark the frontier of the Empire. In medieval times, England and Scotland were almost continuously at war and consequently Northumberland has more battlefields and castles than anywhere else in Britain, including at Alnwick (used as a set in two Harry Potter films), Bamburgh, Dunstanburgh, Warkworth and Chillingham, my next destination.

Originally a monastery, Chillingham Castle played a significant strategic role. Located smack on the border, it was used as a staging post for English armies entering Scotland, but was also repeatedly attacked and besieged by Scottish armies and raiding parties heading south. In 1617, James I, the first king of both England and Scotland, stayed at the castle on a journey between his two kingdoms. As relations became less violent following the Union of the Crowns, the need for a military stronghold in the area declined. The castle was gradually transformed: the moat was filled in and battlements were converted into residential wings. A banquet hall and a library were built. Nowadays it's run as a country house hotel and boasts of being the most haunted place in Britain.

On the face of it, Chillingham's claim to its haunted status has sound foundations. After all, it's got the most gory history. The number of people who were maimed, tortured, tormented, thrown in the lake and hanged here is just horrific. William Wallace, a knight and Scottish patriot who led a resistance against the English occupation of Scotland during the Wars of Scottish Independence and was sentenced to death for treason in 1305, stayed here on his way to be hanged, drawn and quartered at Smithfield in London. If I'd been strangled by hanging, released while still alive, emasculated, eviscerated, my bowels burnt before me, beheaded, then cut into four parts and my preserved head placed on a pike atop London Bridge, I'd want to get my own back by haunting anyone and anywhere I could. However, I've never believed in ghosts and unless I can be convinced otherwise at Chillingham, I'll continue to be a dyed-in-the-wool sceptic.

To crown my visit, when I pull up the long drive and come to a stop at the foot of the castle's front steps, Sir Humphry Wakefield, second Baronet, who bought the then-dilapidated castle in the 1980s, tells me I'll have to catch my own supper on the castle's lake. I can't wait.

'You love fishing, don't you?' Sir Humphry, a distinctly less bloodthirsty chap than his predecessors, is kitted out for the sport in flat cap, wax jacket and good, stout shoes.

'I like it, I do. But the fish don't like me much.'

A short while later we're in a Land-Rover driving through the castle grounds with two of Sir Humphry's staff. One of them, the gamekeeper, Jim, is dressed like Sir Humphry in a flat cap, but his jacket is a mass of rips and tears. Watching the two of them is not unlike watching the *Fast Show*'s Ted and Ralph, albeit without the undercurrent of unrequited love. There's great respect for each other, and not a little hidden affection. As he hands me a whippy fly rod, the gamekeeper says the beautiful lake that fringes the park is well stocked with brown trout.

'There's lots of bodies on the bottom, they tell me.' Standing on a small wooden bridge, I cast my first line.

'Ah yes, but the flesh has gone from them, I think,' says Sir Humphry.

It's an idyllic spot, crawling with flies and teeming with fish, although none of them seems interested in me. While we're fishing, Sir Humphry explains the history of the castle. Dating back more than eight hundred years, Chillingham was built for one purpose and one purpose alone: killing. In the heart of Northumberland the castle was the first line of defence back in the days of William Wallace, when the castle was ruled over by Edward I, popularly known as Longshanks. 'In 1246, my wife's ancestors, whose main concern was fending off the Scots at another castle, decided to take Chillingham as a weekend retreat.' With the castle came a herd of wild white cattle, which had been hefted in the area since Roman times and which were considered to be 'unstealable meat', safe from Scottish marauders. Attracted by the cattle, Sir Humphry's wife's fore-bears attacked the castle and seized it for themselves.

'The whole border area was not unlike Afghanistan. The tribes were fighting each other all the time. In 1513, some forty thousand Scottish soldiers arrived with canon and masonry smashers to destroy the castle . . .' Sir Humphry suddenly stops talking. He's had a bite.

'That looks like a nice wee fish.' I watch as he reels in his line.

'This is a *very* nice wee fish. It's edible.'

'Supper?' says Jim. 'It's a tradition in Northumberland: fish doon the trousers.' He shows me how to slip the trout down the front of my trousers, but I decline. Meanwhile, Sir Humphry continues to relate Chillingham's gruesome history, which began in the thirteenth century. According to legend, at this time the dungeon and torture chamber were run by one man. John Sage was formerly a soldier of Longshanks who was said to have succeeded in reaching the rank of lieutenant before being wounded by a spear to his leg. The injury earned him the nickname Dragfoot and the torturer position for which he became notorious.

Dragfoot was said to torture more than fifty people a week, his favourite instrument of torture being a cage in which he would enclose his victim before placing it over a fire. Other methods included boiling alive, the iron maiden and the use of an oubliette – a deep, claustrophobic dungeon with a narrow and inaccessible opening at the top. The name comes from the French *oublier*, meaning to forget, and most prisoners cast into an oubliette would simply be left to die.

In his torture room, which still exists fully equipped today, Sage had a torture rack upon which he strangled his girlfriend, Elizabeth Charlton, during sex. It was meant to heighten sexual pleasure; instead it killed her. Unfortunately for Sage, Elizabeth's father was a Border reiver, one of many clan leaders and local outlaws. Allied with the Scots, he threatened Longshanks with an attack against the castle if Sage were not executed. Realizing he was outnumbered and short of the cash to finance a defence, Edward called for Sage to be hanged. The execution took place from a tree along the Devil's Mile within the grounds of Chillingham Castle and in front of a large crowd. As was common at public hangings, the crowd cut off souvenirs from Sage's body as he died, including his toes, fingers, nose and testicles.

Many of the stories surrounding Dragfoot are unverified. No one knows how much of it actually happened, but it keeps the spook-hunters happy. According to one story, following the execution Sage's body was dismembered and buried at a crossroads 'so his ghost wouldn't know the way to heaven, and would therefore choose the road to hell'. Lovely.

'The more one looks, the more one sees what a wild, blood-thirsty place it was,' says Sir Humphry. 'Many of the family who lived here got their heads cut off by the king for pushing their luck or trying to take over.'

Meanwhile I continue casting, watching in vain as fish rise to nibble on my fly but decide not to bother. I miss one fish, but console myself that he was just a wee chap. It's very frustrating, but that's part of the joy of fishing. If you're a busy person, it's the only way you'll get to stand still for three hours in the countryside. And it forces you to concentrate entirely on only one task for that time, which can be very liberating for the mind. While I'm pondering the Zen of fly fishing, Sir Humphry hooks another trout, although Jim deems he's too small to be worth keeping and releases him back into the water.

A few hours later we sit down to dinner, the trout cooked by Jim on the kitchen Aga with boiled potatoes, carrots, green beans, and bread and butter. With some lemon squeezed over it, the fish is delicious. At a kitchen table large enough to seat fifteen and surrounded by an eclectic mixture of mismatched and beautiful crockery, our conversation continues about the history of the area. Northumberland, I have discovered, is a magical place, a wilderness of open spaces and castles that feels more remote and untouched than any other part of England.

Travelling through Britain, I've noticed that the country is in much better shape than many of the doomsayers would have you believe. Give or take the odd mobile phone mast, the landscape is just as beautiful and untouched now as it would have been at any time in the last century. There's more traffic, for sure, but we've done a good job in maintaining and protecting the parts of the landscape and the buildings that matter historically.

'It has survived, but one's got to watch it like mad,' says Sir Humphry. 'The moment tourism arrives, the developers arrive, the woods and hills become full of twinkling lights and smoke, and we lose our wilderness. One is fighting against people who need and want money – and why shouldn't they?'

Sir Humphry has a point, I think. 'So many people want to come to the wildernesses of Northumberland, Yorkshire and Scotland to see a world that's unspoilt,' I say, 'but the paradox is that the more of them come, the less there will be that's unspoilt. They can't help destroying the thing they love.'

'Luckily, people went off to the Lake District for the lakes, to Scotland to see the mountains and to Yorkshire to see the Dales. And they left us in peace.'

Sir Humphry is right. There is a remarkable 'untouchedness', as he describes it, about Northumberland and if we can keep it that way, then it will remain as special as ever. Sir Humphry has played a big part in maintaining the 'untouchedness' of his little corner, although it involved battles that in their own bureaucratic way rivalled the more violent and bloodthirsty clashes fought in this area some eight hundred years ago.

'The first battle was the idea of taking it on,' he says. His family having lived in the Lake District for four hundred years, Sir Humphry bought the castle in 1982 with his wife Catherine, a distant descendant of the Greys, the family that with their descendants, the Earls of Tankerville, had lived at Chillingham since the thirteenth century.

When Sir Humphry acquired Chillingham it was a wreck. Thought too expensive to maintain after the death of the seventh Earl of Tankerville, it had been abandoned since 1933. In much the same way that Victorian gentry directed that their horses be shot after their death, the eighth earl decided the castle should die rather than pass out of the family. During the Second World War, it was used as an army barracks and much of the decorative wood was stripped out and burned by billeted soldiers. After the war, the castle fell into disrepair. Lead was removed from the roof, causing extensive weather damage to large parts of the building.

'It had a wonderful family link since the 1200s and that was romance to me. And the architecture was romance. It was a sleeping beauty.'

Pigeons had taken over, leaving a ton – literally – of droppings in each room. The roofs had fallen in and it was easier to collapse the floors, let the muck drop and cart it out than try to clean it out in the normal way. Sir Humphry approached the National Trust, but it wanted more than £28 million to take on the castle. Then, when he announced that, instead of restoring the castle to its Victorian state, he was going to return Chillingham to its medieval roots, English Heritage objected, and there was even talk of legal action. Sir Humphry argued that there were a thousand Victorian palaces in Northumberland alone and many more throughout the country, but very few medieval or Elizabethan castles with their defensive details. Underneath the rotted Victorian plasterwork, he found arrow slits, huge chimneypieces and even intact Elizabethan plasterwork. So he persisted, against the wishes of English Heritage.

'When the Victorian décor was cleared, each room sang out what it wanted. There was a dominance of medieval in some rooms and a dominance of Elizabethan in other rooms, so we followed that. Every avenue we cleared, every garden we reinstated, every roof we put back, I had the feeling the castle was thanking me for doing it.'

I think Sir Humphry made absolutely the right decision. It's a beautiful building, all crenellated battlements and stone-flagged floors. Constructed around a courtyard, with a massive tower at each corner, suiting its purpose as a serious, no-frills border fortress, the castle had windows all facing on to the courtyard until Elizabeth I's reign, when it began its transition from fortress to grand country house. Embellished with Renaissance-carved stonework, arcading in the courtyard and large mullioned windows, it gained not one but two fashionable long galleries. Further changes were made in the eighteenth and nineteenth centuries. Had Sir Humphry reinstated the Victorian features and plasterwork, it would have been a reproduction of that period's crafts, not original because none of it remained intact. None of it would have been real. However, the arrow slits and the medieval features it has now are totally authentic because they survived the centuries. And where changes are apparent, such as arrow slits that became rifle slots and then windows, Sir Humphry has left the changes intact so that visitors can see the development of the castle's various features. Surely that's much better?

The back-to-the-bare-bones restoration has uncovered the insertion and removal of floors and walls, as well as an entire staircase hidden within a wall. In one upper room, concealed within a walled-up fireplace, Sir Humphry found a cache of more than one hundred Tudor documents, including papers relating to James VI of Scotland's succession to Elizabeth I.

As for Chillingham's reputation as the most haunted place in Britain, I'm still sceptical, but I'm not sure about Sir Humphry. 'You're an ex-soldier,' I say. 'You're pretty unsentimental about the business of battle. What do you think about the idea of ghosts?'

'This place is packed with vibes, but I think they're generally good vibes. In past centuries the castle was a centre of black magic, so when I came here I called in a wonderful priest and asked him to get rid of the spirits. He looked round and at the end of the weekend, he said: "No, they're too strong. I can't touch them." '

Seven years later, the priest returned. 'I asked him what was happening now. He said the spirits were still here, but they were rooting for me and were absolutely happy.'

Sir Humphry believes the spirits have protected him on several occasions when he's had dramatic accidents during the restoration of the castle. Instead of being filled with evil spirits who had come to a nasty end here, Sir Humphry believes Chillingham is home to the spirits of more colourful characters. 'I think what happens when you die off, the regimental sergeant major says: "All this way." But certain people who have had a very interesting life down here, played around with the Royals, had great battles, heard great music and had great love, they say to the sergeant major: "Thank you, but I'll stay right where I am. I don't want to go there and I don't want to be told what to do." So I think this place is packed out with people who've had a wonderful life.'

It's a nice idea. The people who've had good lives become the spirits, rather than those who are aggrieved that their lives haven't turned out as they wished. However, it's got an uncomfortable whiff of elitism about it. A very aristocratic view of spirituality, you might say.

'So some say: "I've had such a good time, I'm not ready yet to shuffle off this mortal coil." '

'Exactly,' says Sir Humphry. 'They say: "You don't speak to an officer like that." '

This makes me really laugh. You spend your whole life fighting against the pernicious effects of rank and breeding and then, when you die, you discover some sort of cosmic class system is going on in the afterlife. 'That's so naughty.'

According to Sir Humphry, the castle is home to some very famous ghosts, the best known of which is the Blue Boy, who as midnight rang out would cry and moan in agony. Apparently, the noises always came from a spot in the castle's Pink Room, near a passage cut through a 10-foot-thick wall into the adjoining tower. As the bloodcurdling cries died away, a bright halo of light would form close to an old four-poster bed. Anyone sleeping there saw, gently approaching them, the figure of a young boy dressed in blue, surrounded by light. Witnesses apparently said his clothes were like those seen in paintings dating from the 1660s, when Charles II was on the throne. To add to the spookiness quotient, the story continues that during the 1920s the bones of a young boy and some fragments of a blue dress were discovered next to the skeleton of a man behind a wall where the fireplace is now located. This was close to a trap door opening to the stone arches of the vaults below. The remains were removed and interred in consecrated ground. Since then the figure has apparently never been seen again, although to this day there are reports of guests in the Pink Room being awakened by strange blue flashes in the middle of the night.

Another apparent ghost, Lady Mary Berkeley, searches for her husband, who ran off with her sister. Lady Mary, desolate and brokenhearted, lived in the castle by herself with only her baby girl as a companion. The rustle of her dress can supposedly be heard as she passes by on the turret stairs.

Although I think the notion of haunted castles is ridiculous, bedtime is looming and I have an important question to ask of Sir Humphry. 'Having been very kindly invited to stay, if I was at all concerned about ghosts, which rooms should I avoid?'

'Only the rooms around the Pink Room.'

'Fine. I have, however, invited along some chaps who claim to be ghost-hunters. They say they can detect ghostliness and all that with their equipment. Would you mind that?'

'Not at all. I'd love it. The technical ghost-hunters who've been here in the past find their dowel rods reeling and the non-technical ones get full of excitement, vibes-wise. So we've got someone for everybody.'

I thank Sir Humphry and descend to the dungeon, where the parapsychologists I've invited have covered several tables with equipment that allegedly detects spirits.

'What's going on here then? Sensors? What are they logging?'

Mark Turner, a trained engineer, is a rather intense young Scot who speaks with very sibilant 's' sounds and who used to run a removals business. He's the chief paranormal in-vestigator. 'We're looking for anomalous noises outside the hearing frequencies,' he says.

Ah. *Of course.* 'Why would you expect something like that to happen here?'

'Although we know there have been many paranormal experiences here, the first thing we have to do is discount noises for which there is a simple scientific explanation. Fear can be contagious, you know. Then if there is anything para-normal going on, we want to capture it so that we have objective evidence. If it falls within the realms of science, then we'd be able to capture it. But if it falls outwith the realms of science, then obviously we wouldn't be able to capture it with the equipment that we have.'

We're standing in a room where many people have met a grisly death. I ask Mark if he thinks there might be some resonance of that.

'Could be. It could be stored in the brickwork. It could be the people were so traumatized they don't actually know they're dead.'

'Wow. Really? They died too quickly to resolve something? Aren't we heading into a religious sphere here?'

'Definitely. Fear of judgement, possibly, since Christianity was brought in. Possibly some deed in life has kept them here.'

I look around the dungeon with its implements of torture hanging on the walls. 'I think you'd have to behave appallingly to be stuck in this room for five hundred years.'

'I beg to differ. I love this place. It has a fantastic atmosphere.'

'So you'd be happy to haunt this room?'

'I'd be perfectly happy to haunt this room.'

'I see . . . okay.'

Given that we're standing in what is statistically – how they measure these things is a mystery to me – the most haunted place in England, surely they'd be expecting their meters to go mental.

'We'd like them to go mental,' says Domenic, a Glasgow maintenance worker by day and a ghost-hunter specializing in electronic voice phenomena by night. 'But it doesn't have to go mental for us to detect any presence in the building.'

Mark interjects: 'We always say that just because we're here, it doesn't mean they are going to pop out and show us the place is haunted.'

'Ah, right. They might just decide not to bother that night?' How convenient.

'Could be.'

Eventually my scepticism gets the better of me. 'It's like your man who bends the spoons. If I had huge psychic powers, I would use them to warn people who had incipient heart disease or whose baby needed more folic acid or who required more exercise to avert a heart attack in five years, rather than using my powers to amuse people with bendy spoons. So I'm a wee bit cynical.'

'Cynicism is healthy.' Why did I know Mark was going to say that? 'We have to question everything.'

'We certainly do. We have to question it with a *big* question mark.'

'Absolutely.' Softly spoken Mark is unflappable.

'Hmmmmm.' I don't like this.

'We're not trying to prove anything. We are just trying to investigate.'

'Okay . . . anyway, I'm going to bed. Shall we see what you've got in the morning?'

I sleep like the proverbial baby, not least because of Sir Humphry's generosity with his whisky. After breakfast I convene with the investigators, eager for my cynicism to be shattered. They're waiting in the castle garden, tired after only three hours' sleep. During their long night, they investigated in and around the Pink Room, and at several other locations in the castle. I ask Mark if they caught any ghosts.

'We did pick up some interesting voices.'

'Did you?'

'We picked up a voice in the Grey apartments. When we asked for a name, it replied Edward.'

'You're kidding? Can I hear that?'

They play the recording and – lo and behold – there is a noise that sounds a bit like a raspy voice gasping 'Edward'. But then I've also seen dogs on television that sound like they're saying 'sausages'. If you want hard enough to hear something, you probably will.

'What do you think it is then? Is it Edward the First on the way to slaughter our people? Is he still hanging around here?'

'It's certainly possible.'

'Really?'

'We didn't actually hear the voice at the time, only later on the recording because it's on a different frequency.'

'You couldn't hear it with your ears?'

'No.'

That's odd, or maybe just convenient.

'The interesting thing that we got last night was severe temperature drops. In the chapel.'

'Wouldn't that happen anyway in the middle of the night?'

Mark assures me that his technical equipment compensates for draughts and normal temperature variations. 'The interesting thing is that a girl died of pneumonia in that room. A lot of the temperature drop we experienced is her, trying to warm up.' He says it with complete conviction.

'I'm not going to pretend,' I say. 'I think this is rubbish.'

'Why?'

'Because there's absolutely no evidence that it means anything whatsoever. We've come a long way. We've had the Enlightenment. We've sent men to the moon. That impresses me, but all you've done is ask questions – like do we survive death? – without answering them.'

Then Mark drops the bombshell: 'I don't believe in life after death.'

'So where do these noises that you say you've recorded come from?'

'I don't know. All I know is we've picked up a voice. We're investigators. We don't have the answers.'

That's a bit more interesting, but to me the two of them are still as mad as a box of frogs. 'I have to say I disagree with you and Sir Humphry. I'm not convinced at all, but thank you for showing me what you do. Maybe one day you'll prove me completely wrong. If you get Frank Sinatra coming through, singing as he did in 1953, please get in touch. It would make me a very happy man.'

Chapter Fifteen

Situated almost smack on the border, Chillingham Castle was my last stop in England. Heading north, all roads now lead back to the auld country. It feels good to be returning to Scotland and to have my final destination in sight. I've always liked the feeling of the north, the trees thinning out, the accents sounding clearer, the attitudes becoming more egalitarian and the jokes honing in on bursting pretensions. Ah, home at last. Well, nearly.

Normally, if I was driving back home on the vile, stinking M74, I'd see a towering landmark in the distance: the 300-foot cooling towers of Chapelcross, Scotland's first operational nuclear power station, a structure almost exactly as old as the motorways and my trusty Jaguar XK150. For years, the sight of those four huge funnels looming on the northern horizon would quicken my heart. It wasn't just my approaching homeland; I've always liked cooling towers, particularly the lacy crisscross bits at the bottom, which makes them look as if they were being held to the ground like hot-air balloons. These huge structures remove heat from the water that circulates in the power station's cooling water system. Using a process called natural draft wet cooling, they draw heat out of the cooling water using the latent heat of evaporation, creating the huge clouds of water vapour often seen discharging from the top of the cooling tower. And now, seeing as I'm going by B-roads, I can get up close – real close – because I'm going to get to see inside the cooling towers only a few hours before they're brought crashing down to Earth.

Built at the height of the Cold War in the late 1950s, about 4 miles from the Solway Estuary, Chapelcross was officially opened in May 1959. The sister plant to Calder Hall in Cumbria, now part of the Sellafield complex, its four Magnox reactors powered eight 30 MegaWatt turbines to produce enough electricity, according to British Nuclear Fuels Ltd, to supply every home in south-west Scotland, the Borders and Cumbria (admittedly a fairly sparsely populated area, and no mention was made of where industry got its power). In 2004 it was closed after forty-five years of 'safe and successful operation'. Those are BNFL's words, not mine, because in May 1967 Reactor Two suffered a partial nuclear meltdown that closed it for two years while a clean-up operation took place. There was a second accident in 2001, when a basket of discharged fuel elements was dropped during a refuelling operation. In neither accident was there any evidence of injuries or harm to the local population. However, the site also housed a facility for making tritium, a vital component in hydrogen bombs, and was therefore considered a defence site, which meant that for many years it was not subject to all international safeguards.

As you can probably tell, I have very mixed feelings about nuclear power. At a time of global warming and declining fossil fuel supplies, it provides an ostensibly clean and plentiful energy supply. But it's not without considerable dangers and

265

because historically it's been linked to the defence industry, we've never really been able to tell its true costs. Take Chapelcross: it will need a century to decommission the site, many times longer than it took to build the plant, and it will be thousands of years before the spent nuclear fuel it used is no longer a health or environmental hazard.

At the time Chapelcross was being constructed, few of the locals knew anything about nuclear power. The only association was with Hiroshima and Nagasaki, but they trusted politicians, who told them nuclear power plants were quite different and totally safe. In the immediate post-war period, neither the locals nor the politicians had been educated in the principles and consequences of nuclear fission. All most of them cared about was creating employment in a moribund, isolated economy. Whatever misgivings they might have had soon evaporated when they heard it meant jobs for all. When the power station was built, it created two thousand jobs and transformed the fortunes of the nearest town, Annan. As well as electricity, it has apparently generated more than £1 billion for the local economy since it went into operation.

The general feeling from the local community is a feeling of fondness for a site that is not only a landmark but has brought the area economic stability and employment. The landmark is fondly recognized by locals as 'home' when they come back from a journey. The towers are even used as a guide on over-head aviation paths and by birds flying home. And for two local residents, Bill and Mary Thompson, it was also the place they met, fell in love and started their lives together.

In 1958 Bill was working in Greenock and moved to Annan to work for four years on the Chapelcross plant in the mechanical maintenance department. He lived in a camp of a thousand construction workers and engineers and has fond memories of his time there, including playing in the football team and the day the first reactor 'went critical' – that is, started producing energy. But his fondest memory is the day early in 1959 when he was called in to repair a coffee machine in the canteen at which Mary worked. At that time, Mary lived on a farm in the nearby hamlet of Creca and had taken a job as a cook at Chapelcross when it was built, quite literally, at the end of her garden. Bill repaired the machine, met Mary, romance blossomed and, by September 1959, they were married. A true Scottish romance.

For the next three years, Bill and Mary worked at Chapelcross, then Bill got a succession of jobs at nuclear power plants around the country, taking Mary with him to Hunterston, nearby in south-west Scotland, and to Dungeness in Kent.

'When the towers come down tomorrow, what will it feel like for you?'

'A sad day in some ways,' says Mary, now sixty-seven years old and clutching her handbag over a safety vest. 'I saw it being built from the very first brick. But that's life, isn't it?'

'When I would come down from Greenock on a motorbike,' says Bill, 'I could see the towers from the top of a hill at Hetland in Dumfries and I'd know that in twenty minutes I'd be back in my digs, so it's a landmark I'll miss.'

I'd heard that Bill had proposed to Mary in the shadow of the towers, so I wanted to know exactly what happened. 'Is there not a wee plaque or something to mark the spot?'

'It wasn't very romantic,' said Mary.

'Was he a bit shy?'

'Actually he was. I used to take my coffee in a workshop in

which Bill and his brother Jack would fight over who would sit next to me and who would get the coffee first. One day when Jack was getting the coffee, Bill said: "I'm going to marry you."'

'What did you say?'

'I said, "Oh, are you really?" And that's how he proposed. He's no romantic at all.'

I think it's quite nice. At least he was definite about it. None of that 'I quite fancy you, what do you reckon?' malarkey.

'And there was nae bun in the oven,' Bill insists, which immediately makes Mary giggle.

'You're in the spare room, boy,' I say.

As for the demolition, Bill and Mary, who have retired nearby, are concerned about the implications for the six hundred people who now work at the plant.

'It's just progress.' Bill shrugs his shoulders. 'But the people of Annan have very mixed feelings.'

Bill, Mary and I have an appointment to meet in a field a safe distance from Chapelcross to watch the towers come tumbling down together, but before that I'm going to see the preparations up close.

The security surrounding Chapelcross is phenomenal. There's a siren that goes off several times a day just to prove it's still working. I drive up to big steel sliding doors through which I couldn't ram a tank, let alone the XK150. Even though Chapelcross is no longer active, it's still considered a potential terrorist target. Waiting for me on the other side of the gates is Dave Wilson, deputy site director. A civil engineer and project manager, he's been working on the decommission for three years and could be at Chapelcross for many more years to come. I can see that he feels torn between sadness and pride over the demolition. If it all goes to plan, it will be a job well done, but it will also be the end of a considerable feat of construction and engineering.

'These are magnificent.' I am standing beneath the cooling towers with Dave. In the background, some of the plant's buildings are partially dismantled and covered in scaffolding. 'I've seen them so many times before. It's such a landmark when you hit Scotland. But not for much longer.'

'No. They've been here fifty years and tomorrow they'll be gone in about ten seconds. That'll be it. The landscape changed for ever.'

'Presumably they'll be falling this way.'

'Yes.' Dave laughs. Where we are standing is the only patch of bare ground around the towers. If they fall in any other direction, they could demolish parts of the plant that houses highly radioactive components. Most definitely. Very slightly this way.'

Dave points at the legs at the bottom of each tower, which are wrapped in plastic. 'The explosives on each of those legs will go off.' He points further up the tower, where I can see a spiral of plastic, also encasing explosive charges. 'And all around the tower, so the whole tower will fall in on itself but very slightly this way.'

The four towers will be demolished in sequence with a two-second delay between each of them. It seems a great waste to decommission a power station that has been reliably supplying power for half a century, but it's old technology, with four reactors capable of producing around 200 MegaWatts of power, whereas a single modern reactor can produce 1,000 MegaWatts on its own. It's no longer economical.

'What will happen to the rest of the site?' I ask.

'We go into the decommissioning phase. We take away all the redundant buildings. We take the fuel out of the reactors. We remove all the radioactive waste, process it and package it for storage or disposal. And then we'll clear the site, except for the four reactor buildings.'

'Where does the waste go? That's what I and everyone else worries about.'

'Low-level waste goes to a repository in Cumbria. As for intermediate-level waste, the current UK strategy is to store that on site until a repository is available.' Dave says the Nuclear Decommissioning Authority is 'working on providing' a repository. What that means is that it's very difficult to find any nation that wants a repository on its soil because the intermediate-level waste is so toxic. 'It's not going to happen in the very near future.'

'What confuses people like me is why it can't be dissipated or burnt or chemically cleansed in some way to make it less dangerous.'

'The graphite in the cores has been irradiated for a very long time and now has a high concentration of radioactive isotopes. Over time that will decay, but it will take about a hundred years before most – but not all – of the reactor core is safe for man access.'

'Where will it be in the meantime?'

'It stays there.' Dave points at the buildings.

'Blimey.'

'It's government strategy.'

'But it'll have to be protected all that time. Is that not colossally expensive?'

'Not that expensive. The cores are covered in eight metres of concrete to make it biosafe.'

With the level of science education that most of us have, it's difficult to know whether to feel safe or at risk, but Dave tells me that he's very comfortable about the technology and the risks involved. But then he's employed by the nuclear industry.

So what about the iconic cooling towers? 'For the town and people around here, this must be like losing their church steeple.'

'It will be a sad day for the community when they go. There's a whole generation that's grown up with these things on the landscape.'

It certainly will be sad for the locals, but before that happens I'm eager to see as much of it as I can. 'Can we crawl in before it falls doon?'

'Why not?'

Up close, the towers appear far more dilapidated than from afar. A lot of the structures around their base have been bull-dozed and crushed to gain access. Rubble lies everywhere; I suppose there's no point in tidying it into neat heaps when you're about to bring tens of thousand of tons of concrete down on top of it. Stepping between the legs wrapped in plastic sheeting to protect the explosive, I look up into the tower.

'Oh my Lord!' The size of it is overwhelming. This is definitely no place for the faint-hearted. I shout and hear my voice echoed three or four times.

Having been stripped of all superfluous materials, including a lot of asbestos, the towers are now hollow structures, bristling with tons of explosive, all ready and prepared for the demolition. Not that it's called demolition any more. Demolition has been through the political-correctness wringer and the company that's masterminding the operation calls it a 'dismantling service'.

To see the inside – a sight I'm sure that everyone who's driven past it would dearly love to see – is quite a privilege. There are about 1,600 holes in each tower filled with explosive; beyond them I can see the sky in the distance, but it looks as if it's half a mile away, which I suppose is almost the case.

'You've only got this view, looking all the way out, since we pulled out the internals,' says Dave. Normally there's a big disc collecting the water that's streaming down the insides of the towers.

It's quite extraordinary. I find it hard to believe that the 25,500 tons of concrete in the four towers will very soon crumple into a pile no wider than the width of the funnel.

'Why don't we put some aluminium foil in here before you demolish it?' I suggest. 'Then when the explosives detonate, there'll be burn marks up the sides and in ten thousand years, when the archaeologists come to excavate the site, they'll think something huge landed here.'

Dave wisely ignores my prank, so shortly before 9 a.m. the next day, as the countdown to the blast begins, I join Bill and Mary Thompson to see a huge part of their past disappear for ever. Watching from the farm where Mary grew up in the shadow of the towers being built, the event is all the more poignant.

'I hope you don't think I'm being insensitive when I say I can't wait to see it come down,' I say. 'I know it means a lot to you, but it's going to be something special when it comes down.'

Mary and Bill nod knowingly.

'I guess there'll be a last siren before it blows.' As I say it, the siren starts. 'Here we go. Lordy, lordy.'

Mary starts to talk, but is stopped by the sound of a loud crack and the sight of the first of the towers starting to collapse. The left-most tower looks as if it's dropping to its knees. That'll be the legs blasted away, I think. There's another loud crack, a puff of smoke appears at the base of the tower to the right of the first tower and it, too, drops by about a tenth of its height as its legs are detonated. Then, a second detonation on the first tower crumples the chimney in on itself, a dark cloud of dust puffing into the sky through the space where concrete used to stand. The other three towers follow suit. In less than twenty seconds, the towers are gone.

I'm overcome with how beautifully they came down, spiralling elegantly to the ground. And when the dust settles, there's not a brick near any of the other buildings. It's quite extraordinary.

Beside me, Mary has burst into tears. I'm not surprised. She's watched the towers come down from the garden behind the house in which she'd seen them erected.

'There's a change,' says Bill, putting his arm around Mary. 'Quite an emotion there, love.'

'Yes.' Mary looks shaken.

'It's not often the past just disappears like that,' I say. 'Usually it slips away, doesn't it? It doesn't often go bang like that.'

'Like closing a book after you've read it,' says Bill.

'Exactly . . . exactly.'

Perhaps it was seeing Bill and Mary look back on their youth, but I've been inspired to delve into my own past and the place to do it is here: Dumfries and Galloway, a place the Americans would call my ancestral heartland. But before I go in search of my roots, it's time for a little admission. My real name is not Coltrane; that's my stage name, which I took as a tribute to the jazz saxophonist John Coltrane. My family name is McMillan, one of the Highland Scottish clans. The MacMillan clan has been traced back to Loch Tay in Perthshire, but my branch of the clan, as far as my Aunt Gretta could find, traces its roots to Glen Trool, site of one of the battles of the Scottish War of Independence. Incidentally, the two different spellings of McMillan or MacMillan don't necessarily indicate two different families. The name is a translation from the Gaelic and the spelling was defined only in the nineteenth century.

My journey north takes me over the moors, close to Glen Trool, but I pass by without visiting because I am heading for the home of a MacMillan who invented something that almost all of us have at some time in our lives used fairly regularly. It's an extraordinarily clever invention.

If there has been one overriding theme to this trip, it's been the invention of tradition. I've visited many villages and towns in which the locals have either invented traditions or reinvented them to pull the community together. But now I'm about to enter the realm of the tradition of invention. Because if there's one expertise to which we Scots can lay claim, it's invention. I don't want to drone on about all the things that we Scots have invented, but it's a very long and impressive list for such a small country. Unfortunately, for a long time Scotland didn't have the capital to exploit its talent, so most of the Scots who invented things had to leave Scotland to develop them, which is quite sad. This particular invention, however, was invented right here in Scotland. The inventor was a very ingenious blacksmith, who, according to family myth, is a relative of mine. The myth is based on no more than that we are both McMillans or MacMillans from Glen Trool, but nevertheless I'm hoping to determine if there's truth to it. It doesn't really matter, but it would be nice to know if my party boast is hot air or cold fact.

My destination is Drumlanrig Castle, a magnificent baroque country house that's home to the ninth Duke of Buccleuch and Queensberry. With a grand avenue leading to the front of the castle and pink sandstone walls, it's a very impressive structure, but I'm not here to visit the duke or his home. I'm here to meet Rik Allsop, a ponytailed, whippet-legged bicycle fanatic, and to see his bike shed.

Built beside a nice wee courtyard, the bike shed keeps happy the many visitors to the cycle trails that run through the Drumlanrig estate. You can rent and buy bicycles and dozens of accessories, but the really interesting part is at the back of the shop, where Rik has built a museum packed with old bicycles and bicycle accessories, such as acetylene torches.

'Is this it?' I point at a wooden contraption with a hard leather-covered seat and iron rods attached to the rear wheel.

'It's a replica. It was built a few years ago.'

'Jeez. Look – it's got cranks to power the back wheel. I often wondered how it worked . . .' This is a replica of the bicycle made by my namesake, Kirkpatrick Macmillan, in 1842 and believed to be the first rear-wheel-driven safety bicycle.

Like many inventions, the bicycle was not the result of a dramatic breakthrough but of incremental improvements and the amalgamation of several elements. The first known bicycle, called the hobbyhorse and invented in 1817 by Baron von Drais, a German, was effectively a two-wheeled cart with a seat. With two equal-sized wooden-spoked and iron-tyred wheels, it was very uncomfortable and not particularly fast – riders propelled it simply by scooting their feet along the ground.

However, in 1824 Kirkpatrick Macmillan, who was working

with his father as a blacksmith at Courthill Smithy in Keir Mill, about 5 miles from Drumlanrig, saw a hobbyhorse being ridden along a nearby road and decided to make one for himself.

Now, shoeing horses and copying other people's designs is all very well, but if you're a MacMillan you need to bring something a bit more creative to the enterprise, which is why, upon completion, he realized what a radical improvement it would be if he could propel it without putting his feet on the ground. Working at his smithy, he borrowed the principles of his design from the mechanisms used at that time on spinning wheels and Watt's steam engines. Treadles converted reciprocating feet movements into a rotary motion, which was transferred to the rear wheel using rods and cranks. With a steerable 30-inch front wheel and a 40-inch rear wheel (both of them iron-rimmed and wooden), it worked. Although at 57 lb it was so heavy that Kirkpatrick had to push off by striking the ground with his iron-spiked boots, the pedal cycle was officially born in 1839 and Kirkpatrick is now recognized as its inventor.

Thought mad by fellow villagers, Kirkpatrick became known locally as 'daft Pate', but he persisted with his invention, called a velocipede in those days, and would ride it all around the local villages, where it became well known as the 'Devil on Wheels'. In 1842 he rode his cumbersome machine 68 miles over rough roads from his tiny smithy home to Glasgow, where he visited his two schoolteacher brothers. During the journey he clocked up another notable first when he became the first ever cyclist to be prosecuted for a traffic offence. Speeding at 8 m.p.h. through the Gorbals, he knocked down a wee lassie in the crush of a crowd that had gathered to watch the arrival of the Devil on Wheels. According to the story, the magistrate at the Gorbals Public Bar was sufficiently intrigued to ask MacMillan for a figure-of-eight demonstration in the courtyard and, suitably impressed, is said to have slipped him the money for the fine. The *Glasgow Herald*, which reported the case in some detail, commented that 'this invention will not supersede the railway'. Little did they know.

Having raced the stagecoach on his return to Dumfriesshire, MacMillan went back to the quiet life. Sadly he was no entrepreneur and failed to patent his invention, which was soon copied by an English firm and put on sale at £7. Meanwhile, Kirkpatrick, a keen churchman, married and fathered six children, whom he refused to let read on a Sunday. When he died in 1878, a plaque was erected on his smithy home, which read 'HE BUILDED BETTER THAN HE KNEW'.

Like many inventions, there's a degree of scholarly disagreement about the veracity of Kirkpatrick's having invented the first pedal bicycle. Detractors say it is an amalgamation of two other velocipedes built by Thomas McCall, a Scottish cartwright, and say Kirkpatrick's claim is based solely on the research of his relative James Johnston in the 1890s. For a while Kirkpatrick wasn't considered the inventor, because there was a chap from Kilmarnock who sold MacMillan's velocipede as his own. But in the absence of any conclusive evidence to disprove the story, bicycle historians regard my namesake's creation as the first rear-wheel pedal-propelled bicycle and that's good enough for me. Of course, the bicycle would have to go through several improvements – including a chain drive to the rear wheels, suspension wheels with wire spokes and John Boyd Dunlop's invention of the pneumatic tyre – before it became the machine we all know today, but in my book Kirkpatrick was the father of it all.

'I don't know if I'm really related to Kirkpatrick,' I say to Rik. 'But my father, who was not beyond a wee exaggeration, always maintained it was the case – although I suppose every MacMillan thinks they're related to him.'

'If nothing else,' says Rik, 'it disproves the supposed link between cycling and penile dysfunction.'

I suppose that's another way of looking at it. Local carpentry and metalwork apprentices built the replica at the museum. It's absolutely beautiful and, although Kirkpatrick didn't leave me any money, maybe he did bequeath in his genes an appreciation for anything mechanical and a love of making things. So when Rik tells me that in a workshop a few doors along from the museum they're making a second replica of the MacMillan velocipede so that he can recreate Kirkpatrick's journey, I jump at the chance to lend a hand.

The workshop is a proper smithy with a forge, mechanical bellows and a real blacksmith called Ross Berry, a larger-than-life character with a bright red Mohican and several ounces of metal piercings through his nose, lips, eyebrows and ears. With great big arms, he looks like Hagrid with his beard shaved off – exactly how I think a blacksmith ought to look. By appearance, Ross is everybody's idea of a terrifying man, but of course he has the soul of an absolute angel.

'I hope you don't mind getting dirty,' he says.

'Getting dirty? Oh yes. I'm good at getting dirty.'

Over the next couple of hours I am in heaven, discussing blacksmithing techniques, ball-bearing design, shipbuilding, locomotive design and the invention of threads, while assisting Ross. We attach the wooden cartwheels to some metal forks that he has made, then Ross shows me how to taper a metal bar that I later weld to the bike. We attach the treadle, rods and cranks, then fit the handlebars and seat. It's ready.

'It's the wobbliest, ricketiest thing you'll ever see in your life,' says Ross. 'It's amazing how anyone stays on.'

Lifting it down, I'm amazed how light it is considering how much iron has been used in its manufacture. I wheel it outside to where Rik is waiting.

'Fantastic,' he says. 'Is it still hot?'

'No. It's time.'

'Time for a test ride?'

We wheel the bike over the cobbles to the castle, where the grand avenue provides an ideal length of smooth tarmac. Rik climbs on awkwardly, the large rear wheel making it difficult to swing a leg over the back. He pushes off, gets his feet on the treadles and moves down the road at an impressive speed. We watch him disappear down the grand avenue, then he stops, holding a piece of ironwork in his hand. It's the handlebar.

'I told you something would fall off,' he says.

We fix the handlebar, then watch again as Rik rides off down the grand avenue. He's moving at quite some speed.

'That's fantastic,' I say.

'It is,' Ross agrees.

'And MacMillan wouldn't have made the journey on a road like that.' I point at the smooth tarmac.

'Dirt and rocks,' says Ross. 'And no suspension. Relying on wooden wheels staying together.'

It may not be as fast or reliable as a modern bike, but back in the mid-nineteenth century it was a godsend. In those days, the average working man couldn't afford a horse, so rarely travelled more than 5 miles from home. But with the invention of the bicycle, people could suddenly travel 20 miles away and back in a day. It brought together courting couples from villages beyond walking distance and immediately widened the gene pool. It also played a significant role in the emancipation of middle-class and upper-class women. This was not, as some male Victorian doctors suggested, because the exercise could help cure the fairer sex of their myriad nervous disorders; rather, cycling liberated women from the constricting boned corsets, hooped crinolines and voluminous skirts of the Victorian era. French women in knickerbockers led the way, rather too fast at first for their staid British sisters and their male chaperones, but soon the craze spread to Britain and beyond.

It's strange to think of a blacksmith in a wee Scottish town creating something that transformed the lives of millions of people, but my namesake's invention – or at least his part in its evolution – really did change the world.

Chapter Sixteen

I'm so close to home now, I can almost smell it, but before my final approach to Glasgow I take a wee north-easterly detour to Abbey Craig, a volcanic hill overlooking the Carse of Stirling. Stretching west from Stirling, these flat farmlands were formed around 6,500 years ago by the silting up of the Forth Estuary, though they have changed greatly in the last 250 years. Looking out over one of the finest views in Scotland, everything appears very beautiful and very peaceful – but it wasn't always so. The Romans had a big fort here when they were trying to keep us Scots in place, something that's been tried by various nations over the years, not always with the greatest success. The man who started the big revolt against outside rule is standing above and behind me at the top of the Wallace Monument. It commemorates William Wallace, the man who you could say first defined the idea of Scotland as a nation rather than a bunch of tribes who went around stabbing each other, although we still managed to do that right into the eighteenth century.

Wallace battled with the English just below where I am standing. From Cambuskenneth Abbey, an Augustinian monastery built in the twelfth century, he watched the gathering of the army of Edward I before delivering a shattering defeat at the battle of Stirling Bridge. Of course, these days we Jocks don't battle openly with the English any more. We just sneak in the back door, become prime minister and fill the Cabinet.

As for William Wallace, he was succeeded as Guardian of Scotland, the de facto head of state, by Robert the Bruce, one of Scotland's greatest kings. By coincidence, I'm here to meet a man called Bruce who is also very independent, although in his case it's an independent brewery. Scotland is blessed with lots of flora that, with a bit of ingenuity, can be made into beer, for which we're all slatheringly grateful, but it has taken a man called Bruce Williams and his brother Scott to make a business out of Scottish brewing ingenuity. Twenty years ago Bruce was running a homebrew shop in Glasgow when an elderly lady walked in with an old family recipe in Gaelic for *Leann fraoich*. Bruce enlisted a Gaelic-speaking islander to translate this recipe for heather ale, then started working on making the beer palatable.

Experimenting with different varieties and quantities of heather flowers, he made up batches that he would test on his customers. Once the formula was perfected, he began by brewing small quantities for friends and family, but word of the strange beer spread and, with his brother, Bruce opened up a small brewery to meet demand, selling the brew as *Fracoch* (heather) ale. They've grown and now produce 120 barrels a year, some of which they export to America and Canada, but it's still a small business with about a dozen employees at their recently opened new brewery in Alloa.

Rather than seeing the heather ale as a gimmick, Bruce is definitely on a crusade. He wants to bring traditional Scottish brews to the people and has recently diversified into new recipes, including a spruce beer. Made from malt, pine and spruce to an Aberdeenshire recipe, it's Bruce's personal favourite, has a lovely flavour and is used by some chefs in cooking desserts. And at 7 per cent alcohol, it'll blast your socks off.

I meet Bruce, a bit of a free spirit, near the Wallace Monument, where he takes me on a walk to pick spring oak leaves and spruce. Seasonality is absolutely crucial; the pine can be harvested only for a month in the springtime when the new shoots appear on the trees. Only the greenest, freshest shoots from the lower branches can be used. As for heather, it can be picked only when in flower in July and August.

Bruce tugs at a branch on a tree. 'These are the spring oak leaves. The light green colour means there's a lot more flavour to them than later in the year, when the autumn oak is dark.'

'Where does the flavour come from? Is it the resin in the bark?'

'The chlorophyll compounds in the leaves release tannins and other flavoursome things.' Bruce is biting into leaves as he explains.

'You're eating this, are you?' I take a bite. 'Is this a challenge of some sort? Mmm.'

'It's quite like eating a lettuce.'

'It is.' I'm very surprised. 'You're right.'

'Like rocket.'

'Yes, quite peppery.'

'That flavour we are going to try to get out into the liquid by soaking and infusing it in hot water and lemon juice.'

'Like making tea?'

'Exactly.'

Quite how people decided which leaves from which trees could be made into beer intrigues me. After all, I could look at a forest for months and be none the wiser.

'Who would want to drink water all the time?' says Bruce. 'You would put things in it, stew them up and see what happened. They would have discovered that some of the chemicals in the plants have preservatives. Then they found out that certain types of leaves had effects on the human body, such as narcotic, medicinal or toxic qualities.'

I have to confess that when I first tasted heather beer in a pub – and it's delicious, by the way – I thought it was some trendy thing invented by some young buck to promote Scotland. Then I discovered that we didn't have hops in Scotland and that for centuries we used heather because we lacked anything else.

'We didn't get hops until the eighteenth century,' says Bruce, 'so many people assume that before then beer didn't exist. But it did, for four thousand years before that. Until the seventeenth century, heather, myrtle, oak, spruce and pine were used to make beer. Archaeologists discovered a shard containing traces of a fermented beverage made with heather flowers in a Neolithic settlement on the Isle of Rum. That dates back to two thousand BC or earlier.'

As well as spruce and pine, we're looking for elderflower, but we're a bit early in the season. The buds haven't opened yet. Instead I pick some nettles.

'It's my belief,' says Bruce, 'that they used to make up broths using plants such as nettles. And if the broths were left to stand for a few days, they would have discovered that in the right conditions it would ferment the sugars into alcohol.'

'Is that what we would normally call mould?'

'Sort of . . .'

'So that curry you've left for three days, with the hairs on it, could be alcoholic? Maybe that's why there are so many students wandering around looking slightly inebriated.'

Bruce says that if you look at old Egyptian paintings, you can see them drinking soup using a straw to break through the crust on top. That they were drinking the soup to get steamed might explain the straw and the mouldy crust.

But enough theory; it's time to collect my own ingredients to make ale. We're going to concentrate on gathering spruce as it's currently in season. Brewed throughout the northern countries, spruce and pine ales were introduced to Scotland by the Vikings in the ninth century and were very popular in the Scottish Highlands until the end of the nineteenth century. Many early explorers, including Captain Cook, used spruce ale during long sea voyages because it prevented scurvy and ill health. Shetland spruce ale was said to 'stimulate animal instincts' and produce twins. *All,* a Scandinavian word that means strong at sea, is thought by some to be the origin of the word 'ale'.

After picking some ingredients, we head to Bruce's brewery at Alloa, which, thanks to a huge reservoir created by artesian water dropping off the nearby Ochill Hills, has been a centre of Scottish brewing for centuries. At one time Alloa had seven breweries. These days, there's just the one, Bruce's brewery, which is in an 1884 building in which Younger's used to bottle their beer. Across the fields is Stirling Castle. The Wallace Monument is in the distance. Inside the brewery are pipework, giant brewing tubs and Ian McNeill, the brewer with whom I'm going to make some best spruce ale.

Ian explains how the beer is brewed by boiling a mix of pure malted barley, water and young sprigs of pine, like making a giant cup of pine tea. After an hour and a half, fresh shoots of the spruce are added for a short infusion before the mixture is transferred to a tank in which it is fermented for ten days. As we heft sacks of pine sprigs and spruce around the brewery, I cannot believe we're making a beer from bits and pieces gathered in the local woods, but when I stick my head inside the brewing vessel, it smells like running through a forest on an early morning.

While we wait for the brew to do its stuff, Bruce lets me sample some of his experimental brews, including a nettle and ginger beer, a rose petal beer, beers made with tayberries and gooseberries, a heather ale and a myrtle ale. Every one of them is delicious, but I can't help playing devil's advocate. 'Why do you spend all your time making these strange infusions from bits you've picked out of trees when you could make humungous amounts of lager and be a rich man?'

'I just wanted to use local resources, make specialist indigenous beers and learn more about our past – often things that people have forgotten – and in doing that, we hope we'll create a new, specialist market.'

In an age when so much of what we eat is standardized by multinational conglomerates, it's very encouraging to see people making individual decisions about what we drink and eat. Bruce, Scott and everyone at the brewery are passionate about quality and individuality. I'm all in favour of that. Well done, the chaps.

My last stop before Glasgow is just beyond the city limits at Barhead. It's hard to think I'm only 10 miles from the city centre when I look around at the rolling countryside – and smell the country air. It seems they're spreading something very rich today, although I suppose I shouldn't be surprised, considering I'm on my way to visit Tom Thompson, who farms 360 Highland cattle on a 900-acre holding.

Now if there's one animal that perfectly symbolizes the Scottish then it surely has to be the Highland cow: tough, independent, unique and, of course, ginger. So beloved are these cows that the Highland Cattle Society of Scotland was formed in 1884 and shows no sign of diminishing. Despite their aggressive, wild look, both bulls and cows are actually known for their mild temperaments.

But it isn't their placid natures that has made them a kitsch symbol of Scotland, seen everywhere from tins of Scottish toffee and shortbread biscuits to the Highland landscape paintings of Alfred de Breanski. Highland cows, as a breed, have survived as a result of their hardy nature. Small and compact, they're very sure-footed and they don't get foot rot, which is handy for Scotland. They can live on practically anything – they'll even eat heather – and their enormous amount of fur protects them from the elements, helping them cope in harsh, mountainous conditions. The fur also insulates them, lowering their need for fat, so they produce delicious, very lean, low-cholesterol, marbled meat.

As Tom explains to me, these characteristics have made the Highland cow popular not only in its homeland of western Scotland, but also in many farflung parts of the world. Able to breed and thrive on vast expanses of poor mountain land with high annual rainfall and bitter winds, Highland cattle can even be found foraging 10,000 feet up in the Andes, as well as in more clement conditions on every continent. In the southern Alps they're used for conservation purposes, as they'll happily regenerate old scrubland, eating most things and using their horns to clear scrub and brambles in places no other cattle would go. As for breeding, they're renowned as excellent mothers that will calve easily outdoors and require minimum attention. Some are still calving at more than eighteen years of age, having borne fifteen calves.

Probably the least known fact about Highland cattle is that the ginger cows we all know from the toffee tins are not true Highland cows. Originally they were all black, like the Angus. But for some reason, breeders decided ginger was preferable, apparently because hundreds of years ago some lairds cross-bred them to produce a different colour from their neighbours' cattle. The red, gingery coat caught on and is now the most commonly seen colour. Who would've thought?

Despite these obvious advantages, nowadays four-fifths of Highland cattle are bred for showing rather than for their meat, mainly because they're relatively small and therefore produce less meat per carcass than other breeds. I've come to see Tom because he's president of the West of Scotland Highland Cattle Club. Today he's hosting the club's Highland cattle training day, at which novices, experts and judges come together to swap tips and learn new skills in order to make their cattle the prettiest around.

As Tom explains, cattle preening is not just about winning awards; it's part of his marketing strategy. 'We sell our cattle all over the world, so we regard the showing as advertising for them. Hopefully it'll encourage people to come and buy them, and the top ones can make a lot of money.'

It seems strange that these low-maintenance cows are given such a high-maintenance treatment for shows. 'So what do you need to do to them to make them pretty for showing?' I say.

'You probably wouldn't believe me if I told you. Just like a woman, you've got to look after them well, give them special feeding and keep them well groomed. Shampoo and set, a blow-dry, comb-through and lots of brushing.'

Tom doesn't consider himself a grooming expert – his expertise is breeding and keeping Highland cattle – so he has called on the services of championship show trophy-holders. He introduces me to Andrew Kilpatrick, who keeps a commercial breed of Highland cattle and exports a lot of meat to Germany. Talked into buying a Highland cow by his wife Helen, who thought they were very attractive and dreamed of having a herd, Andrew has won four championship trophies and is now a judge. Holding a sharp knife, he shows me how to prepare the cow's horns, which he scrapes roughly with the blade.

'Bloody hell!' I'm surprised at how hard Andrew is scraping.

'It sounds worse to us than it feels to the cow.'

Wondering how he knows this, I try to comfort the cow, which is shaking its head from side to side. 'All right, dear, this won't last long.'

Then Andrew pulls out a large sheet of sandpaper to buff the horns, showing no mercy while the cow moos loudly. Maybe it's the scraping noise that is bothering her – it sounds like nails being dragged across a blackboard – but the poor girl doesn't seem to like it.

As for me, the cow's horns are quite low and I am quite high, so they're just the right height to take out my eye. I instinctively grab the nearest horn and put my thumb over it. To my great surprise, I find the horn is alive. It's warm almost down to its tip.

Meanwhile, Andrew is moving on to the final stage of the horn-buffing treatment. 'You finish up with a wee sand block and then some oil, which you rub in just before it goes on show.'

I'm going to have to repeat Andrew's prettifying on the cow's other horn, but before that he shows me how to groom its coat using a selection of fearsome-looking combs to pull out knots. There are two types of hair, I discover. Underneath the long, shaggy topcoat there's a coat of shorter hair, like a horse's coat. Both of these have to be combed out before I can shampoo the cow. That done, I'm introduced to Liz Shaw, a very energetic and trim woman with a blonde ponytail and a no-nonsense manner. By day she is a nuclear power plant worker; in her time off she's a cattle-showing enthusiast with a particular expertise in bovine shampoo and sets.

With her son Rory, Liz keeps nine cattle. Like a pushy mum at a pageant, this forty-eight-year-old is obsessed with having the most beautiful cows and has her tricks of the trade, which she's agreed to divulge to me. In the past, she's even gone as far as using ten bottles of Paul Mitchell shampoo on a bull.

A few minutes later, I find myself shampooing a cow – as you do. I can't help laughing. Over the course of this journey I've done some silly stuff, but this takes the biscuit. Strangely, I can tell the cow is really enjoying it – to get the shampoo deep into her hair, I'm having to rub very hard, so the old girl is getting a top-quality intensive massage. All she needs now is a copy of *Hello!*, a white towelling robe and some lavender tea for the fully pampered spa experience.

'Rinsing's important,' says Liz, washing her cow beside mine. 'You need to get all the junk out and the hair doesn't shine as much if there's shampoo left in it. Then you have to dry them really thoroughly because the Highlander's hair holds the water.'

'I'm wondering: would I put conditioner on it?'

'Yes, you would.'

Jeez. I was only joking. 'Always?'

'Except when they've got finer hair, when conditioner makes it too soft and you can't get it to do a thing.'

'A bovine bad hair day, you might say?'

'Oh yes.' With that, Liz pulls out a hairdryer and starts giving her cow a blow-dry.

'What do you use in that case?'

'I use mousse and hairspray.'

Liz is a mine of information on how to prepare a Highlander for showing, what the judges look for, and how to come to terms with eating a cow for which you've cared for many years. I feel very uncomfortable talking about steaks or joints of roast beef within hearing distance of the cow.

'It's all right,' says Liz. 'She doesn't speak the same language.'

'Well, you think that, but I think they might sit in their sheds and go: "What's that marbling thing they're talking about, Jim? I don't like the sound of that at all. I think he's talking about my leg there. And steaks and stuff. I think we should make a run for it." '

'Do you know how you get over being attached to them when you go to the butcher's? You don't give them names. If they're a number, it's okay. But with a name, you can't eat them. Well, I can't.'

'This one's called Bob. And he loves you and you mustn't take him away to the bad market. He doesn't want to end up in a freezer at McDonald's.'

'He'll be all right. He's called Fergus.'

I just hope she doesn't mind being called Bob and Fergus, poor cow.

I ask Liz for a critical appraisal of my cow, which I think I've prepared to a very high standard.

'You've done very well, because you've got all the knots out of her coat,' she says. 'But there's a wee bit of a problem here: bubbles left in the coat. Your cleaning was good, but your rinsing was not so good.' Ah, attention to detail. I could have done a better job. 'You'll need to do some more work if you want to win,' says Liz.

Half an hour later, dressed in a white coat and tie, looking like a butcher at the co-op, I'm leading three-quarters of a ton of prime beef, horns and titivated hair to the judging ring.

'Whoa, whoa, whoa,' I say as the cow tries to take off on her own. 'Chill, girl.'

'You've done a grand job,' says Tom. 'She's nicely washed and brushed.'

'Whoa. Jeezo.'

'They're strong animals.'

'It's like being in a rugby scrum.' I try to grip her by the horns, but unsurprisingly she's stronger than me, so Tom takes over and she immediately calms down.

In spite of my best grooming efforts, there's a lot about my cow that is beyond my control. Much of it is down to genetics. The judges are looking for a grand and picturesque head, with a wide, long and bushy forelock between the eyes, which should be bright with courage. The horns should be strong, coming level out of the head, inclining slightly forward and rising to the points. Drooping is considered a very bad fault – where have I heard that before? The neck should form a straight line from the head to the shoulder and the hair should be thick, long and gracefully waved.

'What exactly are you looking for?' I say to Andrew as he watches the cows walk round the judging ring.

'I'm looking for someone leading the animal with its head up and on a short rope, an animal that walks with confidence and calmly.'

'How do you think I did in my preparation?'

'For an absolute novice, Robbie, you've done excellently. And I was very impressed that when you made your first approach to the animal you grabbed it by the horns.'

'Instinct really. I was worried about my eye.'

'It must be in your genes.'

There could be some truth in it. My folk were all cattlemen, most of the cattle being stolen from the English, apparently.

Andrew announces his choice of winner, a beautiful pale-coated yearling that's being led round the ring at a very steady pace by a young schoolgirl. From the little I know, I'd immediately agree with his choice. The beauty and poise of this cow in comparison to the others stands out even to a newcomer like me.

As soon as the prizegiving is finished, the barbecue is fired up and laden with beefburgers, sausages and a very appetizing rack of beef. I'd like to stay for it, but I've got a meal waiting for me in Glasgow, and the last stage of my journey to finish before it.

I'm in a dilemma: driving into Glasgow is normally a very simple business – the M8 ploughs slap bang into the centre of the city. But taking that would be too easy.

The poor old Jag's feeling the strain. She's done remarkably well, covering the 700-odd miles with just a few hiccups, so I've arranged one last little mission, one last little treat for the old girl – and for me.

For more than five hundred years, a ferry service has operated between Renfrew, on the south bank of the Clyde, and Yoker on the north bank. Not only is it one of Scotland's oldest ferry services, it's also one of the most popular, carrying nearly 150,000 passengers across the Clyde each year. Until 1984, it also carried vehicles, but with most motorists using the Clyde Tunnel and Erskine Bridge to cross the river, the decision was taken to make it solely a passenger route. That is, until today.

Following a special request, they've agreed to put the Jag on the *Yoker Swan*, which with the *Renfrew Rose* is one of two Renfrew passenger ferries, and instead of shuttling the 200 metres between graded slipways either side of the Clyde, they're going to ferry me all the way to the city centre. I couldn't think of a more appropriate way to return home. After all, as the saying goes: Glasgow made the Clyde, and the Clyde made Glasgow.

After weeks of sunshine, a light rain is falling as I board the ferry. A perfect Clyde day, you might say. Joe, one of the two crew, leads me up to the bridge, where his crewmate John is behind the wheel.

'What a treat.' I look around with amazement. 'To get on the Renfrew ferry and head off. Everyone will think we've gone mental. "Is that not the Renfrew ferry? Where the hell is that going?" What fun.'

I get terribly nostalgic going down the Clyde. With a GP dad who would assist the police when they pulled dead bodies out of the river, much of my childhood and adolescence was spent in and around the Clyde. In those days the banks of the river were lined with shipyards, building thousands of boats destined for countries all around the world. When I was a boy, Dad would name all the yards – 'That's Barclay Curle's, that's

Whiteinch, that's Broons', all the way down to Denny's at Dumbarton – and because he was a doctor, he knew people who worked on every single yard. He always knew when something heavy was being lifted by a big crane, like a steam engine going to India, or when there was a launching. And if it wasn't a weekend, Dad would get me out of school. I'd see his head poke round the classroom door. 'A bit of a family emergency,' he'd whisper to the teacher. 'I'll have to take Robin out of school.' And Dad would beckon me out of class.

The next thing I knew, we'd be at a dockside, shouting 'Ya beauty' as chains swung and clanked all around us and the noise of 20,000 tons of metal sliding into the water completely enveloped us. There's absolutely nothing like it.

Without the Clyde, Glasgow would not have manufactured thirty-five thousand ships or exported fifty thousand steam locomotives. In its heyday, you could hardly move along the river for cranes and boats. It's not a rose-tinted view of the past to say that. It really was crammed with boats. And in those days, the shipyard workers were allowed to catch salmon in their lunch hours. I'm pleased to say that since work has begun to clean up the Clyde, salmon have now returned, but unfortunately little has replaced the dockyards. But there is a scrapyard for cars – the metal probably destined for China – and a lot of money is being spent regenerating the waterfront.

The Clyde teaches us that we have to accept change. Like most heavy industries, shipbuilding has moved to where labour costs are much cheaper, but there are lots of other things we can do. It's easy to be romantic about the shipyards, but I wouldn't like to get up at four in the morning to batter five thousand rivets into a ship's hull. During the war, men were hammering out dreadnoughts twenty-four hours a day, getting

295

paid a pittance, surviving on bread, dripping and tea, and living in the kind of housing in which nowadays we wouldn't put a dog. Let's not get too rosy-eyed about the Clyde's past, but let's not forget it entirely.

I dearly hope that the redevelopment of the waterfront will include things like affordable housing, cycle paths, public parks and space for cafés and restaurants, so that it becomes a living waterfront for everyone, a bonny place to live and not an empty dormitory with executive apartments that only the affluent can afford.

'This is great,' I say to John as we progress up the river. 'I really should do this more often.' I glance at the ship's wheel. 'I don't suppose I could have a shot?'

He lets me take the wheel as we pass a derelict space where Brown's shipyard used to stand and where HMS *Hood*, the *Lusitania* and *Aquitania* were built. The last ship launched here was the *QE2* in September 1967. It was so huge they had to use tugs to slow its entry into the water. Many in the crowd on the opposite shore were swept away by the wave. I can't help saluting as we pass by.

'You don't often get the Renfrew ferry past Broon's yard,' I say to John and Joe. 'This is better than winning a BAFTA. It's better than winning an Oscar.'

We're soon approaching the centre of Glasgow and, with the delicate stuff looming ahead of us, I hand the wheel back to John. 'Back to you, sir. On you go. Thanks very much. I really appreciate that.'

'You're very welcome.'

I'm going to burst into that song if I'm not careful – 'The Clyde, the Clyde, the wonderful Clyde' – but I stop myself. We're heading into the centre of town now. You can tell because all the graffiti is improving. It's been the perfect way to come home.

But before I put my feet up on the sofa and settle down for a long-awaited cup of tea, I'm going to change into something more, well, Glasgow – a dark suit and a white shirt – and have what I always have when I come home to the city: a nice curry.

Now you might think that this was someone else's idea – a great meal to end the journey – but if there was anything in this whole journey that was down to me, it is this, the curry at the end. Abso-bloody-lutely. Manchester might have a mile of curry, Birmingham might be the home of the balti, but if you want to eat the best version of Britain's national dish, the place to come to is Glasgow, which for decades has had a long-term love affair with food from the Indian subcontinent. In fact, it's believed that Sultan Ahmed Ansari, who owned the Taj Mahal in Glasgow fifty years ago, invented chicken tikka masala when a customer complained that chicken tikka was too dry. With the help of another national favourite – a tin of tomato soup – mixed with some herbs and spices, the tikka masala was born. Although no one can trace the exact origins of this dish, Glasgow's claim is thought to be the most authentic in the industry. And if you need any more evidence, Glasgow is twinned with Lahore, so it's no wonder we rule the rogan josh roost.

Going for a curry in Glasgow was a habit for the locals long before the rest of Britain caught on. I remember going to London in my teens and seeking a curry, only to find that there was not much on offer outside the noticeably Asian areas, and even their curries didn't taste as good as the curries in Glasgow. Maybe it's because most Glasgow Indian restaurants are Punjabi, whereas those in Manchester and Bradford are mainly

Pakistani, and in Birmingham mainly Kashmiri. Punjabi curries tend to have more powerful, fruity, rich and pungent sauces that appeal particularly to the Glasgow taste buds.

Having won the prestigious Curry Capital of Great Britain award three times, everyone now knows how to make a curry up here in Glasgow, and the restaurant I'm in has been part of the Curry Capital winning team for some time. Conveniently located at Finnieston on the banks of the Clyde, India Quay is a real family business. Head chef Sanjeev Sanghera is second generation in a proud lineage of passionate curry cooks and visibly proud that he's representing Glasgow in the competition again. He's also working hard to change perceptions of curry restaurants. With whitewashed walls, lots of glass and wood, his cosmopolitan new restaurant is more like restaurants in India and nothing like the British stereotype of flock wallpaper, dark carpet and sitar music. Unlike the Indian restaurants of old, India Quay strives to have a menu in which every dish is very distinctive, not just differently coloured. Sanjeev's signature dish is lamb desi and I'm really looking forward to learning how to cook it. To complicate matters, as part of the Curry Capital contest each restaurant in the competing cities has to run a charity dinner. And you guessed it, that's exactly what's on at India Quay tonight.

Once in the kitchen, I soon discover the scale of the pressure we are under to make the evening's service a success. With nearly a hundred invited guests attending, it's not the best time to learn the ropes. Sanjeev puts me to work, but I see that he's not as mild-mannered in the kitchen as he seemed earlier when we were sitting having a chat in the restaurant.

'Could you chop all these first?' Sanjeev pushes a huge pile of onions in front of me. 'And I want them nice and small.'

'Okay . . . okay.'

'Like this.' He holds up some very consistently sized chopped onions.

'Okay. Can I get a harder knife?'

'Don't you start with me.' Sanjeev turns away, then passes me some peppers. 'When you've done the onions, can you chop these. And when you're done, give us a shout.' Sanjeev turns to his stove, where he's frying onions in mustard oil, then looks at my onions. '*Nice and small, please*, I said. Are you nearly done? C'mon, the rest of it is almost burning.'

Sanjeev is assisted by three other Punjabi chefs, none of whom speaks English. Deepa is Sanjeev's right-hand man, cutting up ingredients and laying everything out; Gurdev is fryer chef and responsible for pakoras; and Ravi is the tandoori chef, mixing all the spices and making naan bread. Meanwhile, my chopping is so slow that Sanjeev leans over me, chops some ingredients himself, adds them to the pan and tells me to join him at the stove. Needless to say, lacking chef skills, my efforts to fry, stir and mix don't come quite up to scratch, while Sanjeev adds a bewildering list of ingredients, including ginger, fenugreek, chillies and tomatoes. It all smells heavenly.

As the guests pour in, the pace in the kitchen gets more hectic, and I find out that even frying onions isn't as straightforward as I thought.

'Just keep mixing,' says Sanjeev.

'Yes, yes.'

'If you don't keep mixing, it will stick and burn.'

'Okay.'

'Keep it above the flame.'

It's fearsomely hot. I look round at one of the assistant chefs, who's staring at my pan. 'Are you waiting for me?'

'Yes. When you're ready . . .'

'Your gas bill must be horrific,' I say to Sanjeev. 'Everything's full on all the time.'

'It would be horrific if every curry took as long to cook as yours. Keep stirring.'

A lamb dish usually takes about ten minutes, Sanjeev tells me, whereas chicken dishes take about six minutes. 'Almost done?' he says.

'Not quite.'

'One sec – before you make a mess here.' Sanjeev takes over.

A minute later my lamb desi is ready to be served – my only regret is that I won't be the one eating it – and I am being led over to the tandoori oven to make naan bread. The oven is so hot it feels as if you could melt steel in it. A naan bread takes only forty seconds to cook in this 400-degree furnace.

This is turning into the generation game. I can hear Brucie saying 'Didn't he do dreadfully?' as Sanjeev shows me how to turn a lump of dough into a thin wedge of naan to put into the oven. Inevitably it all goes horribly wrong for me, the dough folding in on itself, then landing on the floor as I burn my arm on heat blasting out of the oven.

'This is revenge for the empire, isn't it?' I say. Sanjeev laughs, then gets me to put a naan that one of his assistants has made into the oven. 'Speed is everything, isn't it? If you put your hand in too long, the skin will be away.'

'That's why a lot of these guys have no hair on their arms. It's all singed off.'

Sanjeev tells me the oven is set to its lowest temperature today because they knew I'd be in the kitchen. Having stoked steam engines that were cooler than the tandoori oven, I find it hard to imagine how hot it must be at its upper temperature.

'We're getting more orders coming in now,' says Sanjeev. 'Maybe you should go back out into the restaurant.'

At least I tried. You know what they say: if you can't take the heat . . . Hard as it was, I learnt a lot. And anyway, I don't want to scupper Glasgow's chances of retaining the title. After working in the kitchen, burning my hand and watching everyone else eat the competition dinner, I'm finally getting to eat my curry. One thing's for sure: I'll never look at a naan in the same way again. As for the curry, it's just fantastic. Unfortunately, Glasgow doesn't retain its title and comes second. Better luck next year, lads, eh?

It's lovely to come home. It's been an amazing trip, much better than I'd anticipated all those months ago when Hamish and I first had our brainwave over that drunken dinner. In every way it's turned out to be so much richer, more interesting, more varied, less inward-looking, more spectacular and altogether more inspiring than I'd expected before setting off. I've learnt a lot and I've laughed with some great people. Although we often think of Britain becoming increasingly homogenized and uniform, I've found it doesn't take that much to find people celebrating wonderful and unique things with passion and pride.

The journey itself has been an awakening. Like many people, for some time I've thought we lived in a world dominated by the accoutrements of modern culture: iPods, electronics, celebrity fixations, reality TV and the rest. But I've discovered that most communities are filled with a life that is much deeper, more meaningful and more lasting than the ephemera of conspicuous consumption, and we shouldn't worry so much about the small changes that sometimes seem to dominate, because invariably they're making our lives richer without replacing the activities, habits and conventions we've always cherished. In some ways, we British have changed very little over the years. We remain unashamedly eccentric, we love a good party and most of the time we're very inclusive.

Nevertheless, having just spent six weeks to make a journey that if I'd taken the motorway would have taken maybe eight hours – I'm delighted to be home. Once a Glaswegian, always a Glaswegian, I suppose. And having seen some spectacular sights and marvelled at some stunning landscapes, I now know just what lies out there, none of it very far from the motorways. Next time you're taking a journey, why not avoid the right fork you've always taken at that junction and turn left instead. Veer on to the B-road, cruise in the slow lane and who knows what you might find.

Index